THE WORLD BANK: OVERVIEW AND CURRENT ISSUES

THE WORLD BANK: OVERVIEW AND CURRENT ISSUES

ELISABETH P. MCLELLAN (EDITOR)

Nova Science Publishers, Inc.
New York

Library of Congress Cataloging-in-Publication Data

McLellan, Elisabeth P.
The World Bank: overview and current issues / Elisabeth P. McLellan.
p. cm.
Includes bibliographical references.
ISBN: 1-59033-550-3.
1. World Bank. 2. Economic assistance. 3. International finance. I. Title.

HG3881.5. W57 M35 2002
332.1'532—dc21

2002040987

400 Oser Ave, Suite 1600
Hauppauge, New York 11788-3619
Tele. 631-231-7269 Fax 631-231-8175
e-mail: Novascience@earthlink.net
Web Site: http://www.novapublishers.com

Printed in the United States of America

CONTENTS

PREFACE

The advances of technology and business have made the world and its nations increasingly interconnected and interdependent in an era of globalization. In such an environment, the events in one country can and will have a definitive influence on the conditions in others. Examples abound in the stock market, capital flows, living standards, and pollution. The World Bank assembles the collective financial resources of its member nations and uses these funds to address the concerns of its clients. It is a development institution that has a primary goal of reducing worldwide poverty by promoting economic growth in individual countries. To this end, the Bank sponsors an array of programs that contribute to the fight against poverty by funding economic reforms, fighting corruption, and assisting war-torn nations. From the client nations, the Bank requires an budgetary agenda that balances both economic efficiency and social programs. It is this requisite balancing act that has brought the World Bank a great deal of criticism from anti-globalization protestors who feel that the Bank mandates hinder social advances in poor and struggling nations. Nonetheless, the Bank continues to fund and support its lofty goals in nations around the world and has responded to its critics by easing some of its lending restraints.

This book delves into the issues surrounding the World Bank, which holds a tangible and important influence on every nation in this global society. In order to understand and form a solid opinion about the Bank's role, history, and future, one must be familiar with the information presented here.

Chapter 1

WHAT IS THE WORLD BANK*

The World Bank is one of the world's largest sources of development assistance. Its primary focus is on helping the poorest people and the poorest countries.

- In 2002 the World Bank provided $19.5 billion to developing countries and worked in more than 100 developing economies, bringing finance and/or technical expertise toward helping them reduce poverty.

We live in a world so rich that global income is more than $31 trillion a year. In this world, the average person in some countries earns more than $40,000 a year. But in this same world, 2.8 billion people—more than half the people in developing countries—live on less than $700 a year. Of these, 1.2 billion earn less than $1 a day.

The challenge of reducing these levels of poverty, while the population continues to grow—by an estimated 3 billion people over the next 50 years—is enormous.

The World Bank works to bridge this divide and turn rich country resources into poor country growth. One of the world's largest sources of development assistance, the World Bank provides financing that supports efforts of developing country governments to build schools and health centers, provide water and electricity, fight disease, and protect the environment.

---

* Excerpted from the World Bank website: http://web.worldbank.org.

NOT A BANK, BUT RATHER A SPECIALIZED AGENCY

The World Bank is not a "bank" in the common sense. It is one of the United Nations' specialized agencies, and is made up of 184 member countries. These countries are jointly responsible for how the institution is financed and how its money is spent. The "World Bank" is the name that has come to be used for the International Bank for Reconstruction and Development (IBRD) and the International Development Association (IDA), a trust fund managed by the IBRD to provide grants and interest-free credits to the world's poorest countries. Together these organizations provide low-interest loans, interest-free credit, and grants to developing countries.

$8.1 BILLION IN ASSISTANCE

The world's low-income countries generally cannot borrow money in international markets or can only do so at high interest rates. In addition to direct contributions and loans from developed countries, these countries receive grants, interest-free loans, and technical assistance from the World Bank to enable them to provide basic services. In the case of the loans, countries have 35-40 years to repay, with a 10-year grace period.

This type of financing comes from IDA, the world's largest source of concessional assistance. Some 40 rich countries provide the money for this funding by making contributions every four years. The fund was replenished most recently in 2002, with nearly $9 billion from donors and another $6.6 billion from the Bank's resources. At that time, donors agreed on increased use of IDA grants—up to 21 percent of resources—to help address the special difficulties, such as the HIV/AIDS epidemic, faced by the poorest and most vulnerable countries.

IDA credits make up about one-quarter of the Bank's financial assistance. Aside from IDA funds, very little of the Bank's income is provided by its member countries.

IDA credits make up about one-quarter of the Bank's financial assistance. Aside from IDA resourcing, very little of the Bank's income is provided by the member countries.

- **In fiscal 2002 IDA provided $8.1 billion in financing for 133 projects in 62 low-income countries.**

$11.5 BILLION IN LOANS

Higher-income developing countries—some of which can borrow from commercial sources, but generally only at very high interest rates—receive loans from the IBRD.

Countries that borrow from the IBRD have more time to repay than if they borrowed from a commercial bank—15 to 20 years with a three-to-five-year grace period before the repayment of principal begins. Developing country governments borrow money for specific programs, including poverty reduction efforts, delivery of social services, protection of the environment, and promotion of economic growth that will improve living standards. In fiscal 2002 IBRD provided loans totaling $11.5 billion in support of 96 projects in 40 countries.

RAISING CAPITAL

The IBRD raises almost all its money in the world's financial markets. With a AAA credit rating, it issues bonds to raise money and then pass on the low interest rates to its borrowers.

The World Bank Group

In addition to IBRD and IDA, three other organizations make up the World Bank Group to support critical functions to its poverty reduction mission. The International Finance Corporation (IFC) promotes private sector investment by supporting high-risk sectors and countries. The Multilateral Investment Guarantee Agency (MIGA) provides political risk insurance (guarantees) to investors in and lenders to developing countries. And the International Centre for Settlement of Investment Disputes (ICSID) settles investment disputes between foreign investors and their host countries.

GLOBAL GOODS

Over the past few years, the World Bank has put significant resources into activities meant to have global impact. One is debt relief, and under the enhanced Heavily Indebted Poor Countries (HIPC) Initiative, 26 poor countries have received debt relief which will save them $41 billion over time. The money these countries save in debt repayments will instead be put into housing, education, health, and welfare programs for the poor.

The World Bank, along with 189 countries and numerous organizations, has committed to to an unprecedented global partnership to fight poverty. The Millennium Development Goals define specific targets in terms of school enrolments, child mortality, maternal health, disease, and access to water to be met by 2015.

Among numerous other global partnerships, the World Bank has put supporting the fight against HIV/AIDS at the top of its agenda. It is the world's largest long-term financer of HIV/AIDS programs. Current Bank commitments for HIV/AIDS amount to more than $1.3 billion, with half of that for sub-Saharan Africa.

The Variety of Work on the Ground

The Bank is currently involved in more than 1,800 projects in virtually ever sector and developing country. These are as diverse as providing microcredit in Bosnia Herzegovina and raising AIDS awareness in communities in Guinea, helping educate girls in Bangladesh and improving health care delivery in Mexico, helping East Timor rebuild upon independence or helping India to rebuild Gujarat after a devastating earthquake.

International Development Association (IDA)

IDA helps the world's poorest countries reduce poverty by providing "credits," which are loans at zero interest with a 10-year grace period and maturities of 35 to 40 years. These countries face complex challenges in striving for progress toward the international development goals. They must, for example, respond to the competitive pressures as well as opportunities of globalization; arrest the spread of HIV/AIDS; and prevent conflict or deal with its aftermath. To help these countries improve their prospects, the policy framework emphasizes:

- Accelerating broad-based growth through sound macroeconomic and sectoral policies, especially for rural and private sector development.
- Investing in people through strong support for the social sectors (see figure), including gender mainstreaming and efforts to counter the

challenge and social impact of communicable diseases, especially HIV/AIDS.

- Building capacity for improving governance - including in public expenditure management - and combating corruption.
- Protecting the environment for sustainable development.
- Fostering recovery in post-conflict countries.
- Promoting trade and regional integration.

IDA's Evolving Role: Greater Emphasis on Participation and Partnerships

Responding to recent changes in the international development environment, IDA works more closely with borrowers and other development partners. The Poverty Reduction Strategy Papers, prepared in a participatory manner by IDA countries, offer an opportunity to align donor strategies more closely with country strategies.

IDA's Stepped-up Effort in the Social Sectors
285 Projects ongoing (compared with 184 a decade ago)

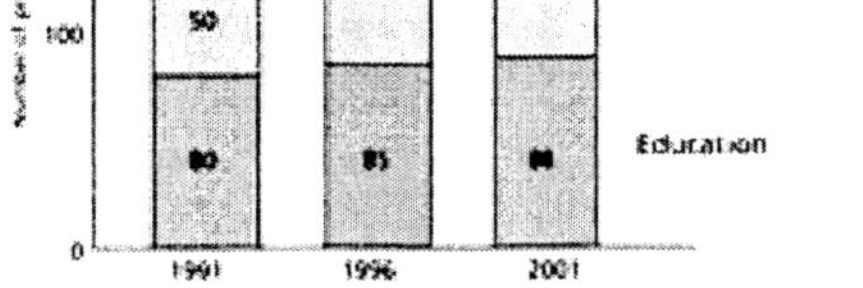

IDA commitment value of ongoing social sector projects

1991: $7.7 billion
1996: $13.1 billion
2001: $13.9 billion

The Bank took important steps in the spring of 2001 to increase transparency and broaden participation in the formulation of IDA's operational approaches. Documents for the donor meetings on the 13th Replenishment of IDA (IDA-13), which will fund lending in fiscal, are publicly available. And in June 2001, for the first time in IDA's 41-year history, representatives of borrowing countries joined donors in discussions about IDA's future directions.

Increasing Aid Effectiveness through Performance-Based Allocations

Research shows that aid is most effective in spurring growth and poverty reduction in countries that have a strong commitment to reforms. IDA leads all development institutions in directing its assistance to countries that pursue poverty-reducing policies. IDA employs a performance-based allocation system to channel its resources to countries that are undertaking reforms. Through targeted allocations, effective leveraging of resources, and country-based strategies, IDA is helping the poorest countries participate in the global economy, and promoting equity and inclusive growth for their poorest citizens.

Basic Facts About the International Finance Corporation (IFC)

The International Finance Corporation (IFC) promotes sustainable private sector investment in developing countries as a way to reduce poverty and improve people's lives.

IFC is a member of the World Bank Group and is headquartered in Washington, DC. It shares the primary objective of all World Bank Group institutions: to improve the quality of the lives of people in its developing member countries.

Established in 1956, IFC is the largest multilateral source of loan and equity financing for private sector projects in the developing world. It promotes sustainable private sector development primarily by:

- Financing private sector projects located in the developing world.
- Helping private companies in the developing world mobilize financing in international financial markets.
- Providing advice and technical assistance to businesses and governments.

Ownership and Management

IFC has 175 member countries, which collectively determine its policies and approve investments. To join IFC, a country must first be a member of the IBRD. IFC's corporate powers are vested in its Board of Governors, to which member countries appoint representatives. IFC's share capital, which is paid in, is provided by its member countries, and voting is in proportion to the number of shares held. IFC's authorized capital is $2.45 billion.

The Board of Governors delegates many of its powers to the Board of Directors, which is composed of the Executive Directors of the IBRD, and which represents IFC's member countries. The Board of Directors reviews all projects.

The President of the World Bank Group , James D. Wolfensohn, also serves as IFC's president. IFC's Executive Vice President, Peter Woicke, is responsible for the overall management of day-to-day operations.

Although IFC coordinates its activities in many areas with the other institutions in the World Bank Group, IFC generally operates independently as it is legally and financially autonomous with its own Articles of Agreement, share capital, management and staff.

Funding of IFC's Activities

IFC's equity and quasi-equity investments are funded out of its net worth: the total of paid in capital and retained earnings. Strong shareholder support, triple-A ratings, and the substantial paid-in capital base have allowed IFC to raise funds for its lending activities on favorable terms in the international capital markets.

About Multilateral Investment Guarantee Agency (MIGA)

Our Mission

The Multilateral Investment Guarantee Agency (MIGA) was created in 1988 as a member of the World Bank Group to promote foreign direct investment into emerging economies to improve people's lives and reduce poverty. MIGA fulfills this mandate and contributes to development by offering political risk insurance (guarantees) to investors and lenders, and by helping developing countries attract and retain private investment.

Principles

MIGA is led in its mission by four guiding principles: focusing on clients — serving investors, lenders, and host country governments by supporting private enterprise and promoting foreign investment; engaging in partnerships — working with other insurers, government agencies, and international organizations to ensure complementarity of services and approach; promoting developmental impact — striving to improve the lives of people in emerging economies, consistent with the goals of host countries and sound business, environmental, and social principles; ensuring financial soundness — balancing developmental goals and financial objectives through prudent underwriting and sound risk management.

Members

MIGA membership, which currently stands at 157, is open to all World Bank members. The agency has a capital stock of SDR1 billion. In March 1999, MIGA's Council of Governors adopted a resolution for a capital increase of approximately $850 million. The agency received another $150 million in operating capital from the World Bank.

Development Impact

Projects supported by MIGA have widespread benefits: local jobs are created, tax revenue is generated, skills and technological know-how are transferred. Local communities often receive significant secondary benefits through improved infrastructure, including roads, electricity, hospitals, schools, and clean water. Foreign direct investment supported by MIGA also encourages similar local investments and spurs the growth of local businesses that supply related goods and services. As a result, developing countries have a greater chance to break the cycle of poverty.

MIGA's guarantee coverage requires investors to adhere to social and environmental standards that are considered to be the world's best. Without World Bank Group involvement, projects often go ahead without adequate safeguards.

Unique Strengths

MIGA both supports and draws on the extensive resources of the World Bank Group, applying unparalleled knowledge of emerging economies to the projects it guarantees. MIGA's unique strengths also derive from its structure as an international organization that acts as an umbrella of deterrence against government actions that could disrupt investments, and allows it to influence the resolution of potential disputes. MIGA's capacity to serve as an objective intermediary enhances investor confidence that an investment going into an emerging economy will be protected against non-commercial risks.

Record

Concerns about uncertain political environments and perceptions of political risk often inhibit investment, with foreign direct investment (FDI) often going to a handful of countries and leaving the world's poorest economies largely ignored. MIGA is an important catalyst, increasingly promoting FDI — a key driver of growth — into developing countries through its guarantees, technical assistance, and legal services.

Since its inception, MIGA has issued more than 500 guarantees for projects in 78 developing countries. As of June 2001, total coverage issued exceeded $9 billion, bringing the estimated amount of foreign direct investment facilitated since inception to more than $41 billion. The agency mobilized an additional $153 million in investment coverage in fiscal 2001 through its Cooperative Underwriting Program (CUP), encouraging private sector insurers into transactions they would not have otherwise undertaken, and helping the agency serve more clients.

MIGA's technical assistance services also play an integral role in catalyzing foreign direct investment by helping developing countries around the world define and implement strategies to promote investment. MIGA develops and deploys tools and technologies to support the spread of information on investment opportunities. Thousands of users of take advantage of MIGA's suite of online investment information services, which complement country-based capacity-building work.

The agency uses its legal services to further smooth possible impediments to investment. Through its dispute mediation program, MIGA helps governments and investors resolve their differences, and ultimately improve the country's investment climate.

MIGA complements the activities of other investment insurers and works with partners through its coinsurance and reinsurance programs to expand the capacity of the political risk insurance industry's income. To date, MIGA has officially established 18 such partnerships.

ABOUT THE INTERNATIONAL CENTRE FOR SETTLEMENT OF INVESTMENT DISPUTES (ICSID)

On a number of occasions in the past, the World Bank as an institution and the President of the Bank in his personal capacity have assisted in mediation or conciliation of investment disputes between governments and private foreign investors. The creation of the International Centre for Settlement of Investment Disputes (ICSID) in 1966 was in part intended to relieve the President and the staff of the burden of becoming involved in such disputes. But the Bank's overriding consideration in creating ICSID was the belief that an institution specially designed to facilitate the settlement of investment disputes between governments and foreign investors could help to promote increased flows of international investment.

ICSID was established under the Convention on the Settlement of Investment Disputes between States and Nationals of Other States (the Convention) which came into force on October 14, 1966. ICSID has an Administrative Council and a Secretariat. The Administrative Council is chaired by the World Bank's President and consists of one representative of each State which has ratified the Convention. Annual meetings of the Council are held in conjunction with the joint Bank/Fund annual meetings.

ICSID is an autonomous international organization. However, it has close links with the World Bank. All of ICSID's members are also members of the Bank. Unless a government makes a contrary designation, its Governor for the Bank sits ex officio on ICSID's Administrative Council. The expenses of the ICSID Secretariat are financed out of the Bank's budget, although the costs of individual proceedings are borne by the parties involved.

Pursuant to the Convention, ICSID provides facilities for the conciliation and arbitration of disputes between member countries and investors who qualify as nationals of other member countries. Recourse to ICSID conciliation and arbitration is entirely voluntary. However, once the parties have consented to arbitration under the ICSID Convention, neither can unilaterally withdraw its consent. Moreover, all ICSID Contracting States, whether or not parties to the dispute, are required by the Convention to recognize and enforce ICSID arbitral awards.

Besides providing facilities for conciliation and arbitration under the ICSID Convention, the Centre has since 1978 had a set of Additional Facility Rules authorizing the ICSID Secretariat to administer certain types of proceedings between States and foreign nationals which fall outside the scope of the Convention. These include conciliation and arbitration proceedings where either the State party or the home State of the foreign national is not a member of ICSID. Additional Facility conciliation and arbitration are also available for cases where the dispute is not an investment dispute provided it relates to a transaction which has "features that distinguishes it from an ordinary commercial transaction." The Additional Facility Rules further allow ICSID to administer a type of proceedings not provided for in the Convention, namely fact-finding proceedings to which any State and foreign national may have recourse if they wish to institute an inquiry "to examine and report on facts."

A third activity of ICSID in the field of the settlement of disputes has consisted in the Secretary-General of ICSID accepting to act as the appointing authority of arbitrators for ad hoc (i.e., non-institutional) arbitration proceedings. This is most commonly done in the context of arrangements for arbitration under the Arbitration Rules of the United Nations Commission on International Trade Law (UNCITRAL), which are specially designed for ad hoc proceedings.

Provisions on ICSID arbitration are commonly found in investment contracts between governments of member countries and investors from other member countries. Advance consents by governments to submit investment disputes to ICSID arbitration can also be found in about twenty investment laws and in over 900 bilateral investment treaties. Arbitration under the auspices of ICSID is similarly one of the main mechanisms for the settlement of investment disputes under four recent multilateral trade and investment treaties (the North American Free Trade Agreement, the Energy Charter Treaty, the Cartagena Free Trade Agreement and the Colonia Investment Protocol of Mercosur).

Under the ICSID Convention, ICSID proceedings need not be held at the Centre's headquarters in Washington, D.C. The parties to an ICSID proceeding are free to agree to conduct their proceeding at any other place. The ICSID Convention contains provisions that facilitate advance stipulations for such other venues when the place chosen is the seat of an institution with which the Centre has an arrangement for this purpose. ICSID has to date entered in such arrangements with the Permanent Court of Arbitration at The Hague, the Regional Arbitration Centres of the Asian-African Legal Consultative Committee at Cairo and Kuala Lumpur, the Australian Centre for International Commercial

Arbitration at Melbourne, the Australian Commercial Disputes Centre at Sydney, the Singapore International Arbitration Centre and the GCC Commercial Arbitration Centre at Bahrain. These arrangements have proved their usefulness in many ICSID cases and have helped to promote cooperation between ICSID and these institutions in several other respects.

The number of cases submitted to the Centre has increased significantly in recent years. These include cases brought under the ICSID Convention and cases brought under the ICSID Additional Facility Rules. In addition to its dispute settlement activities, ICSID carries out advisory and research activities relevant to its objectives and has a number of publications. The Centre collaborates with other World Bank Group units in meeting requests by governments for advice on investment and arbitration law. The publications of the Centre include multi-volume collections of Investment Laws of the World and of Investment Treaties, which are periodically updated by ICSID staff. Since April 1986, the Centre has published a semi-annual law journal entitled ICSID Review-Foreign Investment Law Journal. The journal was recently rated as one of the top 20 international and comparative law journals in the United States.

Since 1983, the Centre has also co-sponsored, with the American Arbitration Association (AAA) and the International Chamber of Commerce (ICC) International Court of Arbitration, colloquia on topics of current interest in the area of international arbitration. Other conference activities involving the Centre are described in the ICSID Annual

Chapter 2

IMF AND WORLD BANK: U.S. CONTRIBUTIONS AND AGENCY BUDGETS

Jonathan E. Sanford

ABSTRACT

Along with other member countries, the United States makes contributions--sometimes annually, sometimes every few years--to help support the operational programs of the IMF and World Bank. None of these contributions is used to finance the international agencies' administrative expenses. Their administrative budgets are financed with income derived from operations or from investments. This paper shows how much the United States has contributed to these international agencies in recent years. It also shows how much the international agencies budget (and the source of those funds) for their administrative expenses and their operational budgets.

U.S. CONTRIBUTIONS TO THE IMF AND WORLD BANK

The United States does not contribute money to the IMF every year. Likewise, it makes annual contributions to only some World Bank affiliates. For the IMF and most World Bank agencies, member countries make contributions or subscriptions only when they believe the agency's capital base needs expansion.

International Monetary Fund

In fiscal year 1999, Congress appropriated 10,622.5 million Special Drawing Rights (SDRs[1])-- approximately $14.5 billion to the IMF's general resources. It also subscribed an additional SDR 2.462 billion - approximately $3.5 billion - to a special IMF lending agreement called the New Arrangement to Borrow (NAB). Nothing was proposed or appropriated for fiscal 2000. Since the IMF's inception, the United States has subscribed SDR 37.149 billion-- $52.306 billion-- to the IMF's general resources and SDR 10.962 billion-- $15.434 billion-- to the New Arrangements to Borrow and its predecessor, the General Arrangements to Borrow (GAB). The United States has the largest vote (17.53%) in the IMF because of its SDR 37.149 billion quota.

World Bank

The United States made no contribution (none being requested by the Administration) to the ***International Bank for Reconstruction and Development*** (IBRD) in fiscal 1999 and fiscal 2000. Since its inception, the United States has subscribed $31.96 billion to IBRD capital stock, giving it the largest single vote (16.52%) of any member country. Of that amount, $1.998 billion has been paid in; the rest is subject to call if the IBRD needs money to pay off its bondholders upon its liquidation.

For the same reason, it made no contribution those years to the ***International Finance Corporation*** (IFC), the World Bank's private sector finance affiliate. Since its inception in 1956, the United States has subscribed $569.4 million (all paid-in) to the IFC. It has the largest single vote (23.8%), a total almost as great as the combined vote of the four countries with the next largest votes.

Congress made no appropriation in fiscal 1999 for the ***Multilateral Investment Guarantee Agency*** (MIGA), the World Bank affiliate that measures or guarantees foreign private investors against non-commercial risk from their investments in developing countries. The Administration requested $10 million for MIGA in fiscal 2000. The conference report for the fiscal 2000 Foreign Operations Appropriations Bill would provide $4 million for MIGA. Since MIGA was established in 1989, the United States has subscribed $222 million, enough to

---

[1] Special Drawing Rights are the IMF unit of account. An SDR is notionally a basket of currency. One hundred SDRs is composed of $58.21 U.S. dollars, £10.50 British pound sterling, ¥2,720.00 Japanese yen, and E35.19 euros in German and French currency. Because of the

earn it the largest vote (15.92%) in the body. This is almost as much as the combined total vote for the next four largest member countries.

The ***International Development Association*** (IDA) is the World Bank affiliate that receives a contribution from the United States each year. Other World Bank agencies finance their operations with money borrowed on private capital markets or by leveraging their capital base. IDA makes loans on highly concessional terms to the world's poorest countries. It uses money contributed by the world's most prosperous countries to fund its loan program. Every three years, the IDA donor countries meet to determine how large the next replenishment of IDA's resources should be and what share of the total each donor should contribute. In fiscal 1999, the Administration sought and Congress approved an appropriation of $800 million to fund the U.S. annual share of the most recent IDA replenishment. For fiscal 2000, the Administration requested $803.43 million for IDA. Congress appropriated $625 million.

IMF and World Bank Administrative Budgets

Calculating the budgets of the IMF and World Bank is a more complicated issue than it might seem on its face. The international financial institutions (IFIs) have two kinds of budgets, each financed separately. The first is their administrative budget-- what they spend for staff, travel, and other expenses. The second is their operational "budget"-- what they allocate annually for loans and other forms of assistance. Member countries do not provide any direct support for the IFIs' administrative budgets. Their contributions go to support the IFIs' operational programs.

IMF Administrative Budget

During its fiscal year ending April 30,1999, the IMF budgeted SDR 392.1 million ($520.62 million) for administrative expenses. These were offset in part by $40.5 million in reimbursements from governments or other organizations. It also disbursed $43.9 million for capital improvements on its facilities.

The IMF finances its administrative expenses with money earned through its lending operations. It does not use money from its quota resources or other funds contributed by governments to defray its administrative costs. The IMF lends

interaction pattern among these currencies, the SDR is more stable in value (thus a better unit for keeping IMF accounts) than is any single national currency.

money to its borrowers at a higher interest rate than the rate it pays for the money it borrows to finance these loans. It borrows mainly from the quota sources subscribed by its member countries. The IMF also sometimes borrows supplementary funds elsewhere. To date, it has tapped only official sources (governments or central banks), though it has authority to borrow as well from private sources.

The IMF Executive Board determines each year the interest rate it will charge (rate of charge) its borrowers, calculated in terms of the interest rate paid on SDR. For example, the Board might set the rate of charge at 105% of the SDR rate. The IMF pays countries interest (rate of remuneration)-- generally at the SDR interest rate-- for its use of funds drawn from the lines of credit they established when they subscribed their IMF quotas. During its 1999 fiscal year, the IMF paid interest to the United States and the other countries whose currencies it used to fund its operations at an average 3.82%. It charged most borrowers an average 4.09% for loans financed with quota resources. For loans financed from the new Supplemental Reserve Facility, however, the IMF charges its borrowers the basic rate plus a surcharge ranging from 300 to 500 basis points (i.e., 0.3% to 0.5%).

During its 1999 fiscal year, the IMF received SDR 2.625 billion ($3.696 billion) in operational income and it spent SDR 2.104 billion ($2.962 billion) in remuneration or interest costs. From its net operational income of SDR 827.67 million, it covered all the IMF's administrative expenses and had SDR 435.6 million left over. The Executive Board decided to transfer that amount to IMF reserves.

World Bank Administrative Budget

Each affiliate of the World Bank has its own administrative budget and its own source of funds. No money contributed by governments is used to pay for World Bank administrative expenses.

The ***IBRD's*** administrative expenses totaled $849 million during its fiscal 1999. It financed its administrative costs entirely through operational and investment income. Its income during its fiscal 1999 amounted to $9.642 billion[2] and its total expenses-- including administrative expenses-- amounted to $7.995

---

[2] It received $7.649 billion in income from loans (interest and fees) and $1.716 billion in income from its investment portfolio. It also received another $256 million in income from money invested in its pension plans and $18 million from other sources.

billion.[3] From its net income of $1.647 billion, the IBRD contributed $129 million to charitable activities (such as the campaign in Africa against river blindness). From the remaining $1.518 billion, the IBRD Executive Board gave $352 million to IDA, $90 million to the trust fund for Gaza and the West Bank, and $100 million for the trust fund for Heavily Indebted Poor Countries (HIPC). The Board put the remaining $976 million into the IBRD's retained earnings.

IDA has no staff of its own. It reimburses IBRD for the cost of personnel and administrative services devoted to IDA projects. In FY1999, IBRD charged a $518 management fee to IDA for these services. However, it also credited IDA with $150 million as its share of the income earned by the World Bank pension plan. Consequently, IDA's 1999 net administrative costs totaled $368 million. This was less than the $409 million in net cash generated during fiscal 1999 by IDA operational activities. No money contributed by IDA donor countries was used to cover IDA administrative expenses.

The ***IFC*** has the same president and Executive Board as the IBRD and IDA but it has its own operational staff. Its administrative expenses during its fiscal 1999 totaled $250.02 million. The IFC earned a net $468.76 million in fiscal 1999 from interest charged for loans and $265.2 million from income on equity investments. It also had $101.96 million in income from other sources (mainly fees charged to customers and income from its pension plan) and it set aside $332.94 million as provision against future losses on its loans and investments.[4] The IFC also contributed $3.4 million to special programs. After all costs were accounted for, the IFC's net operating income for the year was $249.26 million. This was retained in its reserves.

MIGA also has its own operational staff. In fiscal 1999, MIGA earned $24.98 million from premiums and fees, $20.43 million from income on its investments, and $3.74 million from its pension fund investments. Its administrative costs totaled $15.24 million and it set aside $23.27 million against future claims. After meeting all its costs, MIGA had a net income of $10.38 million for the year, which it held as retained earnings. MIGA received $6.07 million in capital subscriptions in 1999 from member countries (a figure subsumed above in its financing costs.) The amount listed as retained earnings for the year was greater than the amount of the new capital subscriptions.

---

[3] This included $6.882 billion in borrowing expenses, $246 million for additions to the loan loss reserve, $849 million in administrative expenses, and $18 million in other expenses.

[4] The IFC received $13.17 million during the year in equity subscriptions from member countries, none of it from the United States. This amount is netted into the cost of IFC borrowing to support its loan and investment operations.

IMF and World Bank Operational "Budgets"

The IMF and World Bank do not have annual budgets from which they finance their operations. Rather, they have financial resources (contributed or supported by their member countries) that they use to fund their programs as the situation seems to require. Their operations are demand driven. Countries apply for assistance, the IMF and World Bank staff evaluate their requests, and the Bank and Fund Executive Boards decide which applications should be approved. At the close of their fiscal year, the IMF and World Bank total up the amount they have committed and disbursed for projects. This is, in effect, their operational "budget".[5] Money in the exchequer not used in one fiscal year may be carried over into the next without restrictions in order to finance future operations.

International Monetary Fund

Because it generally makes loans when countries in extreme circumstances come to it for balance of payments financing, the IMF does not have an annual budget limiting the amount it can lend during its fiscal year. The IMF has a certain amount of money available to it through the lines of credit its member countries have accorded it through their quota subscriptions. As of September 1999, IMF member countries had subscribed quotas totaling SDR 215 billion (about $298 billion.) Not all of this is usable money, however. Countries do not borrow their own currency or the money of other countries with weak currencies when they approach the IMF for emergency assistance.

The IMF reported in September 1999 that its usable currencies then totaled SDR 93.3 billion ($129 billion), while its outstanding loan commitments were SDR 16.4 billion ($23 billion) and the minimum working balances on its accounts were SDR 14.2 billion ($20 billion). Thus, its net uncommitted usable resources totaled about SDR 62.7 billion ($87 billion). The IMF must be ready at any time to lend countries the full value of their reserve position. In September 1999, it had a potential liability of SDR 57.3 billion ($80 billion) from this source. It is unlikely, of course, that all countries would draw simultaneously the full value of their reserve. Still, in September 1999, the IMF could have lent only an additional SDR 5.4 billion ($7 billion) before it would be in a position where it could not

[5] The IMF uses the term "operational budget" not (as here) in reference to the total volume of lending for the year but to a decision by its Executive Board specifying the amounts of SDRs and selected member currencies the IMF can use to facilitate new loans and loan repayments during the next 3-month period.

meet new applications for assistance without utilizing resources that are traditionally reserved to cover countries' reserve asset positions. The IMF has been in that position before. In April 1999, at the close of its fiscal 1999, it would have been able to meet only 89% of the demands of its members if they tried to draw their quota reserve simultaneously. In April 1998, it had only enough uncommitted usable resources to meet 45% of such demands. The IMF membership decided in 1998 to increase the Fund's resources in large part because its liquidity ratio had become so small.

The IMF can also draw on a special SDR 34 billion ($37 billion) line of credit provided by the major advanced industrial countries (the GAB/NAB), provided they give their consent. The GAB and NAB are intended primarily to finance loans to countries that have subscribed to the GAB or NAB. In June 1998, however, GAB member countries authorized the IMF to borrow GAB funds to finance a loan to Russia, the first such loan to a non-contributor to the GAB or NAB.

World Bank

World Bank officials have a multi-year plan which shows how much the regional vice presidents may plan to commit for projects in their region during the next few years. This helps the staff decide how many projects they should consider and it tells the Treasurer's office how much money it needs to raise. The schedule is subject to change, however, if the priority among regions should change, if new rush projects are added, or if the projects currently under review take longer to prepare than anticipated.

Among the World Bank agencies, the ***IBRD*** has the most flexibility in its finances The IBRD finances its loan program with money borrowed at commercial rates in world capital markets. It charges its borrowers an interest rate that is one-half percent higher than the average rate it pays to borrow funds. Member countries subscribe to IBRD capital in two forms. Three percent of their subscription is paid-in capital. The rest is subscribed as callable capital, which is payable upon demand. There has never been a call on callable capital. The Bank would make such a call if it were effectively bankrupt and it needed money to pay off its bondholders. With the backing of its callable capital, the IBRD can borrow funds commercially at advantageous rates. Its Articles of Agreement prohibit the IBRD from lending out more than the total value of its capital stock plus its retained earnings. At the end of fiscal 1999, the IBRD's capital stock was worth $188.22 billion and the value of its outstanding loans (including undisbursed commitments) was $117.23 billion. The IBRD's retained earnings totaled $17.71 billion at that time.

IDA funds its loan program with money contributed directly by its member country governments (plus $100 million or so transferred annually to IDA from the IBRD's net income.) It cannot make loan commitments or disbursements in excess of the amount it has on hand. In the Twelfth IDA Replenishment Agreement (IDA-12) approved by the donors in 1998, countries agreed to contribute $11.6 billion in new money to IDA during the period July 1999 to June 2002. IDA is also scheduled to receive about $9.4 billion in loan repayments during that period. If the World Bank choses to lend out an equal amount of these funds each year, it could make new IDA loan commitments totaling approximately $7 billion annually during these three years. The annual flow of contributions and loan repayments varies, however, as does the volume of IDA lending. During its fiscal year 1999, IDA made new loan commitments totaling $6.81 billion (down from $7.81 billion the previous year.)[6]

The **IFC** funds its operations both with money contributed by its member countries and with money borrowed in world capital markets. At the end of its fiscal 1999, its market borrowing totaled $12.54 billion. It had also borrowed another $350 million from the IBRD. The value of the IFC's capital stock was $2.45 billion while the total value of its outstanding commitments for loans and equity investments (some not yet disbursed) was $12.9 billion at the end of fiscal 1999. New commitments in 1999 totaled $2.8 billion. There is no limit, other than that imposed by prudence and the willingness of the market to provide funds, on the amount the IFC can borrow to finance its operations.

MIGA's member countries increased the value of its capital stock to $1.95 billion during fiscal 1999. In the initial issuance of IFC capital stock, countries had to pay-in 20% of the value of their subscription (10% in cash and 10% in non-negotiable non-interest bearing promissory notes); the rest was callable capital. In the new capital increase, 17.65% is payable in cash and the remainder is callable capital. MIGA writes insurance coverage and guarantees; it does not make loans. MIGA had set aside $340 million as of June 1999 as provision against future insurance claims. At present, MIGA may issue coverage for up to 3.5 times the value of its capital stock. The MIGA charter says the "gearing ratio" may be

[6] In fiscal 1999, IDA disbursed a net $5.094 billion to pay for IDA project expenses. It also made grants totaling $149 million for development activities. It received $4.071 billion in new contributions from donor countries and it used $697 million in earlier contributions (which had been temporarily invested) to finance its loan operations. As noted earlier, IDA received a net cash inflow of $409 million from its operations. It also received a net $114 million (an accounting gain only, as IDA does not trade currencies) as a consequence of currency fluctuations.

increased ultimately to 5 times capital. There is talk currently of raising it to 4 times capital stock. In 1999, MIGA issued $1.3 billion in new insurance and guarantee coverage for private investments in 29 countries. The total issued coverage in 1999 was $5.5 billion.

Chapter 3

WORLD BANK: IDA LOANS OR IDA GRANTS?

Jonathan E. Sanford

ABSTRACT

On July 17, 2001, President Bush proposed that the World Bank implement a plan where half of all its assistance to the world's poorest countries would be grants rather than low-interest loans. He said this would enable the Bank increase its levels of assistance for education, health, and other programs aimed at poverty alleviation. It would also keep poor countries from falling further into debt. The increased funding would be tied, he said, to clear and measurable results. The International Development Association (IDA) is the part of the Bank that currently makes low-cost loans (long repayment periods, very low service charge) to poor countries. IDA loans are funded with money contributed annually by donor countries.

Although there has been widespread support for the concept of IDA grants among other donors, multilateral agencies, and the public, many have indicated that they prefer a much smaller program than the President has proposed. Many are concerned about the long-term financial impact a large grant program might have on IDA. IDA funds a substantial portion of its new lending (40% of all commitments planned during the period 1999-2001) with repayments from prior loans. (These are often called "reflows") Over time, if reflows are not available to help cover the cost of future IDA assistance, the cost of the World Bank's concessional aid program to poor countries will gradually rise. The President did not indicate, in his original proposal, that the Administration would support increased funding for IDA to help support the cost of new grants. In December, the Administration said it would be willing to raise the U.S. contribution level by up to 18% if certain institutional changes were made in the World Bank, but it did not link the projected increase to the issue of grants. Some people are concerned that the grant proposal is ultimately a plan to "defund" the World Bank, to bring about the ultimate termination of IDA either because it is too costly to donors or because it does not have sufficient funds.

In 2000, a congressionally-appointed study panel, the Meltzer Commission, made several proposals to replace World Bank IDA loans with grants. One of these would create a large grant program (funded with new contributions) to address poverty alleviation and policy reform issues. A second proposal, though, would basically dissolve the World Bank and use its residual assets to fund a special program – at no cost to anyone – addressing global needs. Many of those with reservations about the President's proposal hear echos of the Meltzer Commission's recommendation – particularly the second recommendation – in his grant plan.

The issue is being negotiated in the series of talks currently taking place on terms for a new replenishment (IDA 13) of IDA resources. In the foreseeable future, the costs and the benefits from a 50% grant program are not dramatically different than those available from the present IDA program. Most of the costs and benefits occur thirty to forty years hence, in a context which may or may not be similar to that faced by developing countries today. Some analysts believe that the underlying controversy may be less about IDA finances and more about influence in the international financial institutions. Should the Europeans develop a common policy front on IFI matters (as they have in this case), they will be the "largest single member country" and their leadership role will be substantially enhanced.

BUSH'S PROPOSAL AND THE RESPONSE

On July 17, 2001, prior to his trip to Genoa for a meeting with the top leaders of the seven leading industrial countries (G-7), President George W. Bush called on the World Bank and other multilateral development banks (MDBs) to provide a major share of their assistance to poor countries in the form of grants rather than low-cost loans. Speaking before several hundred World Bank employees, Bush claimed that his plan would help poor countries without adding to their heavy burden of debt. "I propose," he said, "that up to 50 percent of the funds provided by the development banks to the poorest countries be provided as grants for education, health, nutrition, water supply, sanitation, and other human needs." This would be, he said, compassionate conservatism at the international level. Alluding to protestors who have been calling for a major cancellation of debt owed by poor countries, the President said that his proposal "doesn't merely 'drop the debt' – it helps stop the debt." The increased funding would be tied, the President said, to clear and measurable results.[1]

The White House noted later that the President sought to convert to grants half the money the Bank lends to poor countries annually through its concessional loan facility, the International Development Association (IDA). A few countries borrow both from IDA and from the Bank's regular loan window, the International Bank for Reconstruction and Development (IBRD). Because these "blend" countries would not be eligible for grants, the President's plan would actually involve only about 40% of total IDA funding.

A grant program would have clear benefits, the Administration argued, for economic development and long-run poverty reduction. Besides, spokesmen said, a grant program would allow better assessments ex-ante of project effectiveness. Grants could be tied to clear and measurable policy instruments, to require more prior commitment to achievement of program goals and to link the actual payment of the grant to clear ex-post output measures.[2] The Administration did not explain at the time what the President meant by the comment that grant aid should be tied to ex-ante assessments or that the payment of the grant should be linked to ex-post output measures.

The President's summit colleagues had little comment on his proposal. The G-8 called on the World Bank and other MDBs to take further steps to help poor

---

[1] Quoted in Michael Phillips, "Bush Wants World Bank to Make Grants–Switching from Loans has Large Catch if U.S. Fails to Boost Contributions." *Wall Street Journal.* (July 17, 2001), p. A2. For the full text, see George W. Bush, "Remarks by the President to the World Bank," Washington, D.C. July 17, 2001. Available from the White House web site at http://whitehouse.cov/news/releases/2001/07/20010717-2.htm.

[2] White House. (2001) "Fact Sheet on U.S. Proposal to Increase World Bank Grants to the Poorest Countries."*U.S. Newswire* (Washington) July 20, 2001. The U.S. Treasury Department later released a fact sheet supplying additional points supporting a grant program. It claimed that the President's proposal would make possible a major new increase in funding for education. This would be consistent, it noted, with the President's theme that no child should be left behind, that every child must be educated. "It is often difficult for [the world's poorest countries] to generate the economic returns with which to pay back funds borrowed for education and other development priorities," the Department observed. It makes little sense, either for the borrower countries or the MDBs to be financing projects "with loans that cannot be repaid," it said. More assistance could be provided, with grants, it argued, for health, education, nutrition, water supply and sanitation projects in poor countries benefitting children. In a subtle change, it noted that, under the President's proposal, "*up to* fifty percent" of IDA assistance to the world's poorest countries could be provided in the form of grants rather than loans. [Emphasis added.] U.S. Treasury Department. Fact sheet titled "Increasing Grants and Improving Education in Poor Countries." Dated July 10, 2001 but released after the President's speech.

countries.[3] They did not mention, however, the issue of IDA grants. In a separate communique, the G-7 countries – the major MDB donor countries comprising the G-8 less Russia – said that they might be willing to discuss the concept further. “We support a meaningful replenishment of IDA and, in that context, we will explore the increased use of grants for priority social investments, such as education and health.” They made no comment on the President’ proposal.[4]

Separately, many other G-7 countries expressed opposition to the plan. “It’s not something that we agree with,” indicated Beverly Warmington, spokeswoman for the British Department for International Development. “The World Bank is actually a bank and there are development agencies to give grants. It’s important that the World Bank work alongside them instead of competing with them.”[5] Michael Hofmann, director general for Germany’s Ministry of Economic Cooperation and Development, was also quoted as saying that he thought an important element was missing from the President’s proposal. If it had been accompanied by an announcement that the President would ask Congress to increase the American contribution by a specific amount, he said, “then the whole thing would have had a very different melody.” If none of the G-7 countries really want to increase their IDA contributions, he said “such a suggestion can mean only one thing: reducing the business of the bank.” The French noted that, while they supported the idea of grants, the U.S. proposal went further than they could support. The German government told a meeting of World Bank donors (negotiating terms for a new IDA replenishment) in June 2001 that it could not go beyond 10% grants without breaking a promise to its parliament.[6]

Others have also expressed doubts about the President’s plan. Jerome Booth, an emerging markets fund manager, argued, for instance, that the proposal for

---

[3] Communique. Group of 8 (G-8) heads of state and government. Genoa, July 21, 2001. Available from http://www.G7.utoronto.ca/g7/summit/2001genoa/finalcommunique.html, provided by the G-7 resource center at the University of Toronto.

[4] Communique. Group of 7 (G-7) heads of state and government. Genoa, July 21,2001. Available at http://www.G7.utoronto.ca/g7/summit/2001genoa/g7statement.html.

[5] Joseph Curl. “Bush asks billions for poor nations; Takes proposals to World Bank.” Washington Times. (July 18, 2001), p. A1.

[6] Sanger, David E. (2001) “Rich nations Offer a Hand, But the Poor Hope for More.” New York Times. (July 21, 2001), p. 7. This may be a consequence of the German system of budgeting for IDA contributions. The United States Congress appropriates money for IDA contributions (budget authority), which is available for many years and can be drawn by IDA when needed (outlays) to help fund disbursements for IDA projects. By contrast, according to World Bank sources, the Germans vote money each year for their share of IDA’s expected annual disbursements. Considerable care must be taken to match the amount voted with the amount IDA will actually need to draw in the coming year from the German pledge. The German government has less reason to be concerned than does the U.S. Administration that its will refuse to provide the money.

50% IDA grants was either a preposterous example of ignorance about IDA finances or a ploy to cut the World Bank down in size. He suggested that the effort to expand the flow of grants through IDA might be an attempt by the Administration to cover the fact that the United States was reducing its overall level of bilateral foreign aid.[7] Others questioned whether the IDA donor countries would be willing to contribute the additional funds necessary to make the new plan feasible.[8] Columnist Milan Vesely claims that the new proposal was "posturing." He noted that Condoleezza Rice, the President's National Security Advisor, had said that the grant plan would have no financial impact on IDA for ten years. He observed, that she had not said when or whether the Administration planned to ask Congress for money to help fund future costs.[9] Nancy Alexander , spokesperson for an NGO critical of globalization, suggested that, when combined with the World Bank's proposed Private Sector Development Strategy, the President's plan for IDA grants poses serious risks to the well-being of poor people by reducing their access to the education, health, and clean water services it presumably wishes to support.[10]

On the other hand, the Administration's proposal for 50% IDA grants has elicited strong support from many groups that are deeply concerned about poverty and strongly in favor of programs to promote equitable and sustainable development. Cardinal Bernard Law, Archbishop of Boston, announced that the U.S. Conference of Catholic Bishops "welcomes President Bush's initiative on poverty alleviation." In particular, he said, the Conference welcomed the proposal that "up to 50% of funds provided by development banks to the poorest countries

---

[7] Jerome Booth. "Burdens that can't be passed on." Euromoney, September 2001, pp. 341-43. This article was published in the London-based magazine about the same time that the British government was seeking to persuade other IDA donor countries to resist the Administration's plan. Booth is head of research for Ashmore Investment Management in London, an emerging markets fund manager, and a frequent commentator in the press.

[8] See, for example, remarks to this effect by Mikesell, a professor of economics at the University of Oregon, in his summary of the Commission report. Raymond Mikesell, "Review Article: the Meltzer Commission Report on International Institutions." *Economic Development and Cultural Change* 49:4 (July 2001), p. 887. Likewise, remarks by C. Fred Bergsten, formerly a former high Treasury official during the Carter Administration. Quoted in Alan Friedman, "'Shadow' Group Seeks to Open G-8 to Poor Nations." *International Herald Tribune*. (July 20, 2001), p. 18.

[9] Milan Vesely, "Will Bush Back Words with Deeds?" *African Business*, London. September 2001, pp. 2021.

[10] Nancy Alexander, Director of the Globalization Challenge Initiative, telephone interview with author, January 24, 2002. See the GCI publication "Growing Dangers of Service Apartheid: How the World Bank Group's Private Sector (PSD) Strategy Threatens Infrastructure and Basic Service Provision." *News and Notices for IMF and World Bank Watchers* 2:5 (Winter 2002). Available from www.challengeglobalization.org.

[be] given in the form of grants rather than loans."[11] John Ruthrauff, senior policy analyst for Oxfam America, stated that "Oxfam America supports the Bush administration's position that half of the IDA funds be grants."[12] Increased grant assistance is particularly important, he said, in order to meet the 2015 development goals, help countries invest in their growth, and avoid increasing their debt. David Beckmann, President of Bread for the World, an aid advocacy group, expressed a somewhat more restrained level of support. "Bread for the World supports President Bush's proposal that some of the next replenishment of IDA should be grants," he stated, "with the understanding that the U.S. government will also agree to provide additional funding for the next replenishment."[13]

This chapter explores the different ways a switch from IDA loans to IDA grants might affect recipient and donor countries and the IDA program itself. The report looks at the role which debt repayments for old loans now play in funding IDA's current loan program and identifies some arguments for and against a switch from loans to grants. It also discusses some earlier proposals for shifting

[11] Cardinal Bernard Law. *Statement on the President's Initiative on Global Poverty Alleviation and Increase in World Bank Grants to the Poorest Countries.* Office of Social Development and World Peace, United States Conference of Catholic Bishops, July 19, 2001. Available at: http://www.nccbuscc.org/sdwp/international/gloprov.htm. Cardinal Law is Chairman of the Conference's Committee on International Policy. Catholic Relief Services and Cafod, the overseas development and relief agencies of the Catholic Church in the U.S. and U.K., expressed later a somewhat more muted level of support for the grant plan. The U.S. plan would prevent the accumulation of unsustainable debt by poor countries, said spokesmen for the two organizations, and it would make maximal use of development funds. However, the plan is viable only if donors agree "to offset the cost of reduced repayments to the World Bank resulting from the conversion of loans to grants." The United States could be most persuasive in its advocacy of a grant program, they said, if it would make an "upfront commitment of funds" to allay suspicions that its proposal was merely "posturing in support of the world's poor while continuing to starve them for development resources." They noted that, compared to the size of its economy, the United States provides less foreign aid to poor countries than does 21 other donor countries. See: Loans-to-grants plan needs upfront funds." *Financial Times* [Europe and US editions], January 22, 2002, p. 14. Letter to the editor from the executive officers of both agencies.

[12] John Ruthrauff. *Oxfam America Position on IDA Loans and Grants.* Electronic message to author, January 11, 2002. His statement was approved by Oxfam America's top leadership. It might be noted, though, that Oxfam International, the London-based organization, has expressed more conditional support for the President's plan. Kevin Watkins, a senior policy advisor, was quoted as saying that "We broadly support increased use fo grants in very poor countries, but not the US proposal because of its failure to guarantee funding in the long term." The real problem with the United States, he said, was "that they never put their money where their mouth is." Alan Beattie, "NGOs pressed to back US grant scheme; World Bank move to Replace Loans." *Financial Times* [London Edition], January 17, 2002, p. 9.

[13] David Beckmann. Electronic message to author, January 11, 2002.

IDA to a grant basis and suggests issues that may be relevant to reaching an agreement among the donor countries on this matter.

Initiation of a program of IDA grants might offer opportunities for increased flows of assistance for education, health, and other social programs. However, as discussed below, the operational effects of a shift from IDA loans to grants may be felt only in the second decade after the change occurred and its full impact would be phased in slowly over a period of up to 40 years. A grant program might allow donors to require that recipients give them more opportunities for monitoring program implementation than might be available for programs financed by loans. However, it might also force the donors to choose between increasing their contribution levels or seeing the IDA program shrink in size. Likewise, the change might offer recipient countries some relief from their debt payment burden over the next forty years (since they would not have to repay the grant.) The efficiency of grantfunded programs might be enhanced but the recipient country might also feel less "ownership" for programs when it has little say in their implementation. Some observers believe that this may have a negative effect on its willingness to continue funding for the program or to keep the original policies in place once the donor withdraws and the program becomes its responsibility.

THE DIFFERENCE BETWEEN LOANS AND GRANTS

The Terms for IDA Loans

The World Bank provides assistance to its countries through two loan "windows." Legally, they are separate organizations, though in fact they share a common staff, management, policies, and rules. The International Bank for Reconstruction and Development (IBRD) lends mainly to middle-income countries using funds borrowed at commercial rates in world capital markets. Most IBRD borrowers have annual per capita incomes well below the $5,280 ceiling on eligibility. IBRD loans are repayable over a 10 to 20 year period at interest rates slightly higher than those the Bank pays to borrow funds.

The International Development Association (IDA), by contrast, makes loans to the world's poorest countries. Most IDA borrowers have annual per capita incomes well below the $885 ceiling for eligibility. Some small countries – mostly island countries – with marginally higher income levels and low creditworthiness may also qualify. IDA loans are funded with money contributed by donor countries. The United States presently contributes about 20% of IDA's new resources. As IDA's uncommitted funds are used up, the donors negotiate new plans every three years to replenish its resources. IDA lends without interest and with principal repayments stretching (after a 10 year grace period) over a 20 to 30 years. The borrower pays a 3/4 of 1% service charge to IDA, which the World Bank uses to cover IDA administrative costs. There is no grace period for the service charge obligation. Except for fast disbursing adjustment loans (which go out over 1 to 3 years), IDA loans are disbursed over a period of 8 to 10 years, as work on their projects is completed.

An Earlier Debate on Loans or Grants

There is no impediment in the IDA Articles of Agreement to grants. The IDA Articles specify that "Financing by the Association shall take the form of loans." However, subsequent language authorizes IDA to provide other types of financing in "special circumstances." Deciding whether such circumstances exist is the responsibility of the Executive Board.[14] Perusal of the IDA Articles and IDA operations will show that a number of activities possible only in "special circumstances" (local cost financing or non-project assistance, for example) are now common (if sometimes implicit) procedures.[15]

As Edward Mason and Robert Asher noted, in their official history of the World Bank, IDA is "simply a fund administered by the World Bank."[16] It was created because most poorer developing countries could not afford to borrow from the IBRD. A U.S. government advisory board, headed by Nelson Rockefeller, and a panel of experts at the United Nations both proposed, in the early 1950s, establishment of a new international development agency or authority to provide

[14] IDA Articles of Agreement, at Article V, Section 3. *Articles of Agreement of the International Development Association*. Entered into force September 24, 1960. Available from the Bank's web site at http://www.worldbank.org/ida/idaart.htm.

[15] IDA's Articles of Agreement say, at Article V, Section 1(b), that, except in special circumstances, assistance from IDA "shall be for specific projects." In some years, balance of payments support through structural adjustment loans, sectoral adjustment loans, and reconstruction or rehabilitation loans may comprise upwards of a quarter of IDA lending. Article V, Section 3(e) says that, in special cases, IDA "may make foreign exchange available for local expenditures." This is a regular element of many IDA loans and is embodied in the IDA rules allowing potential suppliers in the recipient country a marginal advantage in price when they seek, through international competitive bidding, contracts to supply goods for IDA projects.

[16] Edward Ma son and Robert E. Asher, *The World Bank Since Bretton Woods*. The Brookings Institution. Washington, D.C.: 1973. The discussion here is based on chapter twelve, an account of the history and operations of IDA.

assistance on a grant basis for activities that were "desirable on social grounds [but] could not bear the full burden of loan finance." Eventually the proponents abandoned the concept of grants in favor of concessional-rate loans, on the expectation that this would be more acceptable to the prospective donor countries.

IDA originated in a proposal by Senator A.S. Mike Monroney (D-OK) in 1958 to create a new international body that would finance development in poor countries by lending to them excess foreign currencies of other poor countries that were currently owned by aid donor nations. Though economically impractical, the Monroney plan was transformed by the Eisenhower Administration into an agency capable of making hard currency loans to poor countries on easy-repayment terms. Monroney's original concept, loans of excess foreign currencies, though a dead letter, is included in the IDA charter. Some donor countries supported Monroney's idea that IDA loans might be repaid in local currency. As Mason and Asher note, the IDA charter "did not foreclose it; but no use has been made of the provision authorizing such loans."

World Bank management was reportedly more opposed originally to the concept of IDA loans than it was to IDA grants, fearing that a concessional loan window would confuse potential bondholders and drive up the cost of IBRD capital. Officially, IDA provides aid in the form of "credits" in order to distinguish it from IBRD "loans." During negotiations on the IDA Articles of Agreement, many prospective donor countries spoke in favor of the concept that IDA should have the authority to make grants. Mason and Asher report that the United Kingdom, France, Canada and the Netherlands were leading advocates of this view, while the United States was in staunch opposition. The IDA charter specifies that all the assistance provided by IDA from original subscriptions must be used for loans, but it holds open the possibility that resources from future replenishments may be used for grants if specifically authorized by the donor countries at that time.[17]

A Decision to Make Grants

As noted above, an IDA grant program may be created only with the consent of the donor countries as expressed in the new replenishment agreement. The Bank's Board of Executive Directors has the authority to determine when "special circumstances" exist but it has no independent authority to create a formal grant

[17] IDA Articles of Agreement, at Article V, Section 2.

program.[18] A two-thirds vote of the donor countries is needed to approve a new replenishment for IDA. The Administration will need broad support from other countries to bring about the establishment of an IDA grant program. In recent decades, the United States has provided about 20% of IDA's new resources but, for historical reasons, it has a 14.8% voting share. Altogether, the principal donor countries have a 61.3% voting share in IDA. As a practical matter, it is extremely unlikely that developing countries would oppose a new replenishment for IDA. As noted before, though, most other donor countries are – at best – lukewarm in their support for a major IDA grant program. The poor countries would likely also look askance on the suggestion if they believe it would reduce the flow of aid they receive from the Bank.[19]

At one time, IDA replenishment agreements could not go forward without the consent of the United States (and therefore the consent of Congress). In recent decades, however, the U.S. contribution share had declined to the point where it no longer has a de facto veto over IDA replenishment plans. The United States also has limited leverage with other donors on these matters. In 1997, other IDA donor countries indicated that – if the United States did not bring its payment arrears up to date – they might create a new international agency to replace IDA. The United States would not be invited to join. Many in the United States believed that this would have serious negative implications for U.S. foreign policy. Congress appropriated $1.035 billion in fiscal 1998 to fully clear the IDA arrears. Many observers doubt that the United States will be able to persuade other donor countries to adopt an IDA replenishment plan whose provisions they do not support.

Comparing the Cost of Loans and Grants

Because of the grace period, IDA receives no reflows from its loans for 10 years. In that respect, IDA loans are the same as grants. Beginning in the 11th year and continuing for the life of the loan, however, IDA receives a stream of repayments of principal, roughly (for a 30 year loan) 3.3% of the amount lent

[18] The Articles specify that the Executive Board shall be responsible for IDA's general operations. IDA Articles of Agreement, at Article VI, Section 5 of the IDA.

[19] See, for example, comments to this effect in Alan Beattie, "Give and Take: European countries are worried that US proposals to replace half of the World Bank's loans to some developing countries with grants could undermine the organization." *Financial Times* , London. (July 20, 2001), p. 20.

initially.[20] Those repayments can be (and are) used to fund new IDA loans. If the IDA donor countries wanted to keep the IDA loan program at a constant level in nominal terms – $6 billion a year, for example – they could reduce their contributions annually at the end of the 10 year grace period by an amount equal to the new repayments being received. Ultimately, IDA would be able to provide a constant nominal level of assistance to borrower countries without any new contributions by donors. By contrast, if the donors want an IDA grant program to stay at a constant nominal level, they would have to contribute the same amount each year for as long as the program exists.

One might also compare the difference in the cost to the donors if they decided to keep the IDA program at a constant $6 billion annually for 20 years and to close it thereafter. If IDA were a grant program, the donors would need to contribute $6 billion annually (a total of $120 billion) during those two decades. By contrast, if IDA were a loan program, they would need to contribute $105 billion to support the same size program, since reflows would pick up some of the cost during the second decade. The donors could then choose what to do with the repayments IDA would continue receiving thereafter. If they chose to have the funds returned to them (rather than assigning them for another purpose), the donors would receive $105 billion in reflows during the next 30 years.

The Benefit to Recipient Countries

The net-transfer of resources from an IDA grant program to the recipient countries would be 100%, since no repayments are expected. By contrast, on a face value basis, the net transfer of resources from an IDA loan is zero, since all the money lent must be repaid.

This calculation overlooks, however, the time value of money. Because the repayment terms for IDA loans are very easy, there is a substantial grant element to IDA loans. The net present value of the repayments from an IDA loan must be discounted substantially because of their negligible interest cost and their long payment terms. World Bank accountants estimate that the grant element of an IDA loan in 2001 was 44% or 47% or 67%, depending whether the comparison is made to G-7 official borrowing, private borrowing, or the standard 10% discount rate used by the Development Assistance Committee (DAC) of the OECD.

[20] This assumes a loan with a ten year grace period and thirty years for repayment of principal. The annual repayment figure would be higher for IDA loans with shorter repayment terms. However, these comprise a minority of all IDA assistance.

A grant program is a one-time transfer of money. By contrast, the IDA loan program is a revolving fund. Thus, it can recycle the grant element of its loans indefinitely as the repayments from old loans are used to fund new loans. (The real value of IDA's future loans will likely be lower in the future, because of exchange rate fluctuations and inflation.) Each subsequent IDA loan would have a positive developmental impact, so long as the projects are effectively designed and implemented. For grants, the money that would have been used for loan repayments would stay in the country. Its developmental impact will depend on the government and the economy's capacity for making effective use of those resources.

IDA's Repayment Record

Some supporters of the President's proposal argue that IDA should shift its assistance program to grants, as they believe there is little likelihood anyway that IDA's existing loans will be repaid.[21] Mary Ellen Countryman, White House assistant press secretary for foreign affairs, told the press that President's plan is simply plain speaking. "Let's call it what it is. A lot of the loans aren't getting paid back anyway."[22]

Others point out, however, that by and large, IDA has a good repayment record. Seven countries are currently overdue in their loan payments. Together, Afghanistan, Congo/Zaire, Congo Republic, Liberia, Myanmar, Somalia, and Sudan are $469 million in arrears. Much of this balance has been accruing since the early 1990s (1988 for Liberia).[23] The total amount lent to these countries was $3.8 billion, most of which is not yet due. At the end of its fiscal year 2000, IDA had $85.8 billion in disbursed loans outstanding to all borrowers.

Those seven countries currently have no effective government or their government is at serious odds with most of the rest of the world. The World Bank

---

[21] See, for example, remarks to this effect in *Newsday*, "Poor Nations Need More Grants, but Who Will Pay?" (Editorial). Long Island, N.Y. (July 19, 2001), p. A36. The *Chicago Sun- Times* opined, favoring Bush's grant plan, that there is "little difference between loans that aren't paid back and outright grants anyway." *Chicago Sun-Times*. "Call It What It IS." Editorial. (July 26, 2001), p.35. Felix Rohatyn also seems to believe that IDA loans are likely to be forgiven anyway. He says that grants are more straightforward and "can be tied to a number of conditions to make them more effective for the recipient country." Felix Rohatyn, "Back to Bretton Woods: the anti-globalization protesters have a point, argues Felix Rohatyn, It's time to reform the IMF and World Bank." *Financial Times*, London edition. (August 20, 2001), p. 17.

[22] Quoted in Joseph Curl. "World Bank contributors oppose Bush plan for grants." *Washington Times*. (July 19, 2001), p. A14.

[23] World Bank. *Annual Report, 2000*. Washington, D.C., 2000. Volume 2, p. 88.

expects that – as has been the case before – they will settle their overdue obligations once their current problems have ended or a new government takes the helm. The World Bank stops making disbursements on its existing loans and it ceases all consideration of possible new loans when a country becomes 6 months or more in arrears. Many IDA borrower countries have no real sources of international credit other than the World Bank.

In their argument that IDA loans are not repaid, the advocates of grants may be referring more to the HIPC program. Heavily indebted poor countries (HIPCs) may qualify to have much of their debt owed to bilateral creditors and multilateral banks forgiven. Qualifying for HIPC assistance remains – though it has been expedited for 20 countries in the past year – a rigorous process. Among other things, countries need to be current on their loan payments and adopt major programs of economic policy reform. HIPC debt is being forgiven, not because the borrowers are not paying, but because the donors are concerned about the human and development costs that will ensue as the debtors continue to service their debts. Except for debt expunged through HIPC, the World Bank does not forgive loans.

Reflows as a Share of IDA Usable Funds

The amount which IDA is receiving annually in principal repayments for prior loans has grown substantially in recent years. Ten years ago, during the World Bank's fiscal 1991, IDA reflows totaled $274 million. In 2000, by contrast, the flow of principal repayments totaled $920 million. By 2005, the amount will likely rise to $1.95 billion. As will be discussed, a substantial share of those future reflows has been earmarked to fund new projects that have already been approved. The inflow of these resources has enabled IDA to shift a greater part of the cost of funding its future loans onto reflows, reducing the amounts required from donor countries. Donors make their contributions in the form of non-interest bearing non-negotiable promissory notes. The balances on those notes are encashed as IDA needs money to fund the disbursements on its existing loans. Overall, in 2000, IDA had a cash flow of $5.6 billion supporting its current disbursement program. Of this, $920 million was from reflows and $4.68 billion was drawn from the donor's outstanding promissory notes. On this basis, in terms of its total operations, IDA loan repayments currently account for 20% of the resources available to fund IDA lending operations.

The figure is different, however, for projects funded from the IDA 12 replenishment plan. In that replenishment, contributions from donor countries comprise about 60% of the funds available to fund IDA loan commitments approved during the period 2000 to 2002. Loan repayments account for the remaining 40%. The pool of IDA reflows earmarked to help fund loans funded with IDA 12 resources does not include only the repayments IDA expects to receive during that three year period. It also includes a major share of the loan repayments that IDA will receive during the following decade during which it will be making disbursements to implement IDA 12 loans.[24]

Reportedly, the IDA donor countries plan to use this same procedure in future replenishments to help reduce the budgetary cost to them from the IDA program. At some point, though, they will likely find that most of the loan repayments scheduled for receipt during a future replenishment period will have already been earmarked to fund loan commitments from earlier replenishments. If successive three-year IDA loan plans are funded in part with reflows that are scheduled for receipts during the next eight-to-ten years, the stream of uncommitted reflows will soon be exhausted. Presumably, at some point, the donors will need to decide whether the existing size of IDA's loan program should be maintained through increased payments or whether it program should shrink to a level that can be supported solely by the donors' contributions.

President Bush did not propose that IDA's existing loan portfolio should be converted retroactively into grants. The World Bank is writing off (through the HIPC program) some IDA debt owed by poor countries. However, no thought has been given to writing off all the IDA debt owed by all countries. Reflows would continue to be available from earlier IDA loans. The current talk about grants concerns the nature of IDA's *future* aid program.

EARLIER PROPOSALS FOR IDA GRANTS

General Support for the Concept

The concept of IDA grants had been under discussion for some time. There seems to be a broad base of international support for the basic concept that some IDA assistance should be provided on grant terms. Until President Bush made his

[24] In effect, the current arrangement resembles a plan proposed earlier by the author. Both assume that future reflows can be pledged for use today either because they will not be needed in the distant future (because of developmental success) or because they will be in replaced by increased donor contributions. If these assumptions are not well founded, then the advisability of both plans may be subject to doubt. See Jonathan E. Sanford, "Feasibility of a World Bank Interest Subsidy Account to Supplement the Existing IDA Program." *World Development* 16:7 (1988), p. 787.

proposal, however, few proposals seemed to contemplate that a large share of IDA resources would be allocated on such terms. The IDA eleventh replenishment agreement (IDA 11) said in 1996 that the World Bank could use some of the resources from the replenishment (in selected cases, in exceptional circumstances, and on a limited scale) for grants. The IDA 12 agreement (1999) said that the World Bank could make some IDA grants in connection with the HIPC program. Until late 2001, at least, most of the donor countries participating in talks about a new replenishment of IDA resources (IDA 13) had reportedly been willing to consider a grant program involving perhaps 10% to 20% of IDA funds. Meanwhile, Bank President James Wolfensohn reportedly favored the idea of an IDA grant program totaling up to $1 billion annually.[25]

U.S. Secretary of the Treasury Lawrence Summers proposed, at the World Bank-IMF annual meeting in September 2000, that IDA should provide more grant assistance to its recipient countries. Specifically, he said, precautions should be taken to avoid loading up heavily indebted poor countries (HIPCs) with new debt once the HIPC program had reduced their foreign debt to sustainable levels. "Further restraint on concessional lending may also be warranted," he said, "including though greater recourse to grant financing." IDA should also put more emphasis, he said, on education, health, and other social programs. Summers did not put a number on his recommendation. Treasury officials suggest, however, that, in private discussions, Summers was advocating a 20% grant level at the time.[26]

Discussion of an IDA grant program has taken place in context where, to an increasing degree, most foreign assistance is given to low-income countries on a grant basis. On the average, between 1971 and 1973, 55% of the official development assistance (ODA) the rich countries provided to poor countries on a bilateral basis took the form of grants.[27] Between 1988 and 1989, grants comprised on average 78% of their bilateral ODA. By 1999, almost 90% of the

[25] John Donnelly "Change at World Bank Requires Donor Support; Some May Balk at Higher Costs." *Boston Globe* (July 18, 2001), p. A24. See also Phillips, *op. cit.*

[26] Interview with William E. Schuerch, Deputy Assistant Secretary of the Treasury for International Development, Debt, and Environment Policy, January 10, 2002. Schuerch served in the same position during the Clinton Administration.

[27] Rutherford Poats, Chairman. *Development Co-operation: Efforts and Policies of the Members of the Development Assistance Committee, 1982* .[Annual Report.]. Organization for Economic Cooperation and Development: Paris, 1982 Table II.A.14, p. 219. The rich countries included in these figures include the 22 members of the Development Assistance Committee (DAC) of the Organization for Economic Cooperation and Development (OECD).

bilateral ODA from the richer countries was grant aid.[28] For many IDA donor countries, all of their bilateral foreign assistance is provided on grant terms.

Congress has spoken favorably on the question of IDA grants. In 2000, Congress included language in the fiscal 2001 foreign operations appropriations act – H.R. 5526, later incorporated by reference into H.R. 4811 (P.L. 106-429) – urging the World Bank to make IDA grants a component of its plan to assist heavily indebted poor countries (HIPCs). Specifically, it directed the Secretary of the Treasury to seek the adoption of a new policy at the World Bank specifying that all new assistance should be on grant terms for countries that have reached the completion point in the HIPC process.

In 2001, the U.S. Congress included language in H.R. 2506, the fiscal 2002 foreign operations appropriations act (P.L. 107-115) reiterating this concern. It directs the Treasury Secretary to give "high priority" and to "vigorously advocate" the adoption of policies (during the current talks about the terms for a new replenishment of IDA resources) which would enable IDA to provide grant assistance (rather than loans) for countries eligible for HIPC debt relief. The House Appropriations Committee said, in the report (H. Rept. 107-142) accompanying its legislation, that IDA should provide all-grant assistance to each HIPC beneficiary country for a three year period following its HIPC decision point. The Committee also said that it agreed with the recommendations of the Meltzer Commission (see below) "With respect to its support for multilateral debt forgiveness under certain conditions and conversion of IDA into an agency making poverty alleviation grants." It is not clear from the report language whether the Committee believed that all IDA assistance to all countries should be provided on grant terms or whether such grant assistance should be limited solely to HIPC countries.

Meltzer Commission Proposals

The Commission Report

The President's proposal was also proceeded by other proposals seeming major reductions (and sometimes elimination) in the international financial institutions (IFIs). Most prominent among these was the March 2000 report of the International Financial Institution Advisory Commission, chaired by Allan H.

---

[28] Organization for Economic Cooperation and Development. Development Cooperation. Table [from *Development Cooperation, 2000*, the annual report of the OECD Development Assistance Committee (DAC).] Available from the OECD web site at http://www.oecd.org/oecd/pages/home/displaygeneral/0,3380,EN-home-notheme-2-no-nono-0,FF.html.

Meltzer.[29] Meltzer is an economics professor at Carnegie Mellon University. To some observers, many of the arguments voiced by the President – the points about increased effectiveness and expost evaluation, for example – resemble those made earlier by that panel. U.S. Treasury Department officials maintain that the Administration's proposal for 50% IDA grants was not derived from the Meltzer Commission report. Rather, they argue, it is based on sound development principles. Linking them together, they say, is guilt by association.

The IFI Advisory Commission was created in 1998, as part of legislation enacted that year authorizing U.S. participation in the most recent quota increase of the International Monetary Fund. The eleven members of the panel were appointed by the House and Senate leadership (six by the Republican majority and five by the Democratic minority.) The Commission issued its report on the strength of an 8 to 3 vote, although one member signed both the majority and minority reports. Many of the Commission's recommendations and findings were controversial. Among other things, it proposed that the World Bank should cease making loans (except in certain circumstances[30]), focusing instead on special purpose grants. Two kinds of grant programs were mentioned.[31]

The Commission recommended that the Bank replace its loan program with a program of grants aimed at alleviating poverty and promoting structural reform.[32] It would not fund the traditional types of development projects. Healthcare, primary education, and physical infrastructure were mentioned as possible areas of emphasis. Focusing on the poorest countries, those with per capita annual income levels below $2,500, it would be funded by contributions from the industrialized countries. The new program would be costly, the Commission said, and "[t]he amount of money requested from legislatures to fund explicit grants should rise." In addition, it said that "[t]he United States should significantly increase its support of effective programs to reduce poverty. The six dollars per capita currently spent is too much for ineffective programs but too little for effective programs."[33]

---

[29] Meltzer, Alan H., Chairman. (2002) *Report of the International Financial Institution Advisory Commission*. March 2000. NP.

[30] The Commission said that, until the African Development Bank was ready to assume full responsibility for development lending in its region, the World Bank should continue making IDA loans to African countries. It also said that IDA should continue making loans to the low-income countries in the Middle East which currently qualify for IDA assistance. There is no development bank for that region. Commission report, p. 94.

[31] The Commission plan was also described later, with some elaboration, by Adam Lerrick, who served as Senior Advisor th Chairman Meltzer. See Adam Lerrick, "A better way to lend a hand." *The International Economy* (Washington), November/December 2000, p. 14.

[32] Commission report, pp. 89-93.

[33] Commission report, pages 91 and 96.

The Commission also proposed that another grant program should be created, terminating and replacing the existing World Bank.[34] Under this plan, the Bank would transfer all or most of its callable capital assets to the regional MDBs, to help them broaden their responsibilities. The World Bank's paid-in capital and retained earnings would be transferred, however, to a special trust fund. The income generated by that trust fund would underwrite a grant program addressing global public goods. These include environment, communicable disease, inter-country infrastructure systems, development of agricultural technology, and the creation of improved managerial and regulatory practices. The Commission did not say how large it thought the program should be. In 2000, IBRD paid-in capital totaled $11.4 billion and retained earnings totaled $19 billion. If this were invested in U.S. Government bonds at 5%, the yield would be in the range of $1.5 billion annually.

In both cases, in what may be the Commission's most innovative concept, the grants would be channeled through private suppliers who would be reimbursed for their costs only if independent auditors found that they had met specific quantitative performance goals which had been agreed to in advance. If the goals were not achieved, the service provider would not be paid. In both plans, reimbursement would be on a sliding scale, declining as a share of total costs as the income level and credit rating of the recipient country increased. Programs in the poorest countries would get a 90% subsidy; those in the most prosperous would get a 10% subsidy. The local government would have no role in the actual implementation of the programs, but it would be expected to pick up the cost not covered by these grants.

The two plans outlined by the Commission were intended to hold program managers to a higher standard of accountability and performance than is the case today. This might increase the efficiency and cost-effectiveness of programs. The donor countries might also be able to require that the implementing agencies allow them to monitor programs funded by grants more closely than might be possible for programs implemented by governments and funded by loans.

Critics contend that there are possibly serious drawbacks to these plans. For example, they say, it is doubtful that many private organizations would be willing to implement IDA grant programs if they have to provide the money to carry out the programs themselves, with no real guarantee that they would be reimbursed later. Few charitable organizations have such deep pockets. The cost of borrowing money to implement these programs (based solely on the prospect of a contingent guarantee) may be prohibitive. Too many things can go wrong – the original goals

---

[34] Commission report, pp. 93-95.

of the project may prove unattainable, close monitoring by donors may complicate the process, or factors beyond the implementing agency's control may hinder success. For-profit contractors might be willing to take the risk, critics note, but the cost (likely substantial) of that risk would need to be built into the price they would charge the international agency.

In any case, assistance programs channeled through private organizations will still need the permission and cooperation of governments. Private organizations (particularly those who are paid only if they succeed) may be vulnerable to demands by corrupt government officials or requirements that funds be spent for sub-optimal purposes. In addition, perhaps for legitimate reasons, governments may be reluctant to pay their share of the costs if they have no control over program operations.

The plan for a grant program addressing global public goods might be a valuable undertaking, particularly if it could be done at no cost to contributors. However, the use of World Bank resources in this manner would have major opportunity costs in terms of other alternatives not pursued. The World Bank and the regional banks already address many of these issues (particularly health) in their current loan programs. International agencies, such as the Global Environmental Fund, World Food Program, and World Health Program address many types of global problems.

The amounts available to fund a grant program for global public goods would also be much smaller than that envisioned by the Commission's plan, critics argue. The regional banks would be unable to make much use of callable capital transferred to them by the World Bank unless it was accompanied by the associated paid-in capital. Callable capital alone would not be a sufficient basis for expanding the regional banks' borrowing programs. Without matching paid in capital and additional reserves, such borrowing would increase their exposure. Too much lending funded in this manner could lead to reductions in their bond ratings. Transfers of paid-in capital would be needed before the regional banks could expand their operations and replace the World Bank, as the Commission recommended.

The amount available to fund the trust fund from IBRD retained earnings may also be less than expected. The Bank's Articles of Agreement say that, if the IBRD terminates operations, any funds remaining after all the Bank's debts have been paid shall be returned to the member countries. This presumably includes the accrued net income of the Bank as well as the paid-in capital. There is no assurance – particularly if major countries disagree with the plan – that many assets would remain after the breakup to fund a global trust fund.[35]

Subsequent Proposals

Some observers have expressed concern that the Bush Administration ultimately seeks the adoption of a plan for IDA somewhat along the lines recommended by the Meltzer Commission. If so, they wonder what effect this might have on future U.S. policy towards the World Bank and IDA.

Their concern was heightened by the appearance, in the week following the President's speech, of a proposal to shut down the World Bank and to use its assets to finance grants. On July 26, 2001, the *Wall Street Journal* published an oped article by Meltzer and Adam Lerrick, his principal advisor on the Commission.[36] It argued that IDA's loan program should be replaced by a self-financing grant system. Meltzer and Lerrick note that IDA currently has $108 billion in rich country contributions on its balance sheets, partly in loans and partly in cash.[37] They argue that IDA could invest these cash balances at what they claim is a conservative rate of 8%, producing a perpetual income stream which might be used to fund $8.6 billion in new grants every year without any further need for donor contributions. It is unclear whether they believe the full assets of IDA should be invested in this manner now or if the cash should be invested now and the reflows should be invested later as they are received Both approaches are implied in their article. They say the World Bank's resistance to their proposal is motivated by intransigence, institution arrogance, and its "lack of basic arithmetical skills."

---

[35] World Bank Articles of Agreement, at Article VI, Section 5. Article V, Section 2 says that the Board of Governors has the authority to determine the distribution of the Bank's annual net income. Section 14 says that the Governors shall determine annually what share of the net income should be placed in reserves and what share should be distributed to members. Although the Governors have chosen annually to allocate all net income to reserves, the money nonetheless the collective property of the member country governments and could be distributed to them upon vote of the Governors. *Articles of Agreement of the International Bank for Reconstruction and Development.* Entered into force December 27, 1945. Available from the World Bank's website at http://www.worldbank.org/html/extdr/backgrd/ibrd/arttoc.htm.

[36] Adam Lerrick and Alan H. Meltzer, "The World Bank is Wrong to Oppose Grants." *Wall Street Journal.* (July 26, 2001), p. A14. See also the reply by the Bank's Senior Vice President and Chief Financial Officer, Gary L. Perlin. Letter to the Editor. *Wall Street Journal* (August 6, 2001), p. 13.

[37] In 2000, the face value of IDA's assets was $101 billion, after allowance for $7 billion in debt written off via the HIPC program. Technically, the $7 billion has not been booked against total assets and is being carried on IDA's books as a negative balance in reserves. See World Bank *IDA Special Purpose Financial Statements*, June 30, 2001.

The concept outlined in the Meltzer-Lerrick plan may be feasible. However, critics argue, its potential benefits should be compared with those available through continuation of the existing program, and that the amount of assistance which might be available through their plan is likely to be smaller than they presume. IDA's assets could be invested, as Meltzer and Lerrick propose, but the fair market value of IDA's portfolio is much smaller than they suggest. IDA does not have the contractual authority to recall its loans or to demand early payment of the balance due. If it wants to turn its loan portfolio into cash, those assets will have to be sold to another party.

According to this interpretation, if IDA were able to sell its assets and the purchasers paid what the Bank considers the "fair market price," it might be able to get $56 billion which it could invest.[38] Ten year U.S. Treasury notes currently yield 5%. Investing the full $56 billion on a no-load, no-cost basis, IDA might be able to realize something like $2.8 billion annually to fund a future grant program. On a grant-equivalency basis, this is less than half the size of the current IDA program. It is also about one-third the amount that Lerrick and Meltzer believe might be available from implementation of their plan.

Two other considerations might be assessed. First, potential purchasers may be unwilling to pay the amount the Bank considers to be the "fair market" value of IDA assets. They may worry that the former IDA borrowers will be less inclined to pay the new private owners of their notes, since the new owners are unlikely to make them future concessional loans. In that case, the amount generated by the proposed investment scheme would be less than that estimated above. Second, IDA's assets likely are worth more if IDA remains a functioning organization than they would be if it were liquidated. In the former case, the debtor countries are more likely to pay and IDA would not need to discount the value of its assets as it uses loan repayments to fund future loans.

Professor Meltzer has spoken out strongly in favor of the President's proposal, though he has given it his own interpretation. The plan will work, he

[38] The face value of IDA's disbursed loan portfolio is about $86.6 billion. According to World Bank accountants, its "fair market value" in June 2001 was between $46 billion and $49 billion. The face value of the portfolio must be discounted, not only for net present value, but also for credit risk, seasoning, multilateral and sovereign risk preferences and other factors. The promissory notes from donors and the IDA's liquidity pool (its remaining assets) are fully committed to finance existing loans. If someone buys those loans, the price would presumably be reduced to offset these undisbursed but committed funds, as IDA has already agreed to use them to cover the IDA share of projects currently being implemented. A new owner would presumably acquire this obligation as well as the funds. Thus, the value of IDA's "cash" resources must be discounted in a manner similar to that used for outstanding DA loans. Including the discounted value of these funds would bring the total up to about $56 billion. See World Bank *IDA Special Purpose Financial Statements*, June 30, 2001, p. 24.

says, and claims by Bank spokesmen that donations would have to increase dramatically are incorrect. "Despite what they say, the grant proposals would be more efficient; that is, they would be able to give more aid with the existing resources," he wrote. For instance, he observed, the World Bank could give half the amount it would normally lend and countries could borrow the rest commercially "because they would have the Bank's guarantee."[39] It might be noted that, under this interpretation of the President's plan, countries would pay commercial interest rates for half the money they used to fund a project and IDA grants would fund the rest. On average, the combined rate they would pay would be higher than the World Bank and other MDBs now charge for their ordinary near-market rate loans. Presumably, if the World Bank guarantees the repayment of the commercial loans, the recipient countries would have to pay the Bank its usual fee for such service.

Brett Schaefer also stated, in a report prepared for the Heritage Foundation, that "Clearly the time has come for the World Bank to implement performance-based grants." The Administration should make sure, he said, that new funding for the next IDA replenishment would be used for the grant proposal. He also proposed that the Administration seek agreement among other IDA member countries for an arrangement to use existing IDA resources for the grant proposal as they are repaid. He said that Congress should prohibit any future U.S. participation in IDA replenishment plans until IDA implements the grant proposal. He said that $873 million would be available to fund grants if the full resources of the next IDA replenishment (presumably $11 billion) were invested at 8% for that purpose.[40]

Schaefer's proposal would also go well beyond that proposed by President Bush. He would have the existing IDA program (which lends $6 billion a year) replaced by a grant program about 15% its size (less if – as suggested by critics – a more realistic interest rate for investments were used and allowance is made for reflows already committed to support previously approved IDA loans.).

THE ADMINISTRATION'S ARGUMENT FOR GRANTS

U.S. Treasury Department officials deny, as noted earlier, that the current U.S. proposal for 50% IDA grants is based in any way on the Meltzer Commission report. They note that Treasury Secretary Paul O'Neill was strongly

---

[39] See Phillips, *op. cit.*

[40] Brett Schaefer, "Real Help for Poor Nations: President Bush's World Bank Grant Proposal." The Heritage Foundation. *Backgrounder*. No. 1466. (August 20, 2001).

critical of the Meltzer Commission's findings in his required report to Congress, discussing steps taken to implement the recommendations of the Meltzer Commission.[41] Virtually every argument and finding was refuted, they argued, in detail.

The developmental effects of IDA need to be enhanced, Treasury argues. The other donor countries say they want to do more, says the principal U.S. negotiator, but – except for the United States – none seem willing to increase their contributions. A grant program would intensify IDA's impact at a relatively modest indirect cost to donors. The World Bank found that a 40% IDA grant program would reduce repayments by approximately $570 million a year in the decade following the end of the 10 year grace period (see below), he mentioned. Considering the overall cost of funding IDA, he argued, this would be a rather modest price to pay. He noted that, with the decline in commercial interest rates in recent years, the grant-equivalency of IDA loans has fallen substantially (to about 65%, he calculated) from much higher levels in the 1980s.

In many instances, he argued, grants are a more appropriate way of providing assistance for long-term needs. Investments in social sector programs are crucial, but their growth effects are not realized until many years in the future. Consequently, they generate little income to help countries repay the loans which financed them. Increasingly, he maintained, most foreign aid is provided on grant terms. Some 99% of the official development assistance that DAC countries provide to very low income developing countries now takes the form of grants. Many of the countries most resistant to IDA grants give most or all of their bilateral aid to poor countries as grants. He noted that, while the United Kingdom was strongly opposing the concept of IDA grants, the U.K. Chancellor of the Exchequer gave a speech in Ottawa supporting the establishment of a new multi-billion dollar trust fund to address (through grants) millennium development goals. He also recollected that a Scandinavian country now opposing IDA grants had advocated 100% grants a decade earlier.

There is no intrinsic reason to believe, he argued, that repayments for IDA loans needed to be recycled through the World Bank for them to be used effectively for development purposes. Arguably, he maintained, if the policies and institutions of recipient countries are sufficient, their governments and private sector should be better able to make effective use of the income and benefits generated by IDA projects to promote their own development. In any case, he asserted, the argument that IDA has an excellent repayment record is misleading. In the past decade, the G-7 countries and others have agreed to forgive most or all

[41] Interview with William E. Schuerch, January 10, 2002.

of the repayments due from earlier bilateral aid loans to heavily-indebted poor countries. IDA has become, in effect, a preferred creditor. The donor countries have been willing to forego repayment of their old bilateral loans in order to ensure that debts to IDA can be repaid. Since IDA has no bondholders (like the IBRD) who must be repaid, and since the countries forgiving bilateral debt are the same ones responsible for most IDA contributions, he argued, IDA's high repayment record is not an accurate reflection of its financial situation.

There is no relationship, the Treasury Department asserts, between the President's proposal for 50% grants and the World Bank's private sector development strategy. "Treasury is taking its policy leadership from the President's speech at the World Bank on grants," stated the official principally responsible for implementing U.S. policy.[42] "That speech has a list of purposes for which grants might be used – education, health, water and sanitation, and a couple other things. That list does not include private sector activities or private provisioning of services." He indicated that the IDA deputies had agreed, during their negotiating sessions, that nobody was against the concept of private provisioning of services *per se*, though several countries had reservations. Everybody also agreed, he said, that governments are responsible for these activities and any private programs would need to be monitored by them.

British and Other Views

Clare Short, the U.K. minister for international development, has taken the lead in mobilizing opposition to the U.S. proposal for expanded IDA grants. The Scandinavians and other European countries have also expressed strong reservations concerning the U.S. plan. Reportedly, they believe that poor countries will be less likely to squander World Bank aid if they know they will have to repay it some day. Some also reportedly suspect that Treasury Secretary O'Neill seeks to undermine IDA's financial base through advocacy of the 50% grant scheme.[43] Development Minister Short has reportedly stated that "IDA is very valuable and we are looking to increase our contribution substantially. But if it is compromised [by a large grant program], we would look to give more bilaterally instead." France, Germany and Japan have indicated, by contrast, that with the

[42] Interview with William E. Schuerch, February 6, 2002.

[43] Paul Blustein, "U.S.-Europe Clash Stalls World Bank Aid Plan; Bush Seeks Grants, Not Loans." *The Washington Post*, January 30, 2002, p. E1.

declining international value of the euro and yen, they cannot afford to contribute the same share to the new IDA replenishment as they gave to the last.[44]

The British government issued a statement in February 2002 further explaining its views on the issue of IDA grants or loans.[45] It made four points. First, it asserted, the current system makes more effective use of the limited aid funds which are available to help poor countries. Reflows from old loans are a major element of the procedure for financing IDA. With grants, there would be a gap – billions of dollars a year in the third and forth decades – that would have to be filled by major increases in donor contributions. "It seems reasonable to assume that there will be an ongoing need for IDA finance," it stated. "On this basis, we should be taking a long term-view."

IDA should remain a loan program, the statement argued, because this enhances ownership and promotes effective cooperation among donor agencies. The World Bank and the other international development agencies should work in partnership, not in competition. "A clear and selective strategy for IDA and effective collaboration amongst agencies are two of the great reforms we have all worked on in the past few years."[46]

Third, said the statement from Ms. Short's department, "We do not accept that IDA's current terms are always inappropriate for interventions in health or education, or that cheaper finance would encourage countries to invest in these areas more." Donor countries should not try to dictate to developing countries what their priorities should be, it said. Rather, the donors should encourage countries to establish their spending priorities through a system of broad national consultation, such as is embodied in the Bank's Poverty Reduction Strategy process. Grants should be reserved for special situations – such as post-conflict recovery or regional programs to combat infectious disease – where IDA's normal loan program might be inappropriate.

Finally, the British disputed the argument that IDA countries could not afford to repay IDA loans. The statement noted that IDA's repayment record has been

---

44 Alan Beattie, "Deadlock in dispute over money for poor nations; World Bank Contributions." *Financial Times* [London edition], January 15, 2002, p. 10.

45 [U.K. Department of International Development.]"Loans or Grants: IDA's Concessional Lending Role." ND. Provided to the author by the Office of the U.K. Executive Director to the World Bank and IMF, February 8, 2002.

46 The British also emphasized this point in an earlier statement on IDA. "Substantial grant funds are available from other development agencies–particularly the UN, bilateral donors and the European Commission," it observed. "It is important that the World Bank should work in partnership with these other agencies not in competition with them, with each institution respecting each other's comparative advantages." See: Office of the U.K. Executive Director to the World Bank and IMF. Statement titled "Loans or Grants: IDA's Concessional Lending Role." ND (Provided to author on August 6, 2001.)

very good. IDA loans "provide a bridge," it said, "between grants and non-concessional borrowing." By demonstrating that they can repay concessional loans, countries help lay the groundwork for their future entry into the regular international financial system. Even the idea that IDA grants should be targeted to HIPC countries (after they have relieved debt relief) is a mistake, the statement argued. "If poor countries exiting from HIPC cannot even service new debt on IDA terms," it said, "then HIPC will have failed." Rather than planning for failure, it maintained, the international community should expect that HIPC graduates will grow, develop, and take their place in the world economy.

NEGOTIATING IDA'S TERMS

During 2001, representatives from the IDA donor countries met on several occasions to discuss terms for the next IDA replenishment. The World Bank has reportedly suggested that an appropriate level for the IDA 13 replenishment would be SDR 18.1 billion (about $23 billion), including SDR 500 million for HIPC debt forgiveness. Of this amount, some $12.5 billion would be solicited as new contributions from donor countries. The remainder would be provided from IDA reflows and other sources.

At the first negotiating session in February, the World Bank presented an analysis of the potential effects a grant program might have on IDA finances. The Bank reported that a 20% grant program would drain IDA's resources by some $400 million during the first ten years and $4.3 billion during the next decade. On the other hand, the Bank reported, IDA's financial base could be strengthened if a 20% grant program were matched by a program hardening the repayment terms for 20% of IDA's remaining loans. The Bank suggested that higher interest charges and shorter repayment periods might be appropriate anyway for countries approaching graduation or for countries with per capita income levels near the top of the eligible range.[47]

President Bush's proposal for a 50% grant program changed the context for the negotiations. Instead of 20% being the leading edge, it now became a level far lower than that preferred by IDA's largest donor country. The U.S. representatives reportedly told the other donor countries in October that a failure to move towards grants could jeopardize the size of the U.S. contribution. The 50% proposal

[47] World Bank. *IDA Eligibility, Terms and Graduation Policies.* International Development Association, January 2001. Prepared for the first IDA 13 negotiating session in Paris, February 28-March 1, 2001. Available from the World Bank web site at http://www.worldbank.org/ida/ida13docs.html.

widened the differences among the donor countries. As noted earlier, the British strongly opposed the U.S. proposal while some other countries were reportedly willing to go as far as the 20% figure presented in the February World Bank report. In November, Ms. Short was reportedly seeking to rally other countries to oppose the U.S. proposal and to isolate the United States.[48] As they prepared for the upcoming December negotiating session, the Europeans and Japanese lined up, almost without exception, in opposition to any large scale movement towards grants.[49] The Canadians were reportedly willing to consider steps that would increase the grant element of IDA lending (by lowering or waiving the service charge and extending the repayment period) while preserving the basic principle that IDA assistance must be repaid.

By the December negotiating session, in Montreux, Switzerland, the IDA deputies had reached agreement on all issues save the actual size and proportional distribution of the new replenishment and the share allocated for grants. The United States put on the table in Montreux a two part proposal.[50] "The U.S. is willing to *substantially* increase its individual contributions to the 13th replenishment of the International Development Association (IDA)," it said, "with agreement on two important issues." First, it stated, the United States wanted to see the adoption of a results-based contribution framework. Second, it wanted a substantial increase in the share of grants. "If the conditions were met, " Treasury said, "the full U.S. contribution would represent an 18% increase from IDA-12."[51]

The U.S. proposal was somewhat vague as to the nature of the results-based contribution framework it desired. Basically, it said that the U.S. would increase its contribution in phases contingent on "explicit input actions (such as country fiduciary, investment climate and poverty diagnostics necessary to design and evaluate credible lending programs) and development results in areas most crucial to growth and poverty reduction (such as school enrollment rates, people with clean water, sustained productivity growth, per capita incomes, and poverty

---

48 Alan Beattie, "UK minister aims to halt proposal to replace loans; World Bank aid." *Financial Times*, London edition. (November 17, 2001c), p. 8.

49 Alan Beattie, "Feeling the pressure: World Bank, by Alan Beattie; the bank has been beset by criticism of its direction and management style." *Financial Times*, Surveys edition. (November 30, 2001), p. 4. See also: *Jiji Press English News Service*. "U.S. Out of Step with Japan, Europe on IDA Capital Hike Talks." Tokyo (December 11, 2001), p. 1.

50 U.S. Treasury Department. (2001a) Paper titled "U.S. IDA-13 Objectives." ND Presented to the IDA deputies negotiating session in Montreux, Switzerland, December 8, 2001. Photocopy provided by Treasury Department to author.

51 The 18% increase in U.S. contributions is calculated in dollar terms. In terms of the SDR, the unit of account for IDA replenishments, Treasury officials said the U.S. increase would be closer to 25% because of recent movements in the relative value of the U.S. dollar compared to the currencies of other donor countries.

rates.)" The United States invited other countries to explore ideas for trigger mechanisms along these lines. The Treasury official heading the U.S. delegation commendted later that, in practical terms, this probably would require some type of institutional changes in the Bank, since changes in world poverty levels or the success of IDA programs would not be measurable (even with maximum effort) in just two years.[52]

The negotiations were adjourned from Montreux with no settlement of the outstanding issues. The other donor countries were reluctant to go to, or much beyond, the 10% level while the United States held firm for the 50% goal. The other countries had no clear response to the U.S. proposal for adoption of a results-based contribution system. Many countries were concerned that the changes sought by the United States might alter the multilateral banks in ways that ultimately would hurt the poor. Many still had deep reservations about the long-term impact a large grant program might have on IDA finances. The IDA donor countries plan to meet in late February 2002 for another negotiating session, if they believe that sufficient grounds for agreement on a final plan have been developed. The issue is likely to be discussed at various levels during the series of G-7 meetings scheduled during late January and early February. Some participants in the discussions are reportedly pessimistic. Others believe that adequate grounds for agreement will be found. "There is a general consensus," said a close World Bank observer, "that there will be a consensus."[53] He also noted that, until the British and Americans can work something out, "it will be hard to get a resolution." Ultimately, he observed, "Everybody knows its going to end up somewhere in the middle, but they haven't gotten to that point yet."[54]

As requested by its stockholders, the World Bank prepared another paper for the December session analyzing the potential financial and program impact of

---

[52] Interview with Schuerch, January 10, 2002. He said this was not a plan to make disbursements for IDA assistance contingent on the recipient meeting specific performance benchmarks (as proposed by the Meltzer Commission or Meltzer and Lerrick.) Rather, Treasury had in mind additional improvements in IDA's new (since 1998) country policy and institutional assessment procedure. The latter seeks to target the bulk of IDA resources to countries that score highly on twenty performance criteria. This tries to ensure that most IDA money goes to countries deemed most likely to use it effectively. Reference was made by Schuerch to several papers (not available to the public) prepared by World Bank research staff and to information on the Bank's web page. For the latter, see World Bank. *How IDA Resources are Allocated.* Updated November 2000. Available from the Bank's web site at http://www.worldbank.org/ida/idaalloc.htm.

[53] John Donaldson, senior official in the Bank's external affairs office, in Julian Borger, "Short Blocks US Plan for World Bank Grants," *The Guardian* [Manchester, UK]. January 17, 2002, p. 16.

[54] John Donaldson, in Paul Blustein, "U.S.-Europe Clash Stalls World Bank Aid Plan; Bush Seeks Grants, Not Loans for Poor," *The Washington Post.* January 16, 2002, p. E1.

several different kinds of IDA grant programs.[55] These included grants linked to certain uses, 50% grants limited to countries with annual per capita income levels below $350, both of these options with easier terms for remaining IDA loans, and 50% grants for all IDA-eligible countries. Substantial differences in the financial impact on IDA were noted. However, in certain cases (grants limited to certain uses, softening the terms and perhaps waiving the service charge), the Bank was able to present figures showing that only 10% of total IDA resources would be needed while 50% of the projects or programs in the group could be made available on grant terms. For the categories reserving IDA grants for low-income, however, the share of total IDA resources devoted to grants was upwards of 20% and for the U.S.-preferred option the total was (for reasons explained above) about 40%.

The Bank later reported that the U.S.-preferred IDA-only grant program would have major out-year costs. During the first decade, it said, the cost to donors would be about $30 million annually. During the second decade, the average annual cost would be $570 million. In the third decade, if the donors want to maintain IDA at its existing level, another $1.8 billion annually in new contributions would be required. During the forth decade, to keep IDA the same size, the donors would need to contribute an additional $3.5 billion annually.[56]

WHERE TO GO FROM HERE

Critics hear in the proposal by President Bush echos of the plans put forth by Professor Meltzer and his colleagues. The conditional reimbursement plan mentioned in the President's original speech – no payment to the private supplier of services unless goals are achieved – is similar to that proposed in the Meltzer Commission. The President's call for more IDA aid for education, health, and poverty alleviation programs reminds many of the Commission's plan to scrap the World Bank's other loan priorities in favor of a special concentration on poverty alleviation and global public goods. Also, by not discussing publicly the long-term costs or U.S. additional contributions, the President seemed to suggest in his

---

[55] World Bank. "Grants and Concessionality in IDA13." International Development ssociation, November 2001. Prepared for the fourth IDA 13 negotiating session in Montreux, Switzerland, December 6-7, 2001. Available from the Bank web site at http://www.worldbank.org/ida/ida13 docs.html.

[56] [World Bank]. "Measuring the Costs of IDA Grants." ND. Unpublicized memorandum sent to IDA donor countries after the December meeting. The amounts are larger than those reported in the November 2001 paper on grants and concessionality. Provided to author by World Bank on February 6, 2002.

speech that a major IDA grant program could be instituted at little or no cost to the donor countries. The Treasury Department's later initiatives during the IDA negotiations, including the suggestion that the U.S. contribution might be increased by 18% and the Secretary's criticism of the Meltzer Commission plan, were not publicized or given much public emphasis. In any case, it was (and remains) unclear how the Department's negotiating position comports with the goals announced in the President's speech.

Concern on this score is compounded by statements by some supporters of the President's plan. For example, Schaefer says that "In all respects, the grant system proposed by the Meltzer Commission would be superior to the current World Bank lending system." He believes that President Bush has endorsed the Meltzer plan. In the next sentence, he says that "[t]he Bush Administration recognizes this fact," in the President's July 17 proposal. The President's plan is, he says, "a variation of the Meltzer Commission proposal."[57]

The Global Challenge Initiative (GCI), a long-time critic of the IMF and World Bank, picked up on this point. "Many of the opponents of the U.S. [grant] proposal see the U.S. as potentially destroying the World Bank and supplanting it with a small grant-giving agency that spearheads output-based aid schemes," it stated. It observed that this model had been proposed earlier by the Meltzer Commission. A grant program linked to output-based aid and a broad emphasis on privatization in the health, education, and clean water sectors would substantially reduce future access by poor people to public services and open the field to unregulated activity in these (and other) areas by foreign investors, GCI concluded.[58]

A World Bank official was quoted as telling the press in mid-2001 that the President's decision to put a specific number on his proposal for IDA grants was "distracting."[59] From this perspective, it raised many extraneous issues and made the negotiations on the issue more difficult when he announced a figure much larger than those the other countries had considered. Concern, on the part of other donors, about the size, implications, and possible hidden motives behind the President's seems widespread.

From another perspective, though, the President's bold announcement pushed the discussion into new areas which might not have been explored otherwise. John Taylor, the current Undersecretary of the Treasury, is quoted as saying that the one-half figure is not negotiable and the other donor countries need to come

---

[57] Schaefer, *op. cit.*, pp. 7-8.

[58] See GCI, "Growing Dangers of Service Apartheid," *op. cit.*

[59] John Donaldson, quoted in Anna Willard, "USA to Stand Firm on World Bank Grant Proposal." *Reuters*. (August 6, 2001.)

around to the U.S. position. "We will go all the way to Bush's proposal – I don't see it as a bargaining situation."[60]

This may be an effective strategy, as a final decision on the IDA replenishment must be reached in early 2002 so there will be time for national legislatures to act during the year. Many people believe the Administration is less desirous than are other donors of achieving a large replenishment. On the other hand, Taylor's firm language may be a negotiating ploy, some observers note, especially in the light of a parallel U.S. campaign to win broad multilateral support in its efforts to combat international terrorism.

There would appear to be grounds for compromise on this issue. In money terms, the two sides seem far apart. In other ways, however, the difference between the parties may be smaller. IDA lent about $2.13 billion for health, education, social protection, and water and sanitation projects, about 32% of the total. Likewise, IDA lent $2.87 billion in 2001 to countries with per capita income levels below $350 annually. This comprised about 41% of the total. If half that assistance had been provided on a grant basis, either 15% or 20% of IDA resources would have been required. Either approach could be the basis for a split-the-difference type compromise.

There might be room for a functional compromise. In addition to a modest grant program, the replenishment might provide that a major share of IDA's loans to very poor countries would be repayable in local currency. This would retain the principal that loans must be repaid and – with a maintenance of value provision – the value of the repayments would be retained. The local currency could be used for loans to the issuing country covering local cost financing, recurring costs, or other similar activities. In effect, though loans, these repayments would not require that countries find foreign exchange to cover the cost of projects whose economic benefits will not be realized until many years in the future.

Likewise, there might be room for a procedural compromise which allows everyone to do what they want. Instead of the IDA 13th replenishment being a single account, the donors could establish two sub-accounts, with contributions to either being counted as contributions to the replenishment as a whole. The funds contributed to IDA 13A would be used to fund loans, as in the past. Those contributed to IDA 13B would be used to fund grants. If the other donors channeled 10% of their overall contribution to the grant account and the United States contributed its entire share, the amount available for grants would comprise 28% to 31% of the total replenishment (depending on the final U.S. share.) The grant component would be even larger if other countries contributed a larger share

[60] John Taylor, quoted by Willard, *op. cit.*

or if the World Bank put the entire amount it usually contributes (from IBRD net income) into the grant account. The latter might be done on the understanding that funds would be used for projects fighting AIDS and other endemic diseases, for assistance to the poorest, and for programs addressing global public goods. All have been priority concerns of the Bank and IDA in recent years.

There might even be room for a hybrid compromise. Half the IDA's loans to poor countries might be made on a conditional basis, where the repayments are automatically waived each year (as a contractual right) so long as the borrower meets certain specified criteria. For instance, no repayment would be required if the recipient continued to meet the education, health, poverty reduction or other performance requirements in the original loan plan. This would de facto convert future loan repayments into future grants and establish a 40 year incentive plan for recipient countries.

From the U.S. perspective, it appears that the Administration may need an agreement where 50% of some type of IDA assistance will be allocated as grants. Otherwise, the new IDA 13 replenishment bill may face renewed criticism in Congress as well as opposition by the Administration's conservative supporters. By contrast, with a 50% agreement of some type, the Administration might be able to present the replenishment plan as a victory and a demonstration that the World Bank can be "reformed." This would be particularly so if the new replenishment required broadly-supported institutional changes or the adoption of improved methods for monitoring project implementation and outcomes.

From the perspective of the other donor countries, by contrast, it would appear important that any agreement for IDA grants should not threaten the financial integrity of the program. One possibility might be an IDA 13 replenishment plan in which a larger share of the new resources comes from donor contributions and a smaller share comes from the advanced commitment of future reflows. More reflows could be scheduled for use in financing new loan commitments only when they were actually received. This would leave available for future IDA replenishments a larger share of the remaining future reflows. On this basis, any long-term negative effects that a grant program might have on IDA finances would be limited in their impact and would be spread out over a longer period of time.

Several other observations might be made. First, it is not clear how much grant money the poor countries could afford to receive, particularly if the assistance requires increased spending for social sector programs. Grants will relieve countries of the need to budget for repayments. However, they can add to countries' budgetary costs in other ways. The MDBs usually finance the import costs of projects. The borrower normally pays the local costs as well as the recurring costs for programs or projects once they are established. The recipients would have to find room in their national budgets – often a difficult task – for these costs. Health and education programs generally require larger proportional inputs from the recipients than do many other kinds of projects. If the recipients cannot afford the counterpart and recurring costs of new health and education programs, it may be inappropriate for IDA to set aside large sums for grants to sponsor them.

Second, concern about the long-term implications of the Bank's prospective private sector development strategy need not be an impediment to adoption of a grant program. President Bush said, in his original speech, that performance based assistance should be part of his proposed grant program. However, it is not evident from his speech and subsequent Administration statements that all IDA grants need be provided on this basis. If the parties were willing, the new replenishment agreement could provide that none or only a small portion (perhaps up to 10%) of IDA grants could be used in this manner.

Third, the growth effects of different types of programs may merit consideration. Treasury Secretary O'Neill said earlier in 2001 that he believed the MDBs should put less emphasis on peripheral matters and more stress on programs that encourage economic growth and increased productivity. Investments in human capital (through education, health, and related programs) will improve the productivity of labor in the long run. However, investments in infrastructure (power, transportation, etc.) and capital facilities may boost efficiency levels and promote growth and development somewhat faster. Likewise, programs promoting economic policy reform, better governance, stronger institutions, and recovery from war or natural disaster can have strong medium-term growth effects. Also, improvements in infrastructure and reform are more likely to stimulate inflows of foreign investment. Unless the donors expand the size of the IDA program, more IDA assistance for humanitarian programs will necessarily mean less assistance for other types of programs.

Fourth, steps may be required to protect U.N. grant programs from competition from an IDA grant program. The terms and objectives of an IDA grant program will need to be coordinated with those of the U.N. Development Programme, World Food Program, and other international grant-making programs. Some critics of the President's proposal worry about "mission creep,"a concern that IDA might compete or undercut the other U.N. agencies if it has a sizable grant program. However, there is a great deal of overlap and similarity among the multilateral banks and the U.N. development agencies these days in the types of programs they all finance. The World Bank may have made incursions into the other agencies "turf," but there seem to have been at least as many incursions in the other direction as well. Supporters of the existing arrangement argue that an IDA loan program is desirable, if only because it teaches borrower countries that the repayment of debt has positive consequences. However, questions have been raised as to whether the principal difference between IDA and the U.N. development programs should be their repayment terms and not in the types of activities they support or the skills and priorities they bring to the table. IDA loans or IDA grants, the issue of overlap among the international aid agencies is one which merits closer examination.

Fifth, attention might also be paid to the equity effects of future changes in IDA's repayment formula. The World Bank has suggested, for example, that IDA might "harden" some of its repayment terms in order to offset the costs of a grant program. Caution should be exercised regarding plans for "gearing up" the creditworthiness of borrower countries or for promoting "efficiency" in IDA operations. In themselves, these may be worthy concerns. Countries may enhance their creditworthiness if they are able to pay a gradually increasing interest rate for their IDA loans. The efficient use of IDA resources may also be improved if less needy countries pay more for IDA loans. However, if the proceeds of the higher IDA interest costs are used to defray the costs of IDA grants, then some of the cost of the grant program will have been shifted from the rich donor countries to the poor countries who are only slightly better off than their poorer neighbors.

Sixth, the claim that recipient countries will be more likely to waste IDA resources if they receive assistance in the form of grants rather than loans might be questioned. This argument seems to presume that the Bank's normal oversight mechanisms would break down or the Bank would be more willing to fund weak projects through grants than it would through loans. There is no evident reason why the Bank would use different standards for evaluating or implementing grant projects than it would for loan projects. Likewise, there is no way of knowing beforehand whether the Bank will make better use of IDA resources if it gets them back as loan repayments than the recipient will do if it had them as a grant. Nobody knows whether the governments of IDA-recipient countries will be wise or foolish thirty years from now. An appropriate concern might be whether the poor in those countries are the principal beneficiary of the activities funded by the hypothetical loan repayments. In any case, future country performance issues can be addressed at least as easily through the Bank's country review process as through future loan programs.

Seventh, it seems apparent to most observers that little real progress can be made in a discussion about IDA grants if other participants harbor serious reservations about the longterm motivations of the United States. From press reports and discussions, it seems that some countries worry that the President's grant proposal would "defund" IDA, substantially increasing the future cost of the program and possibly leading to its closure or substantial reduction in size. Few people seem to know about the Administration's statement in December 2001 that it might support an 18% increase in U.S. contributions. Progress in the negotiations might be enhanced if all donors were willing to discuss and include language in the final report describing their long-term plans and expectations. In particular, they might state whether they believe their countries' future contribution levels to IDA should increase (as a decline in future reflows diminishes the amounts of money IDA has available to support new loans) or whether they believe the IDA program should shrink in size as the inflow of future debt repayments gradually declines.

In many respects, it appears that the controversy about IDA loans and grants is not really one about IDA finances. The costs and benefits of a grant program would be phased in gradually and would become significant only thirty to forty years hence. The real benefits from a grant accrue, not at the time of the award, but at the time the repayments for the alternative loan would need to have been made. In fact, IDA could reduce its assistance levels to former grant recipients by amounts comparable to the hypothetical loan repayments and countries would have the same amount available in future years to fund new development projects as they would have if all assistance had been financed through loans. Whether or not they would use it wisely and for anti-poverty purposes is a different concern.

The World Bank reports that a grant program would require billions of dollars in new annual contributions from donors thirty or forty years hence if IDA is to be kept at the same level as before. This presumes that the donor countries continue to include a 50% grant provision in future replenishments. It also assumes that the demand for development aid will be as great forty years from now as it is today and the World Bank will need those IDA reflows in 2040 to fund new IDA loan programs whose repayments would stretch to the end of the century and fund new loans going well into the next. All these contingencies are speculative. If they were agreed on basic principles, the donor countries and the Bank should be able to work them out over the coming decades.

On another level the controversy seems to be, not IDA finances, but the donor countries' relative influence in international agencies. Until recently, the United States has been the predominant voice and influence within the World Bank. Increasingly, however, it seems that the other donor countries are becoming more assertive in their views. In part, this may be due to concern about the direction of U.S. policy. In part, though, it also seems a function of their growing relative size. Already, it appears that the European countries are devising their policies more in consultation with one another than in separate consultations with the United

States. Should the countries of the European Union ever develop a common policy position, they would be in effect the largest single "member country" in the Bank. The debate on IDA grants seems to presage a situation where influence in the multilateral banks will be more evenly distributed and where – unless the United States makes major efforts to increase its financial support and to reshape the way it tries to influence policy – the Europeans in particular will seek and find a larger role. What effect this may have on the organization and operations of the multilateral agencies remains undetermined.

Chapter 4

WORLD BANK: A STEP FORWARD AND A STEP BACKWARD - DO WE NEED THIS INSTITUTION?

*Vikas Nath**
Inlaks Fellow, London School of Economics

ABSTRACT

This chapter charts out the evolution of the World Bank and provides insight of its changing roles and functions, and the consequence of its actions ranging from inequitable development to environmental destruction. It examines why the World Bank has been able to create so much stir in the last 50 years of its existence that led to pressures for "change" from both within and outside the World Bank. The paper takes a critical look on the current reforms process and how it has changed the World Bank's approach to development. It concludes that World Bank inspite of the shortcomings and the slow-learning approach still holds potential to bring about a positive change, and suggest ways by which the institution can improve the effectiveness of its involvement in the global development arena.

* www.vikasnath.org; v.nath@lse.ac.uk

It is not Easy Being a World Bank

After its conceptualization in the Second World War to help rebuild Europe to its reincarnation a global development agency, the World Bank has singularly garnered more controversy and criticism than any other international financial or development institution. It has faced threats and oppositions from conceivers, supporters and its fund recipients alike. Every step taken by the World Bank is closely monitored by several watchguard agencies which have sprung around it. And the Bank today is engulfed with tremendous pressures to either reform itself or perish.

Such pressures are however not new in the Bank's history and they have always been exerted by one or other of these groups- donor governments, national governments, donor agencies, citizen groups and even the workforce within the Bank. "Ya Basta !" ("enough is enough!") were the cries raised by the critics during its Annual Meetings in Madrid which marked the 50 years of World Bank's existence. And the recent Meltzer commission report (2000) portrays World Bank as irrelevant to the mission of promoting development and reducing global poverty.

The fact that the World Bank still exists is a miracle in itself.

Emergence of Bank as a Global Development Agency

In 1944, 43 countries met at a conference at Bretton Woods, USA. It led to the establishment of the International Bank for Reconstruction and Development (IBRD) to give loans for reconstruction of Europe after the World War II. For instance, In 1950, a total of US$28,600,000 was made available by IBRD for the reconstruction and modernization of steel capacity in France, Belgium, and Luxembourg. (World Bank website). The demand for funds however, failed to match the expectations of World Bank, and its lending portfolio failed to grow within the industrialized countries. The constant pressure on IBRD to invest eventually forced it to look beyond the western frontiers to channelise surplus funds from rich to poor nations. The lack of any expertise in dealing with problems of developing countries, plentiful funds in the coffer and the pressure to lend made a heady concoction. A disaster was imminent and it did in form of overnight resurrection of IBRD to become the World Bank- the leading financial institution for global development.

In the move from West to East, the Bank could foresee vast opportunities for investment in long term loans for large infrastructure projects in developing countries. And rightfully too. During the seventies, World Bank lending increased dramatically as it had started to fund large scale dam projects in Asia, road construction projects in Africa and highway projects in Latin America. Electricity supply, often connected to large dam projects, represented almost half of its total annual lending. A niche was finally found for the World Bank's fund.

Economic Colonization: Patented Approach of the World Bank to Global Development

The Bank in its new found role of leading development financing institution started to grow in aura, power and the ability to cast influence on recipient countries. Its investments had started to bear good returns and it was posting profits for its major shareholders each year since 1948. There were years when the annual returns exceeded the annual amount of loans disbursed. Even if the Bank during this period stressed investments in the social sector, the increase in lending mainly came in the traditional sectors like infrastructure development (World Bank 1992, BIC, 1990). This trend continued until the emergence of international debt crisis in the early 1980's. For the first time, there was a real widespread risk that the World Bank's loan may be defaulted. The World Bank, ever watchful of its funds, was on the guard. After a series of closed-door meetings with its main shareholder group of countries (United States, Japan, Germany, France, and the United Kingdom), the Bank once again changed its focus. There was a shift from the traditional project lending approach of the World Bank to a more invasive role of bringing economies of developing countries under its control to ensure that its loans were paid back.

By the end of the eighties, roughly 25 percent of the Bank's lending went into restructuring of economies of developing countries through its structural adjustment programmes (SAPs). The SAPs were nothing short of controlling the budget and expenditures of the recipient countries from remote. Effectively, the Bretton Woods twins -World Bank and IMF had attained a position from where they could dictate macroeconomic policies and wrest sovereign control of economic sectors from Southern governments should the loan repayments default. Even until 1996, about one-quarter of all World Bank loans continued to be in the form of structural adjustment programs. (http://www.corpwatch.org/trac/feature/planet/fact_4.html)

BUILDING CRITICISM: 50 YEARS MAY BE LONG ENOUGH

The impacts that developing countries had to bear to accommodate the policies of the World Bank were multiple and often crippling. It provoked the cries of Basta and fueled the resolve among development practitioners in South and their supporters in North to put an end to the World Bank regime. And as Bruce Rich in his article "The Cuckoo in the Nest" argues that 50 years of World Bank involvement in global development is "long enough". From what follows in the subsequent paragraphs about the Third World deconstruction brought about by the World Bank's policies, it seems that the conclusion reached by Bruce Rich are not far-off from truth.

SAPs: Sapping the Strength out of Developing Countries

In countries with structural adjustment programs, the World Bank loans amounted to 50 percent or more of the total lending. The measures advocated were largely deflationary in nature and included cuts in government expenditure, privatization of national industries, currency devaluation, gutting of social and environmental and social services, and freeing of prices and interest rates. These lending policies effectively reduced many developing nations to pauper states dependent on doles and bailouts by the World Bank or its Bretton Woods twin - the International Monetary Foundation (IMF). Fresh loans were taken by countries to repay back the earlier loans and this translated into heavier indebtedness of borrowing countries. The World Bank nevertheless, continued to post its annual profits while the borrowing countries gradually lost their ability to shape their own future and, thus, endanger the potential for democratic processes and social sustainability.

On the social development front, SAPs increased political and bureaucratic control over the lives of the poorest of the poor. The reductions in public sector spending and cuts in subsidies, and in many cases on basic food commodities destroyed whatever little safety net that existed for the poor. "50 years is enough" - a coalition dedicated to reform of the World Bank claims that SAPs increased the cost of education and health care, and the burden on women. They caused lay-offs wherever the government was a significant employer, reduced capability to pursue environmental and social goals, and forced small businesses and farmers to sell out. In short, the self-exalted policies of the World Bank accelerated inequitable and unsustainable development in developing countries -leaving the poor more poorer and causing environmental destruction. (www.50years.org)

Abetting Environmental Destruction

The projects funded by the World Bank are determined on the basis of security of financial investments and the ability of debtors to repay back the loan. Until late, they were rarely assessed for their environmental worthiness and impact. Projects funded by World Bank in the past are therefore known to have totally ignored social, human and environmental costs. For instance, the Sardar Sarovar Dam in India, which the World Bank continued to fund for many years despite the fact that it would displace a million people, is one example of the Bank's insensitivity to the human costs behind such projects. It withdrew the funding only after global civil society protests and the controversy the project had stirred when it became known that all assessment reports pointed to environmental and financial unsustainability of the project.

Much to the dismay, the World Bank has still not learned the lessons of the past well. It still often finds itself funding projects, which flout the principles of environmental and social sustainability. For instance, its recently approved oil pipeline project in west African countries of Chad and Cameroon, and a resettlement project in China that would displace ethnic Tibetans and Mongol nomadic herders. The Bank admits that under its current portfolio, 2.6 million people worldwide are adversely affected by forcible eviction, loss of land, or loss of livelihood. The Bank's private sector arm—the International Finance Corporation (IFC) - also commits a large share of its resources to environmentally harmful projects. In financial year 1999, 19.1 percent of the investments IFC approved were earmarked for oil, gas, mining, timber, pulp, and paper operations. While it continues to finance environmentally harmful projects, the World Bank is lending less and less for environmentally beneficial ones. According to an informal US government white paper, spending on the environment has decreased from 3.6 percent of the Bank's overall portfolio in FY94 to 1.02 percent in FY98. The World Bank confirmed this trend it its own accounting by stating that the funds committed to environmental projects have decreased by 32.7 percent between FY98 and FY99. (http://www.foe.org/international/worldbank/wb.pdf)

Controlling Foreign Direct Investment : Misuse of Seal of Approval

World Bank is often looked upon by the other aid agencies, financial institutions and the private sector for investment related guidance. Activities where the Bank invests its funds are usually a favorite of other investors, as the presence of World Bank acts like a seal of approval for their investment. It is estimated, that $1 from the World Bank brings in $4 from the rest of the world (New York Times, 1986). Good as it may sound but wrong use of this "seal of approval" can channelize more and more funds into futile and unsustainable projects while depriving fund from more productive areas. To ensure pay back of its own loans, the Bank routinely exhorts Western banks to continue lending to Low Income Developing Countries (LDCs) even after those countries have effectively defaulted on previous loans.

The end result is that LDCs are under tremendous pressure to accommodate policy recommendations of the World Bank to ensure that their chances of getting foreign direct investment (FDI) from other sources are not in jeopardy. Repayment of World Bank loans therefore gains precedence over public spending on providing social services within a recipient country.

WHY THE WORLD BANK EVOLVED IN ITS PRESENT ROLE?

Before we try to understand whether the World Bank is really reforming itself from the image it has created, we need to analyze the factors that led to creation of the World Bank as it is. Why did an institution which initiated the trend of financing development projects in developing countries, and which could very well have channelised its own funds and leverage other funds for the betterment of developing countries failed to do so. The subsequent sections describe some of these reasons.

THE PRESSURE TO LEND

The “pressure to lend” always rests on the shoulders of World Bank. And the constant bid to remain the largest development financing institution has repeatedly forced it to tread in the wrong directions. In my opinion, the pressure to lend has been the most destructive element of the World Bank structure, which damaged its profile both within and outside the organization. The entire hierarchical structure within the Bank is geared to enhance the lending aspect of the Bank. For a long time, the performance of staff within the Bank was assessed more by the magnitude of funds disbursed by them over any other attribute.

The Bank itself has long acknowledged that there is a trade-off between the "quality and quantity" of its lending programmes. (Wapenhans Report, 1991). A greater pressure to lend forces it to lower the requirements for its loans and expedite the loan assessment procedure. When Robert McNamara began boosting lending in the late 1960s and the early 1970s, the bank lowered the standards for its loans. During McNamara's reign Julius Nyerere, ruler of Tanzania, received more bank aid per capita than any other country. The Bank's unconditional support of Nyerere's dictatorial regime was a major cause of the misery borne by the Tanzanian. And in India, in the eastern state of Orissa, experts found an astonishing 67% of men and 64% of women near a World Bank-financed coal-fired power plant suffering from fluorosis. ((http://www.whirledbank.org/development/health.html)

RETURN TO SENDER: INTERPLAY OF INTERESTS BEHIND THE WORLD BANK COVER

World Bank depends on its main shareholders for pledging of funds which the Bank then disburses as loans. The policies of the World Bank are therefore a reflection of the interplay of political and financial interests of each of them. Ironically, industrialized countries are the biggest recipients of the World Bank loans. A large proportion of money lent to developing countries gets funneled back to donor countries in form of procurement contracts. For instance, the net International Development Assistance (IDA) transfers (gross disbursements minus repayments of earlier World Bank loans) to recipient countries totaled 4.47 billion dollars for fiscal 1992. Somewhat more than half of this (2.35 billion dollars) was paid for contracts related to IDA credits, of which the larger part was returned to the industrial countries. More money was doled out by IDA to British corporations for contracts in 1993 than it committed in future loans to Bangladesh, one of the most impoverished nations on earth. Switzerland, which is not even a member of the IDA, received more money that Philippines or Mali. (Alexander, 1998)

The activities of the World Bank and the regional development banks have also become a profitable market for Western companies looking for Third World contracts subsidized by aid. The confluence of undercover interests is instrumental in shaping up what the World Bank what it is today. Blaming the World Bank and overlooking the string-twisters behind will only focus the attention to the symptom and not to the real cause behind unsustainability of its interventions.

IDEOLOGY AND PERSPECTIVES

Ideology and perspectives within an organization gets embedded from top to bottom, and from more influential to less influential. The case within the World Bank is no different. The culture within the Bank for a long time has been largely elitist and inward looking. It was propagated through recruiting staff with homogenized educational and professional background. Economists constituted the main workforce of the Bank and were engrossed in economic models that were far removed from the reality at the grassroots level. This bred a closed-door and uni-dimensional thinking that was hard to break and it constantly reinforced itself by attracting similar thinking groups or inducing similar thinking across its partners organizations.

This ideology is in antithesis to what is required to make World Bank more effective in global development. An open, outward looking, and multi-dimension perspective is more suited to the functioning of the Bank, especially in dealing with a financial crisis and comprehending its social and political dimensions and consequences. (Percy, 1999). The Bank failed to accept wisdom which came from outside its boundaries and selected group of think-tanks. The Bank staff who failed to conform or accept the embedded perspectives has little option but to quit. The case of resignation of Ravi Kanbur, the chief editor of the millennium World Development Report - a flagship publication of the World Bank, and that of Joseph Stiglitz, the Chief Economist, in recent years is a reflection of rigidity within the bank to promote embedded views over the current wisdom. According to Alex Wilks, Coordinator of the Bretton Woods Project, "the resignation of the lead author of this flagship Bank report confirms the view that the World Bank is unable to accept dissenting views, whether from insiders or outsiders."

REFORMS UNDERTAKEN BY THE WORLD BANK

The crowning glory of the Bretton Woods institutions may be taking flak from all directions but it would be imprudent to say that the situation within the Bank has not changed. The increased scrutiny of its actions, and the criticisms it has been receiving has certainly forced it to introspect and undertake remedial measures. The remedial measures are however dual and are often conflicting in their achievements. On one hand, the measures may include reinforcing the outer glass walls of the World Bank headquarters in Washington to protect itself from the fury of the demonstrators, and on the other it has raised the shield of "Reforms". Reforms is now the new mantra chanted by everyone inside and outside. It is therefore imperative to distinguish real reforms from ones, which are little more than a face-lift operation.

Mainstreaming Environmental Concerns

Since the seventies, the World Bank's policy with respect to the environment has undergone a major philosophical change. From the do-no-harm approach, which emphasized minimizing harmful effects of projects, it has moved to targeted environmental improvement that recognizes the linkages between poverty, development and environment (World Bank Website). Environmental review procedures have gained importance in the Bank's lending program and have become mandatory for certain kinds of lending. The Bank now requires all projects to undergo Environmental Assessments (EAs) at the project, regional and sectoral level. More specifically, the projects do get amended or downsized to comply with environmental regulations. In addition to these assessments and safeguard policies, the Bank now provides environmental improvement assistance to developing countries. In the nineties it provided some $15 billion for projects with primary environmental objectives. Environmental lending as a proportion of total Bank lending is now 10 percent and the Bank is tending towards a larger number of smaller projects.

On the other hand, environmental reforms may not be new in World Bank's annals. For example, after massive criticism from the environmental movement of the eighties and documented social and environmental destruction as a consequence of World Bank projects, a reorganization was carried out in 1987. More environmental portfolio managers were hired, new regulations concerning environmental assessments were approved and 'local participation' entered the Bank vocabulary. Nevertheless, these changes did not make any difference in functioning of the bank as the environmental managers had little powers to oppose the project and their involvement, if any, came at a much latter stage. Even until 1995, out of the 228 screened projects approved by the World Bank in fiscal 1995, only ten percent were classified as category A, which require a full environmental assessment. 36 percent were classified as category B, which require some environmental analysis but not a full assessment, and the remaining 54 percent were classified as category C, which require no environmental assessment (World Bank, 1995). Structural adjustment programs and sector loans are not eligible for environmental impact assessments, although such programs may have significant influence on exploitation of natural resources and priority setting within for instance the energy sector. (FIVAS, 1995)

Even today when environmental concerns may have got more embedded in the project cycle, the World Bank still does not give adequate weight to social effects. Social assessments, even today, are not mandatory for any sort of lending. The World Bank did start a discussion on introduction of social assessment policy in December 2000, but it could be a long time before any such policy is in place and begins to be implemented.

PROJECT EVALUATION

Evaluation should be an integral part of all development projects which involve environmental changes and anthropogenic impacts. The World Bank in the recent years has highlighted project evaluation as a part of its project cycle and even has WB has an Operations Evaluation Department (OED) that prepares evaluation reports of projects and overall effectiveness of development lending, but according to one WB report, only 8 percent of a sample of fiscal 1999 projects reviewed had good evaluation plans. (Poverty Reduction and the World Bank: Progress in Fiscal 1999). The recent Meltzer Commission (2000) too has criticized the evaluation process, saying that it was low in credibility, and that success was measured mostly at the time of disbursement. Ending poverty is a long-term goal. But the World Bank reviews just 5% of its programs 3-10 years after disbursements to gauge broad policy impacts, thus doing 'little to measure the effectiveness of outputs over time' (Meltzer Commission)

MOVING TOWARDS A LEARNING BANK

The Bank in a recent move has christened itself from a financial bank to a knowledge bank. By doing so it has ideologically moved ahead- as knowledge is incubated in all human minds and is a factor of growth and development. Nevertheless, knowledge gets constantly enriched with its use and it requires an open mindset to accept the new knowledge products and discard the old. Moving towards a knowledge bank should ideally push World Bank into the area of objective self-assessment and learning from its own past. It should make it more transparent and flexible in its policies and dynamics. If it is able to do so then it could become a true Learning Bank which keeps reinventing to conform to according to the changing needs of the society.

Signs of learnings are certainly visible. Lately, the Bank has accepted some of its past mistakes and is changing the current ways of doing things. The biggest change came in the Bank's forest strategy, formed in 1991 and reviewed last year. The pressure for change came from the recognition that the forest projects were not doing well and that the goals of forest lending were not being achieved, not in the face of the alarming deforestation in developing countries. The OED in 1998 reviewed forest sector policy and pointed out the deforestation consequences of WB funding for large development projects, the depletion of natural resources in countries trying to raise capital to repay debt, and the emphasis on export that contrary to promoting sound forest management was promoting the harvesting of ancient trees and virgin forests. The OED report of 1999 hypothesized that the Bank had not pursued the multi-sectoral approach promised by the 1991 policy, and certain aspects of the policy had not been implemented. (FPIR, http://wbln0018.worldbank.org/ESSD/FORESTPOL-E.NSF/MAINVIEW)

Nevertheless, as mentioned earlier, the process of change within the World Bank is a slow one and the Bank is still not comfortable on how to treat the voices of dissent.

Change in Organizational Structure

There have been significant changes in the organizational structure of the bank. From a homogeneous staff of engineers and financial analysts, located solely in Washington, D.C. It is now opening doors to a multidisciplinary and diverse staff including public policy experts, sectoral experts, and social scientists. Further, 40 percent of the World Bank staff are now located in country offices. This structure makes the World Bank more aligned to the concerns of the developing countries. The change in organizational structure however, has not shifted the decision-making authority to the country desks. Key decisions are still taken from the centralized office while the country desks serve more as communication outposts.

How Fair Is All the Criticism against the World Bank? Do We Still Need a World Bank?

In February 2000, the Meltzer Commission after exhaustively examining documents and interviewing all kinds of experts came up with a number of devastating findings. It pointed out that 80 per cent of the bank's resources are devoted not to the poorest developing countries but to the better off ones that have positive credit ratings and can therefore raise their funds in international capital markets. The failure rate of Bank projects is nearly 70 per cent in the poorest countries and about 60 per cent in all developing countries. Its verdict in brief was that the World Bank is irrelevant to the achievement of its avowed mission of global poverty alleviation.

In my opinion, the world is still better off with having a World Bank rather than not. To be fair, the presence of the Bank has ensured that global development remains a crucial agenda and it receives widespread attention at the international level. Its presence has scaled up the level at which environment and development related issues are debated. There also has been some internal cognizance of its detrimental role and some slow improvements.

Under the leadership of the current President, Mr. James Wolfensohn, the World Bank has started to open up channels of communication with the non-governmental organizations and is bringing some core changes in its functioning. It certainly is trying to move away from the dominant image of providing structural adjustment loans to making poverty-elimination its central mission. It has started to fund new areas of operation such as promoting good governance, better knowledge management and fighting HIV/ AIDs.

It needs to be understood, that quite a proportion of the criticism hurled on World Bank is for its past actions and is based on the current knowledge sets and situations. This may be unfair in many cases, as realities may be very different then. For instance, in the case of Indian Green Revolution in late sixties, the World Bank promoted agriculture which used high yielding seeds together with massive quantities of fertilizer and pesticides despite the fact that it wrecks toxic havoc on the land, causing soil contamination and non-point source water pollution. Under the present circumstances, when India has enough food in the granaries, this accusation against the World Bank may be easy to justify. The views however would have been much different in the sixties when due to low productivity of domestic agriculture, India was depending on US PL 480 food aid shipments to feed its burgeoning population.

Accepting the widespread criticism, there are still areas where the presence of the Bank is making a significant difference. The subsequent paragraphs delineates situations where it may be better to have a World Bank.

Areas Where World Bank is Making a Positive Impact

In Rio Earth Summit 1992, the Bank took several steps position itself as a suitable institution for taking care of global environmental issues. Many of these actions may have been perfunctory but it certainly led to a cascade effect on other aid agencies and financial institutions, and leveraged the objectives of UNCED. Environment became a high priority area for other aid agencies and it continued to be discussed among the top bracket of political leaders in the later years. One of the best examples may be the World Bank's initiative to start the Global Environment Facility (GEF), which is supposed to act as a financial mechanism to help the South contribute to the solution of so-called 'global environmental problems', like emission of greenhouse gases and loss of bio-diversity. The GEF certainly has a lot of flaws and may be against the interest of developing countries but it certainly created markets for new financing models for development, where none existed before. It has raised the levels of intellectual discussions and there is more awareness about these financing models even in the developing countries.

In the area of primary education, the World Bank continues to be the single largest source of money for education programs for the poorest countries of the world. In the 1990s the Bank significantly boosted loans for education, dispensing an average of US$1.9 billion for the period 1991-1999, approximately 8.2% of its overall lending, nearly double the 4.8% that the Bank allocated to education in the 1980s. It needs to be appreciated that the Bank is investing funds in areas where the private sector has not wholeheartedly participated or has totally bypassed.

In 1996, the Bank proposed the Heavily Indebted Poor Countries (HIPC) initiative to help decrease the external debt of the 22 most heavily indebted countries concentrated mostly in Africa. In 1999 the WB and IMF respectively reduced their debt claims by $11 and 4 billion. All this has certainly helped countries like Mozambique, reducing its yearly payments by two-thirds ((http://www.stern.nyu.edu/globalmacro/), and has been welcomed by the severest critics of the Bretton Woods Institutions. As recent in December 2000, the World Bank approved a comprehensive debt reduction package for Senegal, Burkina Faso, Benin, Cameroon, Niger, Sao Tome and Principe under the enhanced Heavily Indebted Poor Countries (HIPC) Initiative.

The "seal of approval" which the World Bank carries to initiate and catalyze financial investments in a country could be positively used. The World Bank can work alongside the private sector and yet ensure that these companies do not overlook the environmental consequences. World Bank funds may therefore become conditional upon private companies ensuring strict environmental standards. Through judicious use of its seal of approval, the World Bank, can then leverage even more funds in environmentally and socially sustainable projects.

RECOMMENDATIONS

In my opinion, the World Bank is expanding itself into new areas without moving out of some of the earlier ones. This implies, that though the institution has started to become more aligned to environmental and development concerns, its earlier areas of intervention and the older approach continues to taint its newly created post-reform image. The Bank runs the risk of running itself too thin if it does not move out of certain areas and continues to focus attention on new areas.

The World Bank should move away from promoting gargantuan infrastructure projects, which serve only the interest of the World Bank and the donor governments. Funding of such projects should only be based on full national participation and taking environmental concerns into mainstream decision-making. Information transparency and objectivity in decision-making can solve a lot of problems for the Bank as it will reflect upon the participation of the recipient government and the key stakeholders of the project. It should increase its funding and focus on financing small to medium scale sustainable project models which build upon the knowledge of local people and do not destroy the social fabric or promote inequitable development.

The recommendations given by the bank should be fair and objective, and free from all suspicion that they are self-serving for the World Bank. And this will require critical self-awareness and elimination of conflict between the Bank's lending interests and serving the poor. Close collaboration with UN and its specialist agencies is much needed to ensure a wider and more equal platform for the participation of developing countries.

Some of the other improvements needed are: making all the Bank operations, evaluations and reports public and subject to scrutiny; working from the Southern perspective on global public goods like biodiversity and AIDS eradication; and increasing voting power and presence of the poorer nations in the Boards of the Bank.

The key challenge for the World Bank however, would be to build core competence in social and humanitarian issues as its traditional basis of operations -loans, investment policies, organizational structure - are not adapted to multidimensional nature of the international development. Until it takes these steps, the reforms will not be able to stop the roll back of the World Bank and it will continue to help itself by doling out even larger sum of money.

REFERENCES

Alexander, N.C. 1998. *Accountable to whom? The World Bank and its Strategic Allies*, Bread for the World Institute, USA.

Bello W. 'Is Bush bad news for the World Bank?', *Corporate Watch*, January 2001.

Bovard J. 1987. Policy Analysis No. 92, *The World Bank vs. the World's Poor.* http://www.cato.org/pubs/pas/pa092es.html

Bretton Woods Project website www.brettonwoodsproject.org

Dhume S. and Hiebert, M. 2000. 'Building A Better IMF', *Far Eastern Review,* April 12, 2001.

Fifty years is Enough website www.50years.org

FIVAS. 1995, *Foreningen for internasjonale vann-og skogstudier Report.* The World Bank, 1995.

Forest Policy *Implementation and Review and Strategy, The World Bank.* http://wbln0018.worldbank.org/ESSD/FORESTPOL-E.NSF/MAINVIEW

Friends of Earth website, www.foe.org

Kanbur R. 2001 *Economic Policy, Distribution and Poverty: The Nature of Disagreements*. January 2001.

Kass S and McCarroll J. 1997. The World Bank's Environmental Impact Assessments, Part I. *The New York Law Journal*. June 27, 1997.

Meltzer Commission Report 2000 on International Financial Institutions http://csf.colorado.edu/roper/if/Meltzer-commission-mar00

Mistry, P. 1999. "Reforming the IMF and World Bank", Wilton Park Conference on "Managing the Global Economy", 16-19 March, 1999.

New York Times. 1986. "How Do You Give Countries Confidence in Their Futures?" An Interview with Barber Conable," *New York Times*, November 23, 1986.

Rich, Bruce. 1994. The cuckoo in the nest: fifty years of political meddling by the World Bank. *The Ecologist.* 24 no1: 8-13.

Wapenhans Report 1991, The World Bank, Washington.

Whirled Bank Website www.whirledbank.org

World Bank website, www.worldbank.org

World Bank. 1992. Annual Report 1992. Washington.

Bank Information Center (BIC), 1990. *Funding Ecological and Social Destruction: The World Bank and International Monetary Fund.* Washington: The Bank Information Center.

World Bank. 1995 a. Annual Report 1995. Washington.

World Bank. 1995 b. Mainstreaming the Environment. Washington.

World Bank, 1999. *Poverty Reduction and the World Bank: Progress in Fiscal 1999*, The World Bank.

Chapter 5

WORLD BANK: FUNDING IDA'S ASSISTANCE PROGRAM

Jonathan E. Sanford

ABSTRACT

During the past decade, the World Bank's concessional loan facility, the International Development Association (IDA), has relied increasingly on loan repayments ("reflows") to fund its assistance program. By committing future reflows to fund current projects as they are disbursed, the World Bank and its member countries have raised to nearly 40% the share of IDA's current loan program funded with reflows. In future years as the stock of future anticipated reflows becomes increasingly obligated to pay for projects approved earlier, IDA will be relying more on its reserves to fund its future lending program. Under current policies, IDA's cash balance will decline from \$11.78 billion (2001) to about \$1.4 billion (2013) and then will roughly stabilize for several decades. The World Bank and its member countries anticipate that loan repayments will account for 70% of the resources needed to fund IDA's loan program between 2032 and 2041.

This effort is complicated by the parallel effort of the World Bank and its member countries to provide debt forgiveness to heavily indebted poor countries (HIPCs). To date, the World Bank has forgiven over \$9 billion in IDA debt owed by HIPC countries. It has booked most of this debt but – because most of the repayments are not due for many years – it has not yet realized most of the loss. The World Bank's plan to make IDA mostly self-sustaining in the future assumes that donor countries will reimburse its HIPC debt forgiveness in full. If the forgiven loan reflows are not restored, IDA will deplete its cash balance in 2009 and need to start shrinking its aid program. The cost of funding the lost reflows will be roughly $500 million to $600 million a year for the next 20 years. The United States typically has provided about 20% of the money to fund HIPC multilateral debt relief, thus making this an important issue for Congress.

Likewise, the Administration and others have proposed that IDA adopt a major grant program for poor countries. The scope and details of the plan are currently under negotiation by donor countries. A grant program will need to be funded by contributions from donor countries or IDA will need to start reducing the size of its future program in anticipation of lost reflow income. Estimates of the size of the cost of the Administration's proposed grant program differ. Much of the difference in the estimates is due to the methods used for presenting the estimates rather than to major differences in the size of the expected costs. CRS and GAO both estimate that the cost of the Administration's grant program could be funded in full if donors contributed between 1.6% and 1.8% more each year (compound interest). As such, they would need to contribute between $64 billion and $71 billion more during the next 40 years. This would be a 40% to 45% increase in the donors' overall contributions to fund the IDA program. Based on prior practice, the United States would likely be asked to provide 20% of that total.

Basically, the goal of making IDA more self-funding through reflows and the goal of reducing recipient countries' repayment obligations are incompatible. The United States and other donor countries may need to decide which goal to favor – whether to fund IDA debt forgiveness and grants with increased contributions or to allow the overall size of IDA's assistance program diminish in future years.

INTRODUCTION

The International Development Association (IDA) is the component of the World Bank that makes concessional loans to the world's poorest countries. IDA gets most of the new money it uses to fund its assistance programs from contributions by donor countries such as the United States, European countries, and Japan. IDA lends on easy repayment terms, with no interest charge and repayments stretched over 35 to 40 years, including a ten year grace period. It levies a 3/4 of 1% service charge on the disbursed balance for its loans to help offset IDA administrative expenses.

This chapter analyzes the way IDA's assistance program is funded and at the effort by donor countries and the World Bank to have loan repayments ("reflows") carry an increased share of IDA costs. It also explores the potential long-term effects that debt forgiveness and a major grant program might have on IDA's finances. IDA has forgiven substantial amounts of debt owed to it by heavily indebted poor countries (HIPCs). The question whether the costs of that debt relief will be borne by IDA or by donor countries has not yet been resolved. Likewise, President Bush has proposed that IDA institute a major program of grants to poor countries. Currently, IDA makes only loans. The costs of this initiative and the way it would be funded have likewise not yet been determined. In its examination of the two issues – debt forgiveness and grants – the paper discusses the likely cost the United States and other donors would need to bear if they chose to support the costs of IDA debt forgiveness or IDA grants themselves.

For fiscal 2003, the Administration has requested appropriations of $874 million for contribution to IDA. Contribution levels will likely remain at this level, or perhaps increase, in future years. In recent years, Congress has also appropriated about $775 million to fund multilateral debt forgiveness to HIPC countries. Proposals for further HIPC debt relief and a new IDA grant program are currently under consideration and will likely require additional U.S. contributions in future years. Future U.S. contributions or changes in IDA or the HIPC program will need the consent of Congress. Shifts in the way these programs are funded could have a substantial impact on prospective levels of support.

FUNDING IDA'S CURRENT PROGRAM

Every three years, as IDA's stock of uncommitted resources declines, donors meet to negotiate terms for a replenishment of IDA's resources. Since IDA was created in 1960, there have been twelve such replenishments. A new replenishment plan (IDA 13) -- to fund IDA operations during the next three year period – is currently being negotiated. Legislation to authorize U.S. participation and U.S. contributions to the plan likely will be submitted to Congress in June 2002.

In the past, most of the money IDA had available to lend during each replenishment period (the three years funded by a replenishment plan) typically came from donors. Funds from loan repayments were also used to support new loans, but the amount received annually from this source was relatively small. During the past decade, however, the volume of reflows has increased substantially. In 1992, the IDA donor countries adopted a new plan (in IDA 10) to enhance through "advanced commitment" the role that reflows will play in IDA's operations. IDA previously waited until reflows were in hand before adding them to the stock of resources available to finance future loans. Under the advanced commitment plan, reflows received during the next decade are counted as support for an IDA replenishment plan if they are used to pay for disbursements on projects approved during that replenishment period. Because IDA only releases funds as implementation goes forward, the disbursements for an IDA project may be stretched out over a six to eight year period.

Even though the amount being received as reflows during a three-year replenishment period is relatively small, the share of IDA disbursements funded by reflows has increased substantially. In IDA 10, IDA loan commitments made during the period 1994 to 1996 were funded with $16.3 billion in new contributions from donors and $3.1 billion in advanced commitments of reflows.[1] In other words, reflows accounted for about 16% of the resources used to fund IDA 10. In IDA 11 (1997 to 1999), IDA's loan program received $9.86 billion in new contributions from donors and $6.5 billion in advanced commitment of reflows. (Another $1.63 billion in IDA 11 projects was funded with money carried over from earlier replenishments.) On this basis, omitting the carryover to avoid double counting, reflows accounted for 40% of IDA disbursements during the IDA 11 period. However, since actual reflows received during those three years amounted to only $2.39 billion, IDA needed to use $3.1 billion in future reflows to fund disbursements on IDA 11 projects.

In IDA 12 (2000 to 2002), new contributions amounted to $12.44 billion while reflows covered $6.4 billion in future IDA 12 disbursements. In effect, reflows provided about 34% of the funds needed to pay for IDA 12 loans. As IDA was scheduled to receive $4.46 billion in reflows during that three year period, IDA would need $1.94 billion in future reflows to pay IDA 12 costs. In IDA 13, currently under negotiation, donors (including the IBRD) would provide $13.7 billion in new money and "internal resources" (reflows plus reserves, a point to be discussed later) would comprise $8.9 billion. On this basis, reflows and other "internal" IDA resources would account for over 47% of IDA 12's total cost.

IDA's ability to commit future reflows to fund its current loan program is facilitated by the nature of IDA reflows. On average, 95% of the amount due from borrowers is repaid on time and in full. Most of the countries not paying have (in effect) no national government or their government is seriously estranged from the world system.

---

[1] Throughout this paper, one SDR is valued at $1.253. This makes easier the comparison of numbers from one replenishment to the other. The World Bank has used this procedure in its consultations with member countries about long-term IDA funding plans.

Table 1. Projected IDA Cash Flow and Cash Balance, 2002-41 (Billions of US Dollars)

	2002	**2003**	**2004**	**2005**	**2006**	**2007**	**2008**	**2009**	**2010**	**2011**
Commitments	6.28	7.35	7.35	7.35	7.87	7.87	7.87	8.43	8.43	8.43
Contributions	--	4.51	4.51	4.51	4.39	4.39	4.39	4.39	4.39	4.39
Contrib old	4.00	2.00	1.62	1.62	--	--	--	--	--	--
Net Op Income	0.81	0.83	0.86	0.89	0.89	0.82	0.76	0.75	0.72	0.70
Reflows	1.30	1.40	1.60	1.80	1.90	2.10	2.30	2.50	2.70	2.90
Total income	6.55	9.18	9.05	9.29	7.67	7.80	7.95	8.16	8.34	8.53
Disbursmts new	1.43	2.91	4.30	5.48	6.40	7.15	7.70	8.10	8.21	
Disbursmnts old	6.49	7.51	6.08	5.32	4.11	3.01	1.11	1.34	0.81	-0.51
Total Costs	6.93	9.39	9.45	10.09	10.07	9.90	8.76	9.55	9.43	8.24
Net annual cash	-0.38	-0.20	-0.40	-0.80	-2.40	-2.10	-0.81	-1.39	-1.10	0.29
Balance	11.40	11.20	10.80	10.00	7.60	5.50	4.70	3.30	2.20	2.50
	2012	**2013**	**2014**	**2015**	**2016**	**2017**	**2018**	**2019**	**2020**	**2021**
Commitments	9.02	9.02	9.02	9.66	9.66	9.66	10.34	10.34	10.34	11.07
Contributions	4.39	4.39	4.39	4.39	4.39	4.39	4.39	4.39	4.39	4.39
Net Op Income	0.74	0.73	0.74	0.80	0.85	0.87	0.94	0.96	0.99	1.07
Reflows	3.30	3.50	3.80	4.00	4.30	4.50	4.80	5.10	5.30	5.60
Total income	8.98	9.19	9.51	9.78	10.09	10.34	10.72	11.05	11.29	11.69
Disburs new	8.40	8.58	8.74	8.98	9.19	9.36	9.61	9.83	10.02	10.29
isb correction	0.73	0.45	-0.51	0.81	0.26	-0.60	0.73	0.52	-0.54	0.67
Total Costs	9.68	9.59	8.80	10.38	10.00	9.33	10.92	10.95	10.09	11.58
Net annual cash	-0.70	-0.40	0.71	-0.60	0.09	1.01	-0.21	0.10	1.20	0.10
Balance	1.80	1.40	2.10	1.50	1.60	2.60	2.40	2.50	3.70	3.80
	2022	**2023**	**2024**	**2025**	**2026**	**2027**	**2028**	**2029**	**2030**	**2031**
Commitments	11.07	11.07	11.85	11.85	11.85	12.69	12.69	12.69	13.58	13.58
Contributions	4.39	4.39	4.39	4.39	4.39	4.39	4.39	4.39	4.39	4.39
Net Op Income	1.10	1.12	1.14	1.17	1.20	1.24	1.24	1.24	1.24	1.24
Reflows	4.83	5.19	5.51	5.87	6.22	5.43	5.79	6.16	6.52	6.88
Total income	10.96	11.35	11.71	12.11	12.52	11.78	12.15	12.54	12.92	13.30
Disburs new	10.53	10.72	11.01	11.27	11.48	11.79	12.07	12.29	12.62	12.92
Disb correction	--	--	--	--	--	--	--	--	--	--
Total Costs	11.17	11.37	11.68	11.95	12.18	12.51	12.80	13.04	13.39	13.70
Net annual cash	-0.21	-0.02	0.03	0.16	0.34	-0.72	-0.65	-0.50	-0.46	-0.40
Balance	3.60	3.58	3.61	3.76	4.10	3.38	2.73	2.23	1.77	1.37
	2032	**2033**	**2034**	**2035**	**2036**	**2037**	**2038**	**2039**	**2040**	**2041**
Commitments	13.58	14.54	14.54	14.54	15.57	15.57	15.57	16.67	16.67	16.67
Contributions	4.39	4.39	4.39	4.39	4.39	4.39	4.39	4.39	4.39	4.39
Net Op Income	1.25	1.22	1.24	1.26	1.29	1.31	1.33	1.35	1.37	1.39
Reflows	6.00	6.39	6.78	7.20	7.62	7.34	7.79	8.24	8.68	9.14
Total income	12.44	12.82	13.25	13.71	14.17	13.94	14.43	14.92	15.41	15.92
Disburs new	13.16	13.52	13.83	14.09	14.47	14.81	15.08	15.49	15.85	16.15
Disb correction	-0.15	-1.52	-1.42	-1.24	-1.17	-1.78	-1.57	-1.50	-1.40	-1.22
Total Costs	13.81	12.82	13.25	13.71	14.18	13.93	14.43	14.93	15.41	15.91
Net annual cash	-1.37	0.00	-0.00	0.00	-0.01	0.01	-0.00	-0.00	-0.00	0.00
Balance	-0.00	-0.00	-0.00	0.00	-0.00	0.00	0.00	-0.00	-0.00	-0.0

Source: Created by CRS using data supplied by World Bank, as discussed in text.

At the beginning of July 2001, IDA had uncommitted financial resources on hand totaling $11.78 billion. It also had $9.24 billion in donor pledges in nonnegotiable non-interest bearing notes which had not yet been encashed. IDA cannot require that its donors turn their contribution pledges into actual money right away. Rather, the donors' notes must be drawn down over a 9 year period according to a specified schedule. IDA's cash balance (uncommited financial resources) has grown gradually over the years because contributions have come in at the scheduled rate, reflows have increased, and disbursements seem to have been somewhat less than originally expected. The latter appears to be due partly to difficulties the Bank has had implementing complex projects in difficult contexts (IDA had over $20 billion in undisbursed loans commitments in 2002, some 19% of all loan commitments to date) and partly to the dip in IDA loan commitments which occurred in the late 1990s.

Table 1 seeks to present a picture of IDA's financial situation for the next 40 years. As with all projections, the data are strongly dependant on the accuracy of the original numbers and the strength of the underlying assumptions. The calculations here are based on data or assumptions provided by the World Bank.[2] Contributions include planned future transfers from IBRD net income as well as contributions from governments. Operations and administrative costs would increase by 2.3% annually, per the expected rate of inflation. Contributions from donors would remain the same in nominal terms. Investment held in the cash balance are assumed to earn 5% annually. Income from the IDA service charge would continue to be 3/4 of 1% of the disbursed balance. Disbursement figures were the only data not specifically defined by World Bank data or assumptions. The U.S. General Accounting Office (GAO) provided estimates for annual disbursements from future replenishments, based on standard World Bank procedures. The author adjusted disbursement levels for years 2002 to 2021 (funded with new and old money) in order to keep IDA's cash balance each year at the level projected by the Bank. Future disbursement data reflows (for 2022 to 2041) were generated by the assumptions built into the model. Estimates for future reflows were calculated using the disbursement data for the first two decades and standard disbursement and repayment formulas.

According to the World Bank, IDA will fund much of its future loan program through substantial reductions in its cash balance. Over the next 12 years, IDA plans to reduce its cash balance from $11.78 billion (2001) to $1.4 billion (2013). During those years, IDA will disburse $1 billion or more annually than it receives in income. IDA's cash balance will remain favorable through most of the 2020s, but will begin sinking in the last years of the decade. According to the model,

[2] World Bank. *IDA Funding Scheme and Financial Projections: IDA13 Replenishment.* Powerpoint slides distributed to IDA donor countries, late fall 2001. Unpublished.

disbursements will need to be constrained in the 2030s if IDA is not to run out of money. IDA's cash balance is its protection against contingencies, its "margin of error" against unexpected events. Whether IDA's future assistance program will be funded substantially by "reflows" in the next two decades is a matter of semantics, given the many sources of funds that have contributed to the current cash balance. A major share of IDA's reflows during the next decade have already been committed to fund earlier replenishments.

The World Bank assumes that IDA resources in real terms will remain the same size they are now for the next 40 years. Loan disbursements and administrative costs will grow by 2.3% annually (per expected inflation), while donor contributions would remain flat in nominal terms. The Bank presumes that, all else being equal, loan disbursements and other non-donor sources of revenue will provide 70% of the money IDA will need to fund its loan program during the last decade (2032 to 2041) of this period.

FUNDING IDA'S PROGRAM: HIPC

This is the point in the present discussion where the issue of debt forgiveness to poor countries through the HIPC program and possible IDA grants becomes important. Both initiatives would reduce the amount of reflows that IDA receives in future years – shifting the burden either to donors (a need for increased contributions) or to recipients (a smaller IDA assistance program). The data provided by the World Bank (shown in Table 1) assume that there will be no significant IDA grant program and that IDA is reimbursed in full (by donor countries) for all the debts it has forgiven the HIPC countries.[3]

Through December 31, 2001, the World Bank has forgiven or is forgiving $10.2 billion in debt owed to IDA through the HIPC program. To offset some of these costs, it received $778 million in reimbursements from the HIPC trust fund. The cost to IDA for debt forgiveness occurs not in the year when the forgiveness is announced, but in the year when IDA would have otherwise received the loan repayment. IDA has booked a net loss of $8.6 billion in HIPC forgiveness (more will be booked in the future), but to date it has only realized a small portion of the loss.

[3] World Bank. *IDA Funding Scheme...*, p. 9. Among the specific assumptions for the Bank's funding plan is a statement that "Costs of HIPC debt service forgiveness [are] covered by IBRD net income pledge and subsequently by additional donor contributions." Future IBRD contributions to IDA are included in the model but not future IBRD contributions to HIPC. The Bank assumes that coverage of past and future HIPC forgiveness by the IBRD and by new donor contributions is a prerequisite (not included in the data) to the arrangements specified in its new 40 year plan.

Table 2. Projected IDA Cash Balance, 2002-2021 Without HIPC Reimbursement
(Billions of U.S. Dollars)

	2002	2003	2004	2005	2006	2007	2008	2009	2010	2011
HIPC lost reflows	0.32	0.36	0.44	0.48	0.52	0.55	0.58	0.58	0.55	0.57
Balance	11.29	10.82	9.97	8.65	5.33	2.24	0.39	-1.96	-3.90	-4.37
	2012	**2013**	**2014**	**2015**	**2016**	**2017**	**2018**	**2019**	**2020**	**2021**
HIPC lost reflows	0.58	0.59	0.57	0.55	0.55	0.55	0.55	0.55	0.45	0.35
Balance	-5.83	-6.96	-6.94	-8.25	-8.83	-8.50	-9.43	-10.05	-9.47	-9.96

Source: Created by CRS using HIPC reflow data from World Bank and Table 1 data.

Table 2 shows (based on Table 1) the effect of that HIPC debt forgiveness will have on IDA's cash balance if the lost reflows from HIPC are not reimbursed and IDA has to absorb the cost from its own resources. For simplicity, only the results of the calculation are presented.[4] IDA's cash balance will become negative in 2009 in that situation. The difference between the annual balances in Table 2 and those in Table 1 represent the cumulative amount IDA would need to receive from some other source if it were to hold the size of its aid program unchanged despite the shortfall in reflows. The World Bank was unable to provide data on the impact that HIPC would have on IDA reflows beyond 2021. The World Bank says that it plans to contribute between $200 million and $220 million to HIPC in the next four years (through 2005), completing its pledge to provide substantial IBRD contributions to that program.[5] This amount is included in the income calculation for Table 2.

There appear to be three ways IDA can deal with that situation. First, it can shrink the size of its annual IDA aid program by an amount equivalent to the lost HIPC reflows. Second, the lost reflows can be reimbursed to IDA by donor

---

[4] Table 2 shows the key changes that would occur in Table 1 if the reduction in reflows caused by HIPC debt forgiveness were added to IDA costs. If that additional cost were added to Table 1, the cash balance (bottom line) figure would change to reflect the data shown in Table 2.

[5] The World Bank promised its member countries that it would contribute $2.15 billion in net present value (NPV) terms over time to the HIPC trust fund. To date, the World Bank has transferred $1.4 billion from IBRD net income (not reserves) to the HIPC trust fund. The remainder would be contributed by 2005. See: World Bank. *Heavily Indebted Poor Countries (HIPC) Initiative: Status of Implementation.* March 22, 2002. IDA/SecM2002- 0155. Prepared for the Development Committee Meeting, April 21, 2002. See paragraph 23. Also available from the Bank web site. The Bank says that this will permit the IDA component of the HIPC Trust Fund to reimburse IDA for IDA debt through the end of IDA 13. The Bank says that it expects that IDA donors will consider the future needs for funding IDA's HIPC costs in the IDA 14 negotiations. During IDA 13 (upcoming), the IDA donors also reportedly plan to contribute $627 million to cover such costs during the IDA 13 replenishment period. This amount is not included in the income data for Table 2. The donor countries reportedly plan to cover subsequent shortfalls in HIPC funding on a pay-as-you-go basis, though final agreement on this point has been postponed until the negotiations on IDA 14 in 2005.

countries. Third, IDA can seek funds from some other source, in the World Bank or in another international financial institution to cover the shortfall.

Reducing the size of the IDA program could save money but it could also have negative effects on recent HIPC graduates and other poor countries. If donors wish to offset the lost HIPC reflows, they would need to contribute $8.64 billion over 20 years.[6] If they fund the loss each year as it occurs, they would need to contribute the amounts shown in Table 2. Alternatively, if they chose to fund the lost revenues up front, they could make a one-time payment of $5.6 billion. Invested at 6.3%, this would generate enough revenue (principal and interest) to offset the lost revenues in each future year. Based on recent precedents, the likely cost to the United States in either case would be about 20% of the total.

The World Bank has substantial assets in its reserves. However, these are assets of its near-market loan facility, the International Bank for Reconstruction and Development (IBRD). Transferring them to IDA may be difficult from a legal and political perspective. It would require a super-majority vote of the membership, it may engender lawsuits by Bank bondholders, it would likely drive up interest rates the Bank would need to pay to borrow funds, and – if a distribution of assets is triggered – it would require an appropriation by Congress to transfer the U.S. share of those assets (several billion dollars) to the IDA.

FUNDING IDA'S PROGRAM: GRANTS

In July 2001, President George W. Bush proposed that up to half the aid the World Bank provided to poor countries in future years should be in the form of grants rather than low-cost concessional loans. The President said that such a change in IDA procedures would help lessen the debt burden on poor countries, provide means for greater effectiveness and accountability, and put increased emphasis on assistance for education, health and sanitation. Critics of the proposal say it could lead to conflict and competition with other international programs, divert attention from poverty-alleviation and other concerns, and require substantial new contributions by donors. If the proposed grant program is not funded, they add, it would substantially undercut the financial basis of IDA and force substantial cuts (or termination) of its aid program in future years. The British and other European governments have been particularly critical of the

[6] The total reduction in IDA reflows due to HIPC for the years 2002 to 2021 is $10.24 billion, with a net present value (NPV) of $5.6 billion. Not all of this cost has yet been booked. The World Bank has identified sources of funding for some of this. However, its unfunded HIPC liability is $8.6 billion in nominal terms, about $4.5 billion in NPV terms.

proposed plan. Negotiations to seek a compromise and resolution of the issue are currently underway.

Many analysts have sought to determine the likely cost and financial feasibility of the President's proposal for IDA grants. The World Bank says the cost would be about $100 billion, in nominal dollars. Of this, $59 billion was actual lost repayments and $41 billion was foregone interest income IDA would have received if those reflows had been invested (until used) through IDA's cash balance. GAO says the cost would be $15.6 billion, in net present value (NPV) terms for the whole $100 billion and $9.7 billion in NPV terms for the actual lost reflows.[7] It is important to note that the GAO and World Bank estimates are basically the same. The Bank's approach counts the cost as it occurs over the 40 year period. The GAO concept accounts for the time value of money. In effect, it presumes that the costs identified by the Bank could be covered if a $9.7 billion fund were established today and the proceeds in that fund were used to offset future losses in reflows as they occur.

Table 3 (below) provides another estimate, based on the analysis in Table 1, of the likely cost (in nominal dollars) of lost reflows due to grants.[8] According to Table 3, the actual reflows lost if IDA instituted a grant program comparable to that proposed by the Administration would be about $64 billion. This is comparable in concept to the World Bank's figure of $59 billion). Costs are counted only in the year in which they are incurred. Table 3 does not include any estimate for the imputed cost of lost income which might be generated by those lost reflows.[9]

The important thing is not the differences among the numbers, which are relatively small given the fact that they are all projections over 40 years. The important thing is the fact that a grant program will have costs, either to the donors (more contributions) or to IDA's beneficiaries (a smaller program) which will need to be considered if the program is put into effect.

---

[7] U.S. General Accounting Office. *Developing Countries: Switching Some Multilateral Loans to Grants Lessens Poor Country Debt Burdens*. April 2002. GAO-02-593. The present author thanks GAO analysts for several helpful suggestions received during his preparation of this CRS report.

[8] The methodology for Table 3 is the same as that for Table 2. It shows the changes which would occur in IDA's bottom line (cash balance) if the lost reflows attributable to a grant program (comparable to that proposed by the Administration) were added to IDA's costs.

[9] Not shown in Table 3 are the likely consequences (according to the model) if IDA tried to do HIPC debt relief and a major grant program simultaneously without offsetting contributions by donors. In that case, IDA's cash balance would become negative in 2009 and the total would reach minus $10 billion by 2021. Without data on HIPC losses beyond that point, it is impossible to determine what the balance would be in 2041. It would likely be more substantial, though, than that shown in Table 3.

Table 3. Projected IDA Cash Balance, 2002-2041 With Unfunded Grants
(Billions of U.S. Dollars)

	2002	**2003**	**2004**	**2005**	**2006**	**2007**	**2008**	**2009**	**2010**	**2011**
Lost reflows	0.00	0.00	0.00	0.00	0.00	0.00	0.00	0.00	0.00	0.00
Balance	11.40	11.25	10.86	10.06	7.63	5.46	4.57	3.05	1.79	1.90
	2012	**2013**	**2014**	**2015**	**2016**	**2017**	**2018**	**2019**	**2020**	**2021**
Lost reflows	0.06	0.13	0.19	0.28	0.35	0.41	0.47	0.54	0.59	
Balance	0.45	-0.78	-0.96	-2.50	-3.35	-3.29	-4.54	-5.53	-5.46	-6.57
	2022	**2023**	**2024**	**2025**	**2026**	**2027**	**2028**	**2029**	**2030**	**2031**
Lost reflows	0.66	0.79	0.91	1.05	1.20	1.33	1.47	1.61	1.74	1.88
Balance	-7.86	-9.09	-10.41	-11.76	-13.11	-15.74	-18.42	-21.08	-23.82	-26.64
	2032	**2033**	**2034**	**2035**	**2036**	**2037**	**2038**	**2039**	**2040**	**2041**
Lost reflows	2.03	2.19	2.33	2.50	2.66	2.81	2.99	3.16	3.33	3.52
Balance	-30.79	-34.44	-37.47	-40.63	-43.97	-47.53	-51.28	-55.21	-59.34	-64.58

Source: Created by CRS using Table 1 data and standard disbursement/reflow formulas.

GAO proposed that, instead of making contributions to defray the cost of grants as they occur, donors might make advanced contributions to a special fund. The principal and interest in that fund could be used to defray the future cost of lost reflows due to grants. GAO said that the cost of grants could be offset if donor countries increased their contribution to IDA by 1.6% annually over the next 40 years. This is compound interest. Over the course of 40 years, using the financial model presented in Table 1, donors would contribute $64 billion, a 40% increase over planned contribution levels.

Table 3 shows that, unless IDA grants are funded with increased contributions from donors, IDA's cash balance will dip into the negative in the first year in which repayments would have been otherwise due for grants made in 2003.[10] The growing negative balance reflects the cumulative amount IDA would need to receive in donations to keep its aid program at planned levels despite the drop in reflow income.[11] The table assumes that IDA will levy a small commitment fee (here charged as 1.5% of the total in the year the grant is made) to cover

[10] The World Bank estimated that IDA's cash balance would become negative (absent any funding for a grant program comparable to that proposed by the Administration) in 2015. World Bank. *IDA Funding Scheme...*, p. 14. The Bank also estimated that, if IDA instituted an unfunded 10% grant program, the total cost in lost reflows would be about $2 billion and IDA's cash balance (though small) would remain positive through 2021. It made no estimate for the cost or impact on IDA's cash balance for later years (when, by most estimates, the bulk of the losses would be incurred.).

[11] In Table 3, IDA's cash balance is somewhat higher in the first decade than that shown in Table 1 because IDA would receive an up-front commitment fee from grants made during that period. Correspondingly, the IDA cash balance in Table 3 is smaller in later years than that shown in Table 3 because – in addition to lost reflows – IDA would not be receiving the normal 3/4 of 1% service charge during that period on the disbursed balance for aid released as grants rather than loans. The commitment fee used for the calculations embodied in Table 3 is worth considerably less in NPV terms than the usual service fee.

administrative costs. This approximates on an NPV basis the IDA commitment fee for grants which the World Bank reportedly has under consideration.) Over time, as the size of IDA's outstanding loan balance grows more slowly (because more of its aid takes the form of grants), IDA will likewise receive less income annually from the service charge it levies on those loans.

Using data that was not available originally to GAO, CRS did a separate analysis of the amount that would be needed in additional contributions to offset the likely costs of an IDA grant program. This found that the donor countries would need to increase their contributions to IDA at an annual rate of 1.776% during the next four decades to offset the cost of a major grant program. Again, as with the GAO calculation, this would be compound interest. On this basis, using the financial model presented in Table 1, donors would contribute an additional $72 billion to IDA (a 45% increase over current plans) during the next 40 years. This is somewhat more than GAO calculated. However, the differences between the two estimates are not significant due to differences in methodology and the difficulty of estimating costs over such a long period of time. Were the IDA donors to agree on a contribution plan of this sort, to offset the future costs of grants, the World Bank – having more complete data on IDA finances – should be able to determine an annual contribution rate sufficient to accomplish that goal.

The United States currently contributes about 20% of the new money provided to IDA during each replenishment period. Given the relative size of the U.S. economy, it seems unlikely that other countries will agree to increase their contribution levels in order that the United States may decrease its. Should the U.S. contribution share remain at that level for the next four decades, it is likely that the United States will be asked to contribute an extra $13 billion to $14 billion (over and above the $32 billion it would give if donor contribution levels remained flat in nominal terms during that period) to cover the cost of IDA grants.

BALANCING MULTIPLE GOALS

IDA's capacity to fund a major program of assistance to developing countries in the coming decades is heavily dependant on the way the World Bank and the IDA donor countries handle its finances. Under current plans, loan repayments ("reflows") would provide much of the money IDA needs to fund its operations during the next 40 years. Contributions from donors would bear a declining share of the load. In nominal terms, donors would be asked to contribute the same amounts annually during each of those years even though the IDA program would be growing in nominal terms to compensate for anticipated inflation. In real terms, given the effects of inflation, the actual cost of the IDA program to donors would decline by 2.3% annually during the entire period.

In addition to the goal of reducing the cost of the IDA program to donors, many people also hope that the cost to the recipient countries may be reduced as well. The program of HIPC debt forgiveness for poor countries seeks to reduce the amount that poor countries must pay to IDA each year as a consequence of earlier loans. Likewise, the proposal for a major IDA grant program would reduce – if not eliminate – much of the cost that recipient countries must bear as a consequence of IDA aid.

Ultimately, the goal of making IDA more self-financing through reflows and the goal of reducing the recipient countries' debt repayment burdens are incompatible. Any debt repayments that are forgiven (through HIPC) or eliminated (through grants) will reduce the amount that IDA receives in future years as reflows to fund its future aid program. Without additional contributions from donor countries, either to offset the cost of IDA's regular assistance program or to offset the cost of HIPC debt forgiveness or grants, the resources available to fund IDA's assistance program will gradually decline. In that case, IDA will have no real alternative but to shrink the size of its new assistance program in proportion to the amount it is providing its beneficiary countries through debt relief and grant assistance. In either context, the donor countries will need to decide whether they wish to reduce the size of the IDA program in future years or to increase (in real terms) the size of their annual contributions.

Chapter 6

WORLD BANK: MANAGEMENT CONTROLS STRONGER, BUT CHALLENGES IN FIGHTING CORRUPTION REMAIN*

Henry L. Hinton, Jr.

The World Bank[1] lends billions of dollars each year to help countries alleviate poverty and promote economic and social progress. The Bank provides loans that support specific projects as well as loans that support broader economic and social reform. In addition to making loans, the Bank provides advice and technical assistance to borrowing countries. The World Bank currently manages a portfolio of approximately 1,500 projects valued at about $121 billion.[2]

The Bank operates in a difficult and challenging environment in countries where transparency (openness) and accountability are often lacking, and corruption—broadly defined as the abuse of public office for private gain—sometimes flourishes. The Bank must satisfy its dual mandate of providing

---

* Excerpted from the General Accounting Office website: www.gao.gov.

[1] The "World Bank" and "Bank" refer to the World Bank Group of institutions. The World Bank Group is made up of the original "World Bank"—the International Bank for Reconstruction and Development—as well as the International Development Association, the International Finance Corporation, the Multilateral Investment Guarantee Agency, and the International Center for the Settlement of Investment Disputes. Our review focused on the lending operations of the International Bank for Reconstruction and Development and the International Development Association.

[2] Project lending totaled about $13.6 billion, about 47 percent, of the Bank's total lending commitments for fiscal year 1999.

development assistance in these environments and exercising its fiduciary responsibility, including ensuring that corruption is minimized in the projects it finances.

In 1996, the President of the Bank elevated the discussion of corruption by identifying it as a significant deterrent to development and made a pledge to address it more directly with its borrowers. Following the President's announcement, the World Bank adopted an anticorruption strategy in 1997 and introduced an anticorruption action plan in January 1999.[3]

One of the Bank's major goals was to create an operating system that would help ensure that funds are used as intended and spent in accordance with good management practices. The Bank's anticorruption strategy is aimed at improving its systems of management controls, particularly in the areas of procurement and financial management, and ensuring that it is consistent with the standards of effective management control. These standards were defined by the Committee of Sponsoring Organizations of the Treadway Commission and were adopted by the Bank in 1995.[4]

The Congress has directed GAO to review the Bank's progress in strengthening measures to prevent corruption.[5] In conducting our work, our objective was to determine whether the outcomes from the Bank's management initiatives would collectively provide reasonable assurances that project funds are spent as intended. To do this, we focused on examining the progress the Bank has made in meeting the five standards for effective management control. These standards deal with (1) organizational structures, managerial capacity, and systems necessary to establish a sound management control environment; (2) risk assessment; (3) policies and procedures for ensuring that management directives are carried out; (4) monitoring progress in achieving desired outcomes; and (5) dissemination and communication of information.

---

[3] The action plan was the result of a number of initiatives flowing from various units within the Bank. Several items, such as a major financial management improvement initiative, were already underway at the time the action plan was announced. The relative significance of steps in the action plan varies as does their ease of implementation.

[4] The National Commission on Fraudulent Financial Reporting, known as the "Treadway Commission," was created in 1985 by the joint sponsorship of the American Institute of Certified Public Accountants, the American Accounting Association, the Institute of Internal Auditors, the Institute of Management Accountants, and the Financial Executives Institute.

[5] Public Law 105-277, 112 Stat. 2681-167 (Oct. 21, 1998). The Congress also mandated that we review the Bank's personnel procedures, especially regarding the protection of individuals who have alleged that mismanagement, fraud, and abuse of Bank funds have occurred. For our assessment of Bank personnel practices, see World Bank: Status of Grievance Process Reform (GAO/NSIAD-99-66, May 13, 1999).

We did not make a complete assessment of the Bank's management control system but focused on Bank efforts to improve controls that the Bank had identified as weak. We limited our scope to reviewing Bank controls over project lending, which cover about one-half of the Bank's operations. To gain a first-hand view of how these controls are implemented in the field, we also visited four countries that are large Bank borrowers. As agreed with the Bank, we did not name these countries in this chapter or identify the Bank-financed projects we reviewed.[6]

RESULTS IN BRIEF

In its efforts to address corruption concerns, the Bank has undertaken an ambitious and systematic effort to identify and correct key weaknesses in its system of management controls. The Bank has made significant progress in meeting each of the five standards of an effective management control system. However, challenges remain and further action will be required before the Bank can provide reasonable assurance that project funds are spent according to the Bank's guidelines. Surmounting some of these challenges—particularly in building borrower managerial capacity for implementing Bank projects—will be onerous and will require a longterm effort because problems of corruption and weak management are often endemic to the economic development environment in which the Bank operates.

Summarized below is the status of the Bank efforts in meeting each of the five standards of an effective management control system.

- Organizational structure, managerial capacity, and systems. We focused on Bank efforts to improve internal oversight mechanisms, project management, and public institutions in borrowing countries. The Bank has added new oversight committees and staff to better monitor Bank operations and borrower procurement and financial management practices. For example, the Bank has established a new fraud and corruption hotline and hired about 90 new procurement and financial management specialists. However, many of the public agencies in borrowing countries charged with implementing Bank-financed projects are managerially weak and lack skilled and experienced staff. A series of

[6] We reviewed 12 randomly selected projects for 12 different countries approved between November 1, 1998, and July 1, 1999, and a judgmental sample of 6 ongoing projects approved prior to November 1998.

recent Bank studies show that borrowers often have difficulty complying with Bank procurement rules. Significant institutional capacity building will be necessary to ensure that borrowers can carry out their management control responsibilities effectively.

- Risk assessment. The Bank has focused more attention on better assessing the risks associated with corruption and weak managerial capacity of its borrowers. However, the risks identified are not always raised to the attention of senior decision-makers and fully addressed in risk mitigation plans. Moreover, the Bank does not have a system for allocating its anticorruption assistance among borrower countries based on risk.

- Policies and procedures for ensuring management directives are carried out. The Bank has strengthened controls by devoting more attention and resources to supervising its projects more closely. This has included, for example, hiring or training local Bank staff or contracting with consultants to review borrower procurement actions more closely. However, the Bank and some borrowers do not always comply with Bank procedures on project auditing and Bank supervision of borrowers' procurement and financial management practices.

- Monitoring. The Bank has introduced some new tools for monitoring and evaluating the implementation of Bank projects. However, these tools do not provide enough information for Bank management to measure the extent to which some key management control problems are being resolved. For example, Bank studies on the quality of Bank supervision do not fully address key performance problems reported by external and internal auditors.

- Information and communication. The Bank has significantly improved its dissemination and communication of information on its anticorruption efforts, both within the Bank and in borrowing countries. However, some borrower governments and nongovernmental organizations are still not aware of the Bank's hotline and other mechanisms for reporting fraud and corruption.

The Bank is aware of many of these challenges and continues to take actions to address them but does not publicly report progress in implementing these management control improvements. This chapter contains recommendations to improve the Bank's internal oversight mechanisms and risk assessment process, and to assure that the Bank monitors and reports on progress in correcting weaknesses in project management. We also recommend that the Department of the Treasury annually report to the Congress on the results of efforts to strengthen the Bank's management control system.

In commenting on this chapter, the Bank noted that it holds itself to a high control standard and that it had already identified many of the weaknesses we cited through its own self-evaluations and has remedial actions underway. Treasury and the Bank agreed with our findings and recommendations and said that a more aggressive approach is needed in strengthening the Bank's management control systems over project lending and building borrowers' institutional capacity to fight corruption.

BACKGROUND

Concerns about corruption have intensified in recent years as there is a growing realization among international financial donors, including the World Bank, that corruption may undermine development by deterring investment and growth and exacerbating poverty. Although no Bank-wide estimates of the magnitude of this problem have been developed, levels of corruption vary from country to country. World Bank staff estimated that in one large borrowing country, about 20 to 30 percent of all development funds, totaling several billion dollars each year, had been systematically diverted.

The Bank requires borrowers to establish and maintain effective management controls over project funds and to implement projects. For example, borrowing agencies are required to produce a variety of financial and progress reports and to arrange for regular, independent project audits. For its part, the Bank exercises oversight of project implementation through a variety of control activities, including review of financial statements and audit reports, prior review of many procurement actions, and review of the eligibility of many project expenditures.

The Bank and borrowers use the following process to develop and implement projects.

- Project identification and preparation. Project development begins when Bank staff and borrowers identify a project idea. During the subsequent preparation phase, borrowers bear the primary responsibility for examining all aspects of the proposed project and for preparing a project plan for Bank consideration.

- Project appraisal and negotiation. After preparation is complete, Bank staff appraise sponsor proposals (including the arrangements for procurement and financial management). Bank staff negotiate with project sponsors the terms and conditions under which the Bank will commit funds to the project and, finally, prepare a project appraisal document. This document is supposed to contain all of the information the Bank management and the Executive Board need to decide whether or not Bank financing should be provided.

- Board approval. The Bank's Executive Board decides whether to approve each proposed project and, in doing so, exercises oversight over the implementation of Bank policies and procedures—including those that govern procurement and financial management.

- Project implementation. The responsibility for project implementation rests with the borrowers, who must conform to Bank policies and procedures and other conditions outlined in the loan agreement. The Bank monitors and supervises project implementation, including project procurement and financial management, on a continuing basis until project completion and disburses funds contingent upon the borrower providing required documentation. Projects are subject to an annual independent audit arranged by the borrowers. These audits are to include an assessment of the adequacy of the accounting and internal control systems.

The 181 member countries of the World Bank govern it through an Executive Board—the Bank's primary oversight and decision-making body. Twenty-four Executive Directors from Bank member countries comprise the Executive Board. This Board considers and decides on overall policy issues that guide the Bank's general operations and approves specific project proposals presented by the President of the Bank. The United States is the largest contributing member to the World Bank and thus holds the greatest number of voting shares (16.5 percent) on the Bank's Executive Board (voting shares are allocated on the basis of member contributions). Other members holding the largest number of voting shares are Japan (7.9 percent), Germany (4.5 percent), France, and the United Kingdom (4.3 percent each).[7] The Secretary of the Treasury, who represents the United States as

[7] These voting shares apply to projects financed through the Bank's market-based lending.

a governor of the World Bank, has the lead role within the executive branch regarding U.S. policy toward the Bank.

In line with the best practices of major financial institutions in the United States, the Bank in 1995 adopted the management control standards of the Committee of Sponsoring Organizations of the Treadway Commission (COSO). This control framework, known as the "Internal Control-Integrated Framework," establishes a common definition of management controls for all Bank units and provides a standard to assess improvements in these controls. We refer to the components of this framework as the "COSO standards" in this chapter.

The Treadway Commission identified the following five standards that constitute the criteria against which a management control system is to be evaluated. All five standards must be met for controls to be judged effective in any particular area of an organization's operations, thus providing reasonable assurance that funds are spent as intended.[8]

1. **Control environment.** An organization should establish a positive control environment, that is, one with a structure, discipline, and climate conducive to sound management controls. Factors that significantly affect the control environment include the integrity and ethical values of management and staff, the competence of personnel, the way the agency is organized, the manner in which management assigns authority and responsibility, and the attention and direction provided by oversight groups.

2. **Risk assessment.** An organization should properly identify, analyze, and manage the possible risks involved in meeting organizational objectives.

3. **Control activities.** An organization should establish control activities consisting of policies, procedures, techniques, and mechanisms that ensure that management directives are being carried out to meet organization objectives. They include approvals, authorizations, verifications, and reviews of operating performance.

4. **Monitoring.** An organization should continually monitor and evaluate all aspects of internal control to assess the quality of performance over time.

[8] It is recognized that no matter how well designed and implemented, management controls cannot provide absolute assurance that program funds will be used as intended. For example, human mistakes, judgment errors, and acts of collusion to circumvent controls can limit their effectiveness.

Serious management control deficiencies should be reported to higher levels, including top management and the Board of Directors.

5. **Information and communication.** An organization should identify, capture, and communicate information in a form and time frame that enable people to carry out their responsibilities.

In 1999, Bank management used these standards in assessing the effectiveness of internal controls over financial reporting but has not used these standards to determine the adequacy of management controls over the Bank's project lending operations. The Bank concluded that management controls over financial reporting at the International Bank for Reconstruction and Development and the International Development Association funds met COSO standards. The Bank's external auditor concurred with this statement.[9]

Control Environment Has Improved at the Bank but Is Weak Among Borrowers

According to COSO standards, establishing an effective management control environment requires well-managed and properly structured organizations with qualified personnel in place to implement proper management controls and address corruption. We assessed the control environment in terms of the Bank's internal oversight mechanisms, project management, and Bank efforts to improve public institutions in borrowing member countries.

While the Bank has made significant progress in strengthening its control environment by creating new oversight structures and increasing staff with expertise in financial management and procurement, many borrowers still have weak structures and limited managerial capacity, according to Bank records and officials. Consequently, the Bank has increasingly targeted its anticorruption efforts on building borrowers' institutional capacity to fight corruption.

[9] On July 21, 1999, the Bank reported that its external auditor, Deloitte Touche Tohmatsu, agreed with this conclusion.

Bank Internal Oversight Mechanisms Have Been Strengthened but Need Further Improvements

Internal oversight is key for preventing, detecting, and addressing corruption. Although the Bank has long had an internal audit function and a system of management controls, the Bank recognized that its internal oversight mechanisms were weak, according to several officials we spoke to. These officials indicated that the Bank lacked a central focal point for reporting and reviewing allegations of wrongdoing and sufficient expertise to investigate allegations of wrongdoing. In addition, while the Bank expected its staff to exhibit strong ethical behavior, the Bank did not have a strong ethics awareness program. The Bank's external auditor reported in 1998 that the Bank's internal audit department—a key management oversight unit—had a fairly restricted scope of audit coverage and played a limited role within the Bank. For example, about 78 percent of the 206 internal audit reports conducted from fiscal years 1995 through 1997 were focused on administrative compliance issues, such as country mission office procedures, rather than on determining whether project funds were being used as intended.

While the Bank has made progress in strengthening internal oversight units, it still faces challenges in ensuring that all fraud and corruption allegations are centrally reported and effectively addressed.

Progress

In 1998, the Bank established a 24-hour worldwide fraud and corruption hotline, created a new Oversight Committee on Fraud and Corruption for reviewing and monitoring allegations, formed an Investigations Unit comprised of professional fraud investigators, hired new investigative staff, and established a high-level Sanctions Committee to review results of investigations and to make recommendations to the World Bank President on whether certain contractors or individuals should be declared ineligible for Bank-financed contracts. In addition, the Bank strengthened its ethics outreach program and increased staff expertise to investigate allegations of employee misconduct. As of March 2000, the hotline had received 156 calls since its inception in October 1998. Ninety allegations resulting from these calls were referred for investigation to the Oversight Committee on Fraud and Corruption.[10] Of the 90 allegations, 47 were investigated and found to have been either unsubstantiated or did not involve Bank funds. Two

[10] Sixty-six calls did not result in an investigation.

other allegations have been fully investigated and closed while 41 are still being investigated.

In addition, the Bank's internal auditor had increased the proportion of operational audits targeting management controls, procurement, and financial management issues (in relation to administrative compliance audits) in fiscal years 1998-99 to 28 percent versus 22 percent in fiscal years 1995-97. The internal audit department's annual workplan calls for about the same level of coverage of operational audits in fiscal year 2000.

Challenges

The Bank's initiatives to detect, prevent, and investigate fraud and corruption are positive steps; however, the Bank recognizes that further steps are needed to build on the progress made to date.

- First, not all fraud and corruption allegations have been centrally reported to the Oversight Committee on Fraud and Corruption. During our June 1999 visit to one country where the Bank identified corruption to be a serious issue, we found that over 30 allegations of wrongdoing that were reported locally to Bank officials had not been reported to the committee. However, according to Bank officials, the country mission was dealing with these allegations locally and forwarded them to the Oversight Committee on Fraud and Corruption after our visit and followed up appropriately. In November 1999, the Bank issued additional guidelines to help ensure that all field office allegations are reported centrally; however, more time will be needed to assess whether this new guidance is being fully implemented.
- Second, the new oversight units responsible for reviewing, monitoring, and investigating allegations—the Oversight Committee on Fraud and Corruption and the Investigations Unit—are not organizationally independent of the Bank's line management. The Oversight Committee on Fraud and Corruption reports directly to one of the Bank's managing directors. The Investigations Unit also reports to the Oversight Committee on Fraud and Corruption's secretariat. The independence of the investigative function could be affected by the fact that a managing director controls the budget of the Oversight Committee on Fraud and Corruption and Investigations Unit and also makes the final decision on whether an investigation is pursued, including those that may involve employees that report to this director. A January 2000 study by a Bank

consultant confirmed our observation noting that the Investigation Unit did not have the necessary stature or independence. This study recommended that this unit report directly to the Bank President and be given the authority to independently investigative all matters involving fraudulent and corrupt practices.

- In addition, one member of the Oversight Committee on Fraud and Corruption also serves on the Sanctions Committee. Thus, a person who helps decide what investigations should be undertaken also decides what sanctions should be imposed if improprieties are found. Bank managers we interviewed said that this arrangement might create a perception that impairment to independence may exist, regardless of whether it actually affects how investigative duties are carried out. In October 1999, the Bank contracted with a consultant to examine these organizational issues in more detail and propose alternatives to the present organizational arrangement.
- Third, we noted that the Bank's investigation function is fragmented between two units—the Investigations Unit and the Office of Professional Ethics. Each unit currently has its own investigative guidelines; case management system; a hotline and helpline, respectively; and investigative staff. According to Bank officials, this fragmentation has resulted in some confusion over the appropriate duties and responsibilities of these structures and some gaps in investigative coverage, hampering Bank efforts to promptly identify and investigate all allegations of potential wrongdoing. To resolve these problems, the heads of these units plan to work together toward standardizing the procedures and building internal capacity to operate a joint hotline and conduct investigations. In December 1999, the Bank hired another consultant to examine the operations of the Investigations Unit.

Bank Is Improving its Project Management Capabilities, but Some Borrowers Lack Experience and Skilled Staff

A strong control environment within the Bank and borrowing country institutions is critical for effectively implementing the Bank's system of project management controls. For many years, the Bank has had policies and procedures in place aimed at ensuring that project financial management and procurement are sound and that funds are used as intended. Responsibility for ensuring compliance with these policies and procedures is shared by the borrowers, which execute the projects, and the Bank, which supervises the borrower through a variety of approvals and reviews of borrowers' actions.

In recent years, the Bank has recognized that the control environment for its projects had deficiencies. Bank reports and studies issued in 1997 and 1998 indicated that in many cases, both the Bank and its borrowers had insufficient managerial capacity to ensure effective safeguards against the misuse of project funds.[11] In particular, the Bank identified deficiencies in financial accounting, reporting, and auditing in many projects. Furthermore, the Bank did not devote adequate attention to reviewing the borrowers' procurement actions. An underlying cause of this problem was that the Bank did not have an adequate number of skilled staff to ensure that borrowers were complying with financial management and procurement policies and procedures, which were designed to minimize opportunities for corruption.

The Bank has made progress in strengthening its project management capabilities but still faces major challenges in building this capacity among borrower agencies responsible for implementing Bank-financed projects.

Progress

The Bank has undertaken initiatives to enhance the control environment for Bank projects, both within the Bank and among borrowers. In fiscal year 1998, the Bank launched a major effort to hire and train more Bank staff qualified to deal with the financial management and procurement aspects of project management. As a result, the Bank increased the number of qualified financial management staff by about 159 percent (from 34 in fiscal year 1998 to 88 in fiscal year 1999) and the number of qualified procurement specialists by about 78 percent (from 46 in 1997 to 82 in 1999).[12] A financial management specialist and a procurement specialist are now to be assigned to every Bank project, both new and ongoing. Furthermore, the Bank has assigned many of these new staff members to its country missions,[13] where they can be more closely involved in implementing projects and strengthening management controls.

In addition, the Bank has undertaken initiatives to build the financial management and procurement capacity of those agencies in borrowing countries

---

[11] For example, see The World Bank Procurement Function: Adjusting to Emerging Needs (Washington D.C.: World Bank, Apr. 1998), and Loan Administration Change Initiative (LACI) Implementation Strategy Paper (Washington D.C.: World Bank, June 29, 1998).

[12] Figures for financial management specialists and procurement specialists are as of August 1999 and June 1999, respectively.

[13] The Bank had 87 country missions as of the end of fiscal year 1999.

that are responsible for implementing projects. One major initiative introduced in July 1998 is aimed at ensuring that all new projects meet minimum requirements for financial management, including having adequate staffing, internal controls, and auditing arrangements.

Similarly, the Bank has focused on improving borrowers' compliance with Bank procurement rules. These efforts involve assessing implementing agencies' capacity to manage new projects and devising action plans to remedy any significant gaps either before the project begins or during the course of the project.

Challenges

Despite these initiatives, the Bank recognizes that it still faces a major challenge in ensuring strong financial management and procurement capacity among its borrowers as the institutional capacity-building required may be difficult and time consuming to achieve, according to senior Bank officials we interviewed. Also, the Bank's new initiatives to build greater financial management and procurement capacity, which began for new projects appraised in July 1998 (financial management) and November 1998 (procurement) only apply to about 208, or 14 percent, of the Bank's 1,500 projects. Bank studies indicate that management weaknesses persist in ongoing projects. For example, the results of a series of recently completed procurement audits show a lack of understanding of and noncompliance with Bank procurement rules among many (17 of 25) borrowers subject to these audits.

Our review of 12 randomly selected projects approved by the Bank since November 1998 identified 5 projects in which the borrowers' implementing agencies had little or no experience managing development projects, according to Bank records and staff. Thus, their ability to effectively manage the financial and procurement aspects of project implementation and safeguard against corruption appeared limited. Six of the projects we reviewed did not meet the Bank's minimal financial management requirements at the time that the Board approved the projects. Furthermore, for 3 of the 12 projects, the Bank determined that the borrowers' implementing agencies had particularly weak capacity for carrying out procurement in accordance with Bank rules. For four projects, the implementing agencies were not yet functioning and did not have key staff or operating procedures in place. Bank officials told us that it is common practice for borrowers to delay fully establishing project-implementing organizations until after projects are approved by the Board. These officials indicated that most management deficiencies would be corrected, as a legal condition of the loan, before any Bank funds are actually disbursed. However, even with required corrective actions, the ability of these agencies to exercise proper financial management and procurement functions is unproven, given the agencies' lack of experience.

In addition, the Bank remains concerned that project auditors lack institutional independence. Project auditing is a critical element of the Bank's management control system; the Bank uses audits, arranged for by the borrower, to help ensure that project funds are used as intended. The Bank is required to approve the selection of the auditors. However, Bank guidance on auditor selection acknowledges that it is often not possible to ensure the independence of auditors, particularly government auditors that are used for auditing Bank-financed projects in many countries. The Bank guidance states that government auditors are frequently not professionally qualified accountants—many are political appointees, and some are public service administrators. Furthermore, the Bank has been concerned that government auditing institutions sometimes are understaffed, underfinanced, and subject to political pressure.

Until the Bank has assurance that its borrowers' institutions are properly organized, staffed, and experienced in financial management and procurement, the overall control environment for its projects will continue to be weak. Although the Bank has strengthened its capacity to supervise projects, it recognizes that this cannot fully compensate for the weaknesses of its borrowers, given the shared responsibility in implementing management controls. Hence, Bank assurances that funds will be managed appropriately depend on the success of ongoing and future capacity-building efforts.

Bank Faces Long-term Challenges in Improving Public Institutions in Borrower Countries

The Bank has recognized that the key to helping countries fight corruption is to help them create a sound control environment at the country level. Many borrowers lack well-functioning public management systems; accountable organizations; and a strong legal framework to prevent, detect, and redress corruption. The Bank has supported a wide variety of initiatives to strengthen public institutions in its borrowers but faces significant challenges in ensuring that these efforts will be successful over the long run.

Progress

The Bank has introduced new programs to help borrowers establish strong management controls on a countrywide basis. The Bank has helped launch over 350 anticorruption activities in 95 countries. For example, it has conducted detailed surveys to help diagnose the magnitude and nature of corruption in 13 countries, and a major governance pilot program is currently working with teams in 7 African countries to develop and implement targeted anticorruption action plans. The Bank has also provided numerous institutional development grants to borrowers to enhance their ability to deal with corruption. For example, in one country we visited, the Bank awarded a grant to a newly created National Office of Public Ethics. The Bank has also supported capacity-building in the accounting and auditing professions, which are viewed as a critical area of reform for many large borrower countries. A country we visited received two grants to provide procurement and financial management training for agencies that implement projects and for auditing institutions.

Challenges

The Bank faces a difficult and long-term challenge in trying to help borrower countries create effective and well-managed institutions. According to the Bank's Annual Review of Development Effectiveness in 1998, only 40 percent of Bank-supported projects have had substantial impact on institutional development. In addition, the Bank's achievements in institutional building in the financial sector were deemed likely to be sustainable in just 50 percent of countries for a variety of reasons, including "fragile institutional environments," and low capacity to absorb foreign aid.[14] A 1998 evaluation of the World Bank Institute's (the World Bank's research and training institute) efforts to help curb corruption in two African countries questioned the sustainability of these efforts for several reasons, including the lack of needed reforms in public procurement and lack of support and involvement of civil society. Bank officials are optimistic about the prospects for greater impact in its more recent institution-building efforts, because they said these efforts are based on some new approaches. Nonetheless, given the challenging nature of this work, major improvements in borrowing country institutions should not be expected for some time.

---

[14] 1998 Annual Review of Development Effectiveness (Washington, D.C.: World Bank, 1999).

Bank's Risk Assessment Process is More Detailed, but Some Weaknesses Persist

According to COSO standards, an effective management control system requires risk assessments to properly identify, analyze, and manage the possible risks to meeting project objectives. Recently, the Bank has focused attention on better assessing the risks associated with corruption and the weak management capacity of its borrowers. However, our review revealed that weaknesses persist in the Bank's risk assessment process at the project level and country level. As a result, the Bank has approved some projects with limited assurance that all risks and borrower weaknesses have been addressed and that the Bank's supervision of the project will minimize the potential misuse of project funds.

Project Risks and Mitigation Plans Not Always Identified for Decisionmakers

The Bank assesses project risks primarily during the project appraisal and approval process. When evaluating a project, the Bank staff prepares a project appraisal document. According to Bank guidance, this document should include all the information that Bank management and the Board need to decide whether or not Bank financing should be provided, including an assessment of critical project risks. This guidance requires that the appraisal identify each critical risk, note the severity of the risk (ranging from negligible to high), and indicate any measures to be taken to minimize the risk. These risks may include economic, political, and social factors that could hinder the implementation of the project and prevent it from meeting its development objectives.

A series of Bank studies from 1994 to 1998 showed that Bank staff had often not adequately assessed all risks in projects reaching approval stages with Bank management and the Executive Board of Directors. In particular, Bank staff did not always explicitly state the risks posed by the inadequate management capacity of many borrowers' institutions or incorporate appropriate strategies to mitigate these risks. Although the Bank has made progress in ensuring that project risks are better identified and assessed during project design, the Bank faces additional challenges in ensuring that the results of these risk assessments are clearly communicated to the Board of Directors—the key decisionmakers charged with approving Bank project loans.

Progress

The Bank has established new requirements in 1998 to ensure that staff more systematically address risks in the design of new projects. Bank project managers and procurement and financial management specialists are required to analyze the risks to successful project implementation, including administrative, institutional, and financial risks. New project appraisal documents must include an action plan for reducing the risks through capacity-building activities and for mitigating the risks through appropriate levels of Bank supervision. In assessing procurement risks for each project, a Bank procurement specialist is required to rate the level of risk (ranging from low to high) and devise an appropriate supervision plan. This supervision plan is to include the monetary amount (threshold value) above which Bank pre-approval would be required for procurements; it is also to indicate to what extent the Bank will audit procurements to ensure that the borrower has followed Bank rules.

Challenges

Despite improvements in project design requirements, a July 1999 Bank study of new projects approved in 1998 showed that project appraisal documents continued to be unduly optimistic—Bank staff often understated or did not disclose known project risks relating to borrowers' implementation capacity to Bank management and the Board of Directors.[15]

Our review of 12 projects approved after November 1998 confirmed that the Bank's senior decisionmakers still have not adequately assessed the risks posed by potential corruption and weak managerial capacity of borrowers. We found that Bank staff had generally conducted the required assessments of financial management and procurement capacity for the new projects we reviewed. However, in nine cases, Bank staff did not clearly present the results of these assessments in the project appraisal document when seeking project approval from Bank management and the Board of Directors, as required by Bank guidelines. The Bank staff did not indicate the level of procurement risk for seven projects and did not indicate whether the project met the Bank's minimum financial management requirements for seven projects. Consequently, the Board may not have had sufficient information to assess the borrowers' capacity when approving these projects.

Furthermore, we believe that Bank staff did not adequately identify the risks that potential corruption poses to projects when seeking management and Board

[15] Quality at Entry in Calendar Year 1998: A Quality Assurance Group Assessment (Washington D.C.: World Bank, July 1999).

approval. Only 4 of the 12 projects we reviewed identified corruption or undue political interference as a critical project risk (even as a low or negligible one), even though Bank reports had indicated that corruption is a problem in all of the countries included in our project sample.

In addition, in the new projects we reviewed, the Bank often did not identify what steps the Bank will take to manage identified risks and weaknesses. In six of eight projects in which Bank staff had flagged weak management capacity, corruption, or political interference as a critical risk, the project appraisal documents did not describe what specific supervisory actions the Bank planned to take to mitigate the risks. For most projects with these types of risks, the Bank proposed providing additional technical assistance for the borrower agencies (sometimes funded by the projects) or requiring additional borrower actions to address the risks. Given the recognized weaknesses in borrower institutions and the difficulty borrowers have had in building capacity, technical assistance and borrower actions alone may not be sufficient to ensure that project risks can be mitigated.

Furthermore, the project appraisal documents provided to the Board and Bank management did not consistently and comprehensively address how the Bank staff proposed to supervise the projects in order to compensate for specific borrower management weaknesses. Senior Bank officials told us that they have recognized the need for better planning of supervision activities and are devising new requirements for this function. The Bank plans to introduce these new requirements by June 2000.

Country Assistance Strategies Do Not Always Address Corruption Risks

The Bank also assesses risks at the overall country level when making decisions about country assistance and lending levels. In 1992, the Bank introduced a country assistance strategy process as a key tool in examining, among other things, the performance of Bank projects and the policy reform record in countries that receive Bank assistance. The Board considers the results of this analysis, including the risks posed by corruption, poor governance, and an adverse public policy environment, when approving loans and establishing lending levels for each country. In addition, the Bank's process for allocating the Bank's concessional (below market interest rate) loans among borrowers includes consideration of country governance issues, which includes corruption issues.

The Bank acknowledges that historically, like other international financial institutions, it has not adequately addressed the risks associated with corruption and poor governance when making decisions on providing country assistance. According to several Bank officials we spoke to as well as the Bank's anticorruption literature, the Bank had for years been reluctant to address corruption risks openly and directly with borrowers.[16]

The Bank has made progress in addressing the nature and extent of corruption and related risks in some but not all country lending strategies.

Progress

In 1998, the Bank introduced new rules requiring country assistance strategies to explicitly address the state of governance and corruption in the country and its impact on Bank programs so that these issues could be considered in the Board's lending decisions. In the same year, the Bank also introduced new procedures for enhancing the usefulness of key inputs into these country assistance strategies. For example, Bank staff are now required to complete, with borrower assistance, comprehensive risk assessments of countries' national financial management and procurement systems to better identify major risks and weaknesses in institutions, government policies, and legal frameworks.

Challenges

Only about one-fourth of the 31 fiscal year 1999 country assistance strategies that we reviewed included a discussion of corruption-related risks or the role that progress on corruption-related issues would likely have on the Bank's lending decisions. However, Bank officials told us that the treatment of these issues in the country assistance strategies has improved over time. In December 1999, the Bank completed a review of the treatment of corruption and governance issues in Bank country assistance strategies. While the study noted an improvement in the discussion of these issues from fiscal year 1998 to 1999, less than 40 percent of the assistance strategies were rated as satisfactory or better in explicitly assessing corruption risks to Bank projects and proposing remedial measures, if pertinent. This study also found that few assistance strategies included performance benchmarks or lending triggers related to governance conditions or corruption risks. The Bank expects more improvement in the discussion of these issues over time as more country strategies are subject to the new requirements.

---

[16] For example, see *Helping Countries Combat Corruption: The Role of the World Bank* (Washington, D.C.: World Bank, Sept. 1997).

Bank's Process to Prioritize Anticorruption Programs

One of the first steps in establishing a major anticorruption program in a country is conducting an assessment of that country's procurement and financial management systems. However, the Bank has not prioritized, based on corruption risk, which countries should undergo these assessments. In its action plan, the Bank indicated that it would target assessments at countries where corruption risks were greatest. Bank officials confirmed that they did not use a systematic approach or establish priorities for conducting these assessments. Instead, the assessments were generally scheduled based on the interest of the borrowers or the existing knowledge level of Bank staff. As of November 1999, of 143 borrowers, the Bank had completed financial management risk assessments for 57 countries and country procurement risk assessments for 16 countries. Figure 1 shows that few assessments (two procurement assessments and seven financial management assessments) were completed for the Bank's top 10 fiscal year 1999 borrowers. These borrowers collectively received 62 percent of Bank financing in that year.

A senior Bank official told us that the Bank hopes to target future anticorruption efforts, including the Bank's country financial management and procurement risk assessments, to higher risk borrowers and that the Bank is currently developing some comprehensive "good governance" indicators to better guide its efforts.[17] A Bank official indicated that it may take several years to develop these new indicators.

In addition to not targeting risk assessments to higher risk borrowers, the Bank has not scheduled the completion of its country level assessments of procurement and financial management risks to coincide with the approval of the Bank's country assistance strategies. Our review of fiscal year 1999 country assistance strategies did not reveal any cases in which the Bank included a discussion of the risks to development posed by weak financial management and procurement practices in the borrowing countries.

[17] For example, the World Bank Institute has developed six clusters of governance indicators for over 150 countries. The six clusters are (1) voice and accountability, (2) political instability and violence, (3) government effectiveness, (4) regulatory burden, (5) rule of law, and (6) graft.

Figure 1: Anticorruption Risk Assessments among the World Bank's 10 Largest Borrowers

Largest borrowers based on FY 1999 total lending[a]	Country	FY 1999 total lending (billions of dollars)	Country assistance strategy	Country procurement assessment review completed[b]	Country financial accountability assessment or country profile of financial accountability completed[b]
1	Argentina	$3.2	1998[c]	No	Yes
2	Indonesia	2.7	1999[c]	Yes	Yes
3	China	2.1	1998[c]	No	Yes
4	Korea	2.0	None	No	Yes
5	Russia	1.9	1999	Yes	No
6	Brazil	1.7	1998[c]	No[d]	No[d]
7	Thailand	1.3	1998	No	Yes
8	India	1.0	1999[c]	No[d]	Yes
9	Bangladesh	1.0	1999[c]	No[d]	Yes
10	Mexico	0.9	1999	No	No

Legend
FY = fiscal year
[a]Total lending includes investment and adjustment loans.
[b]Completed between 1997 and August 1999.
[c]Progress report.
[d]Review is either planned or underway but was not completed as of August 1999.
Source: World Bank data.

Since the types and level of Bank financing appear to have been set through the country lending process without a full consideration of these important risk management tools, the Bank may have missed an important opportunity to better target its anticorruption risk assessments and leverage its efforts to minimize opportunities for corruption in Bank-financed projects. A senior Bank official told us that the proper sequencing of these events is more likely to occur in the future as the Bank gains more experience.

Increased Emphasis Placed on Control Activities, but Project Auditing and Supervision Remain Weak

According to COSO standards, effective control activities should be undertaken to ensure that management's directives are carried out. The Bank has established various control activities to ensure that borrowers follow Bank rules when implementing Bank-financed projects. The borrowing nation monitors implementation of projects and reports progress and financial status periodically. Independent audits arranged by the borrower are a key component of the Bank's control activities. For every project, the Bank requires the borrower to arrange for an independent auditing firm or institution to conduct an annual financial audit. Audits must include reviews of project financial reporting and testing of internal controls for the project.

To supplement borrower monitoring and project audits, Bank staff conduct various types of procurement and financial management supervision of projects to ensure borrowers' compliance with Bank rules. These activities include, among other things, reviewing project financial accounting, reporting, and auditing arrangements; reviewing bid awards and contracts; reviewing project expenditures; and visiting project sites. In some cases, Bank approvals of certain borrower actions are specifically required under the loan agreements. For example, for major procurements, representing about one-third of the value of total Bank-financed procurement contracts, Bank staff must pre-approve contract awards to ensure that they are fair and verify that contract expenditures are eligible under the loan agreement before Bank funds are disbursed. However, for the remaining procurements, Bank staff are only required to conduct spot-checks to ensure that Bank rules were followed.

In the past several years, the Bank's internal auditor has identified significant weaknesses in some control activities. For example, recent Bank reports have revealed that many Bank-approved auditors produced audit reports that were late and of poor quality, with limited identification of problems. In addition, Bank studies for 1996 through 1998 noted that the Bank had not practiced appropriate financial management supervision and ensured that borrowers complied with the Bank's basic financial accounting, reporting, and auditing requirements. For example, in a September 1998 report on the quality of Bank supervision, Bank reviewers found that financial management supervision, while improving, was less than satisfactory in over 30 percent of the projects reviewed. In addition, other Bank studies indicated that the Bank often failed to conduct required spot-checks of borrowers' compliance with procurement and expenditure eligibility requirements. As a result, a large and growing percentage of the contracts financed by the Bank were awarded without any Bank review.

The Bank has made progress in strengthening project auditing and supervision, but it is not yet clear whether its efforts have been successful.

Progress

The Bank has devoted increased resources and attention to financial management and procurement supervision. In the financial management area, the Bank has increased awareness among staff about the importance of ensuring adequate financial management arrangements and reporting in its projects. It has also upgraded its financial management policies and procedures, established a framework for ensuring proper financial management, and provided additional staff and training for this purpose.

In the procurement area, the Bank has taken a variety of steps to better supervise borrowers' procurement activities and ensure that contracts were awarded in compliance with Bank guidelines. This has included hiring or training local Bank staff or contracting with local consultants to review borrowers' procurement actions. In addition to improving routine procurement supervision, the Bank has undertaken a number of special procurement audits to help oversee the use of project funds. In fiscal years 1998 and 1999, the Bank conducted or contracted for intensive procurement reviews of 54 of its approximately 1,500 projects. Since 1996, the Bank identified cases in 26 projects in 16 countries in which the borrower did not comply with the Bank's procurement rules. Thus, the Bank refused to finance contracts valued at least $114 million. In addition, the Bank has debarred 44 firms and 9 individuals, prohibiting them from conducting future business with the Bank.[18]

For some new projects, the Bank has also introduced innovative approaches to project design and implementation intended to provide more effective controls over the use of project funds. For example, in several new projects we reviewed, community-based monitoring programs are being devised that incorporated input

[18] The information on Bank "misprocurements," that is, expenditures that have not been procured in accordance with Bank procurement rules and related loan agreements, covers the period from January 1996 to November 1999. Data on bank misprocurements occurring before this date are not available, as they were not centrally tracked. Debarment data are through March 24, 2000.

from local citizen and user groups. The Bank believes that since these groups have a vested interest in the outcome of the projects, they will put pressure on responsible officials to ensure the proper use of project funds. In one country we visited, the Bank allocated project funds to hire local consultants to facilitate community involvement in project design and implementation, including monitoring of project expenditures. Project implementers posted detailed information in local villages on the schedule and cost of small infrastructure works financed by the project. Eight of the 12 new projects[19] we reviewed specifically included some aspect of increased transparency or community involvement in the project design to help prevent the misuse of funds.

Challenges

Although there are signs of improvement in the quality of supervision, the Bank is still having difficulties in correcting some of the shortcomings that the Bank's internal units and external auditors have highlighted. For example, according to a 1999 Bank study on procurement reform in two of the Bank's six geographical regions, one of these regions had not conducted the required level of procurement supervision, even though both regions had engaged in significant hiring of new specialized staff and training of existing staff members to strengthen this function. Bank officials indicated that this region is taking corrective measures to ensure that the required level of procurement supervision is completed.

The Bank is also experiencing difficulty in meeting financial management supervision requirements. A 1999 Bank study found that the percentage of projects for which Bank staff meet basic financial management supervision requirements increased from about 70 percent in 1998 to about 80 percent in 1999.[20] However, Bank officials who conducted this study noted that Bank performance in this area was still deficient, considering that the requirements "should have been easily attainable." Bank officials are optimistic that performance of these basic requirements will improve further as the Bank continues to build its financial management capacity.

However, the Bank is also establishing additional requirements that will make financial management supervision more challenging in the future.

We found little evidence that improved financial management supervision has resulted in any increase in the quality of project auditing. The previously cited

---

[19] Approved since November 1, 1998.

[20] Supervision Quality in Fiscal Year 1999: A Quality Assurance Group Assessment (Washington, D.C.: World Bank, Oct. 7, 1999).

1999 Bank study of financial management supervision indicated that Bank staff were generally more diligent about reviewing project audit reports. However, according to Bank managers we spoke to, supervision of project auditors is not considered the responsibility of Bank staff, and Bank staff conduct little quality control of audit work.

BANK CONDUCTS EXTENSIVE MONITORING, BUT PROGRESS IN ADDRESSING CONTROL WEAKNESSES NOT MEASURED

According to COSO standards, an effective management control system requires monitoring of the controls to assess their quality over time and to ensure that problems are promptly resolved. Although the Bank has established an extensive array of mechanisms to monitor project management, it does not clearly measure progress the Bank is making in correcting management control weaknesses. Without a monitoring system that focuses on key areas of weakness, the Bank's management and Board of Directors cannot be certain that the initiatives in the Bank's anticorruption action plan are appropriate or sufficient to safeguard loan funds.

The Bank has a variety of systems to monitor and evaluate the quality of its management processes and controls. At the individual project level, Bank staff regularly (at least semiannually) submit a project status report, which includes the staff's assessment of the progress of project implementation and the status of procurement and financial management, among other issues. These reports are compiled and analyzed annually to provide Bank management and the Board with a detailed report on overall portfolio performance. In addition to this reporting, various Bank units conduct evaluations of Bank project management. The Bank's internal auditor has conducted occasional audits of various aspects of Bank supervision of Bank projects. The Bank's quality assurance unit has taken a systematic evaluation approach, conducting annual studies to evaluate the quality of new project designs and Bank supervision activities. Finally, the Bank's external auditor assesses annually the adequacy of the Bank's management controls over financial reporting.

The Bank has made progress in using new tools for monitoring and evaluating the implementation of Bank projects. However, it faces challenges in ensuring that it corrects acknowledged weaknesses in management control activities.

Progress

The Bank has improved its monitoring mechanisms by assigning responsibility for tracking Bank-wide compliance with quality standards for project supervision to a central operations group. This unit draws upon various monitoring mechanisms in place and has established some new ones. To assess progress on procurement reforms, the unit has sponsored new studies of two regions in 1999, with similar studies to follow in the future. To assess progress in financial management reform, the unit focuses on the quality assurance group's annual review of supervision quality. In addition, in 1999, the unit solicited status reports on project supervision from the regional procurement and financial management advisors in each of the Bank's six regions and compiled annual status reports for Bank management.

Challenges

Bank monitoring efforts do not fully assess the impact of Bank efforts to improve the strength of its management controls over project lending. In particular, the Bank's monitoring efforts do not focus on key deficiencies in management controls highlighted by Bank studies in the past few years. Consequently, we were unable to determine the extent to which the Bank has corrected these deficiencies. In particular, we were unable to determine whether the quality of project audits has improved or whether Bank staff have conducted required reviews of project procurement, financial reporting, and expenditure eligibility.

The Bank does not systematically monitor the quality of project audits. Although the Bank has a system for tracking compliance with auditing requirements, according to Bank officials this system generates unreliable data that cannot be used to reach firm conclusions because Bank staff have not consistently entered these data accurately or on time. The Bank's planned implementation of a new management information system may improve the reliability of these data in the future. Based on our review of the Bank's other periodic monitoring activities, none includes a systematic assessment of audit quality. For example, the Bank's annual study of financial management supervision addresses whether Bank management received and reviewed the required audit reports but not the quality of the audit. Thus, the Bank has not determined the extent to which the reliability of project audits as a management control activity has improved.

In addition, the Bank conducts limited monitoring of the extent to which Bank staff carry out required supervision at the project level, the regional level, or the Bank-wide level. At the project level, Bank staff are not required to report on compliance with key procurement and financial management supervision requirements in their mandatory project status reports. For example, these reports do not indicate to what extent Bank staff conducted required spot-checks of completed procurement actions and project expenditures reports to ensure that the borrower complied with Bank rules. Regional-level monitoring and reporting on supervision performance have also been incomplete. The annual regional reports on procurement and financial management supervision do not provide an analysis of the extent to which each region conducted the required level of supervision. As a result, Bank management cannot use these reporting systems to compile Bank-wide data for assessing whether Bank staff are meeting supervision quality standards.

At the Bank-wide level, the Bank does some monitoring and evaluation of project supervision in the annual review of supervision quality, prepared by the Bank's Quality Assurance Group. However, this review gives an incomplete picture of the quality of Bank supervision because it includes only certain supervisory activities and does not encompass some important Bank supervisory functions where performance has persistently been weak. For example, the review of procurement supervision does not address the Bank's performance in conducting required spot-checks of contract awards made by borrowers.[21] Similarly, the review of financial management supervision does not address the Bank's performance in spot-checking the eligibility of project expenditures. As a result, the supervision quality scores generated by this study mask performance problems reported by external and internal auditors.

The Bank also lacks meaningful performance indicators that could be used to monitor the impact of its institutional development efforts in strengthening management controls in borrowing countries. Only 2 of the 31 country assistance strategies we reviewed established measurable indicators for improving the anticorruption environment. Also, an evaluation of the Bank's anticorruption efforts in two African countries prepared by a World Bank consultant in 1998 indicated that the Bank's performance indicators could not be used to measure the effectiveness of the Bank's interventions and approaches. Bank officials told us that developing indicators to assess progress being made in this area is very difficult, but efforts are underway.

---

21 According to Bank procurement staff, the assessment addresses the Bank's performance in conducting prior review of proposed contract awards but not ex-post reviews of contracts awarded without the Bank's prior approval.

Information and Communication Have Increased, but Challenges Exist in Borrower Countries

COSO standards emphasize the need for information to be communicated in a form and time frame that enable people to carry out their responsibilities. Bank management recognized the need to increase the level and quality of its communications on anticorruption initiatives with its own staff and among borrowers and has launched a major effort to improve communications through a variety of outreach programs. This outreach effort has been conducted through the internet, special publications, Bank-sponsored conferences, workshops, training sessions, and other means.

Despite progress in improving information and communications, the Bank still faces challenges in raising awareness within borrowing countries.

Progress

The Bank has strengthened communication with and coordination on anticorruption issues among international donors, nongovernmental organizations, former government officials, academicians, business leaders, and other organizations. The Bank has also worked in tandem with the Organization for Economic Cooperation and Development, an economic forum of major industrialized countries, to promote global initiatives, such as the International Anti-bribery Convention.

Challenges

During our country visits, we found that some borrowing country staff and members of civil society charged with monitoring Bank projects were not fully aware of the Bank's efforts to establish new mechanisms for countering fraud and corruption in Bank-financed projects. For example, we visited several locations during our field visits where civil organizations involved in monitoring Bank-financed projects were not aware of the hotline or other mechanisms for reporting allegations of fraud and corruption. As a result, allegations of fraud and corruption in Bank projects could potentially go unreported to the Bank's Oversight Committee on Fraud and Corruption or be handled locally without the committee's knowledge. Senior Bank officials confirmed that additional efforts need to be made to increase awareness of the anticorruption activities and resources within borrower countries, particularly project implementing agencies and beneficiaries.

Although the Bank's external auditor does assess the adequacy of some management controls, the scope of the assessment is limited to controls relating to the Bank's financial statement reporting. The scope of the external auditor's annual assessment does not currently extend to controls over project lending. The Bank is planning to extend the scope of its future COSO reviews to include an examination of the efficiency and effectiveness of its operations, which will include its lending operations.

CONCLUSIONS

The Bank lends billions of dollars to developing countries each year in a difficult and challenging environment. Over the past several years, the Bank has made a vigorous attempt to strengthen its management controls and build borrower capacity to better manage Bank-financed projects to reduce opportunities for fraud and corruption on its projects. This effort has entailed making major improvements in the Bank's internal oversight structure, project management, and institutional development strategies. However, these controls, although improving, are not yet strong enough to provide reasonable assurances that project funds are spent according to the Bank's guidelines. Significant weaknesses still exist in each of the key components of the Bank's management control system. Efforts are underway to address many of these weaknesses in (1) internal oversight mechanisms, (2) assessing risks in individual projects and in overall country assistance strategies, (3) allocating anticorruption assistance among borrowers based on risk, (4) monitoring and reporting progress in correcting management control deficiencies, and (5) disseminating information on anticorruption activities within borrowing countries. Additional steps would enable the Bank to further limit opportunities for fraud and corruption and safeguard project funds. Continual management attention would also help sustain the current improvement efforts and ensure these remaining weaknesses are fully addressed. Nevertheless, questions will remain about the adequacy of the steps taken to strengthen these controls unless the World Bank publishes periodic public progress reports.

RECOMMENDATIONS

To help ensure that the World Bank achieves its goal of obtaining reasonable assurance that project funds are spent as intended and that corruption risks are mitigated in Bank-financed projects, we recommend that the Secretary of the Treasury instruct the U.S. Executive Director of the World Bank to work with other Executive Board members to encourage the Bank to

1. integrate investigative functions into a single unit and establish organizational independence of the unit to better address allegations of wrongdoing;
2. include more complete information in project appraisal documents and country assistance strategies on the risks related to corruption and any procurement and financial management weaknesses of borrowers, as well as planned supervisory actions to mitigate the identified risks;
3. target procurement and financial management assessments at countries where corruption risks are greatest;
4. monitor and report on progress in strengthening management controls and correcting past project management control weaknesses, including results of efforts to strengthen project auditing and supervision; and
5. develop a plan to raise awareness of the Bank's anticorruption program among project implementing agencies and beneficiaries.

Furthermore, to ensure that Bank's anticorruption initiatives have the desired impact, we recommend that the Secretary of the Treasury monitor Bank progress in meeting each of the five components of an effective management control system and annually report to the Congress evidence of progress.

Chapter 7

WORLD BANK LENDING: ISSUES RAISED BY CHINA'S QINGHAI RESETTLEMENT PROJECT

Jonathan Sanford and Michelle Chang

SUMMARY

On July 7,2000, China withdrew its application for a $40 million loan from the World Bank to finance a settlement and poverty reduction project in Qinghai province, northeast of Tibet. Chinese authorities said they would do the project their own way with their own funds. The Bank's Executive Board had endorsed a decision by the independent Inspection Panel that China should take remedial steps to address criticisms and face a second vote before the project could be approved. The U.S. Congress approved two amendments in 1999 expressing disapproval of the project.

Qinghai is a region historically claimed by Tibetan peoples, though other ethnic groups comprise the majority of the population. The loan was controversial; many analysts believe the World Bank was cooperating with the Chinese government to move people of Han ancestry into minority regions in order to firmly integrate them into China. Many believe the Bank should have required an environmental analysis and shown more sensitivity to ethnic concerns. The Chinese claimed that the United States and other countries improperly politicized the World Bank loan process.

The Qinghai loan proposal raised many questions. Can the Bank adhere to its rules when a borrower country has other strongly-held priorities? Are its

Executive Board and senior management exercising effective oversight over Bank operations? How much weight should the Bank give to the needs of regional or ethnic minorities vis-a-vis the needs of a country's broader population? How responsive should the Bank be to the preferences of its client? More importantly- who is the client? If the country is the client, then how does the Bank justify the imposition of its social and environmental rules? If the people of the country are the real client, then how does the bank persuade the borrower country to take out loans and adhere to guidelines which it may find of limited value to its larger national priorities?

The Inspection Panel found that the Bank had committed numerous violations of its rules. A review of the Panel's report indicates that it failed to confirm many of the strongest objections that critics had posed to the project. This includes the charge that the project would result in cultural genocide for the Tibetan residents, that it would lead to major soil erosion and water pollution, and that the new settlers were being relocated involuntarily. Nevertheless, the report indicates that the Bank's errors as regards ethnic sensitivity, environmental protection, consultation with affected groups, and public notice were notable. The Executive Board and senior management are reportedly considering steps to assure the public and their member countries that mistakes of this sort will not happen again. Likewise, the situation suggests that the Board may need to establish clearer guidelines so the staff can balance the numerous and sometimes conflicting priorities the Bank has adopted.

This chapter finds that opposition to the Qinghai loan was fueled, in large part, by concern on the part of the partisans of Tibet that time is running out on their hopes for autonomy. Likewise, many observers have reservations about the size and composition of Bank lending in China. The Bank has apparently agreed to lend $1 billion over the next three years to fund new development programs in west China.

INTRODUCTION

On June 24, 1999, the World Bank Board of Executive Directors approved a package of loans to China totaling $160 million to finance a series of poverty reduction projects in Western China. One portion of the package, totaling $40 million, was intended to finance settlement and poverty reduction activities in Qinghai ("Ching-High") province. This province adjoins Xizang province, which is the heartland of Tibet. Many Tibetans believe that Qinghai is part of a broader area in southwest China which they consider to be historically and traditionally

Tibetan. Ethnic Tibetan people no longer comprise a majority of the population in many or most of those areas.

The Qinghai loan proposal was very controversial. Critics argued that it would promote cultural genocide of the Tibetan people and seriously damage the environment in the project area. Critics also complained that the Bank was helping the Chinese move people into the settlement area involuntarily and that it had suppressed public information about the project in order to hamper their efforts to oppose the loan. Before giving final approval to the loan, the Executive Board asked the Bank's independent Inspection Panel to determine whether the Bank had complied with its own rules in the preparation of the project. The Inspection Panel found a number of serious errors. On July 7, 2000, the Executive Board decided that the errors and omissions in the original plan would have to be rectified and it would have to vote again before the Qinghai project could go forward. The Chinese government decided at that point to withdraw its application for the loan. The authorities said that China would implement the Qinghai project its own way with its own resources.

In one sense, the issues raised by the Qinghai loan are moot, since it is no longer an active proposal within the World Bank. In another sense, however, they continue to be matters of broad concern. The controversy about the loan raised questions, in the minds of many observers, about the Bank's ability to design and implement projects effectively and in compliance with its own rules. In particular, it has raised doubts whether the Bank can adhere to its social, human rights, and environmental standards when a borrower country government has other concerns.

This chapter provides a detailed analysis of the Qinghai loan proposal and the events surrounding it. For many people, the Qinghai project casts a long shadow on their future attitudes towards the World Bank and other multilateral development bank (MDB) programs. Much information has been published about the Qinghai project. However, a good deal of the reporting in the press seemed partial and incomplete, focusing more on color and controversy than on the basic documents or issues themselves. Some of the lessons learned from the situation may have been based on inadequate information. This chapter seeks to clarify some of these events and to identify significant implications.

The Qinghai loan controversy highlighted a number of dilemmas or choices which the World Bank and other MDBs may confront during the course of their operations. At the present moment, analysis of the Qinghai project may not yield definitive conclusions, since good arguments can be marshaled on all sides. However, it may be able to show some aspects of these matters which may not have been previously apparent to all observers.

How much weight, for example, should an MDB give to the needs of an ethnic or regional minority compared to the concerns of the broader population of a borrower country? Are development projects in areas which are lightly populated and where the natural landscape has been largely untouched by human activity intrinsically a violation of the environment, even if measures to protect the environment are included in the project design? How responsive should the MDBs be to their clients' needs? More fundamentally, who is the actual client? If the borrower country is the client, how does the bank justify imposing social and environmental requirements which the government does not welcome. If the people of the country are the client and the borrower country government is merely an instrument to serve their needs, then how can the bank persuade governments to borrow money to finance activities which may not be their highest priorities and whose goals they may not folly embrace?

The controversy about the Qinghai loan also raises some possible concerns about oversight. How can the Executive Board and senior management assure themselves that Bank staff are complying with established rules? How can senior management assure the Board, member country governments, and the public that their institution can be trusted to make effective use of the resources provided to them by member countries and to comply with the standards which are presumably the basic justification for that support?

In recent years, the MDB program has been controversial in the U.S. Congress. Some have questioned whether the amounts of money which the Administration has pledged to contribute to MDB programs is appropriate. Appropriations for MDB programs have been substantially less in some years than the Administration proposed. Members of Congress from several different viewpoints have sought to enact legislation aimed at changing the way the MDBs operate, giving greater emphasis to market forces or environmental standards, or direct action aimed at the alleviation of poverty. Congress expressed serious concern, during the period when the Qinghai loan was under active consideration, about the World Bank's judgment in proposing that loan.

The debate about the Qinghai loan underscores some of the difficulties which may hamper effective international debate about MDB operations. The World Bank was parsimonious in the amount of information it released prior to the Executive Board's initial consideration of the Qinghai loan proposal in June 1999. Critics had few other sources for reliable information about conditions in the project area or the proposed project itself. Many of the critics had larger objectives. For them, blocking or reforming the Qinghai project was not an end in itself but rather a step towards building wider public support for a broader agenda. Press treatment of the controversy often seemed less than impartial or thorough.

Because of these conditions, debate on the Qinghai project may not have laid the groundwork for sound generalizations and future policy prescriptions.

This chapter finds that the World Bank seems to have made serious mistakes and errors in its preparation of plans for the Qinghai project. The Bank will obviously be urged to take action to remedy these errors and to restore public confidence. This chapter also finds, however, that the intensity of the international opposition to the Qinghai proposal was much stronger than the types of errors in project design and implementation might lead one to expect. It finds that broader issues, such as Tibetan national concerns about China's current policies towards Tibet and concerns about the future trends in China's relationships with the outside world and the composition of World Bank lending to China, may have played a larger role in motivating public and official concern about the Qinghai project. The chapter discusses, near the end, the recent pattern of World Bank lending to China and it identifies some possible areas of concern.

THE QINGHAI SETTLEMENT PROJECT

The Western Poverty Alleviation loan had three components.[1] Besides the program in Qinghai, it was also intended to finance poverty alleviation programs in Inner Mongolia and Gansu provinces. The latter two are going ahead as planned. The Qinghai project was the latest in a series of settlement projects that the World Bank has funded in low-income, under-populated (and often ethnic minority) areas of Western China. None of the others elicited the kind of attention and controversy as did the project in Qinghai.

The loan package for Qinghai consisted of a \$26.7 million loan from the International Development Association (IDA), the Bank's concessional loan window, and a \$13.3 million loan from the International Bank for Reconstruction and Development (IBRD). IDA is funded through contributions by governments (the U.S. share being about 21%). It lends to the world's poorest countries at very low interest rates over long repayment periods. The IBRD is funded with money borrowed in commercial capital markets with the financial backing of the World Bank's member country governments (the U.S. share being about 17%.) It lends,

---

[1] World Bank. Project Appraisal Document on a Proposed Loan of US\$60 million and a Proposed Credit of SDR 73.8 million (US\$100 million equivalent) to the People's Republic of China for the Western Poverty Reduction Project. June 1,1999. Report No: 18982-CHA. A copy may be obtained from the World Bank web site, (http://www.worldbank.org]. Select "...more special interest," then "July 7, 2000 China to Implement..." then "Documents...", then Project Appraisal Document." Choose PDF version.

without direct subsidy, on near-market terms.[2] Under a longstanding agreement between the World Bank and China, China ceased to be eligible to receive concessional loans from IDA on July 1, 1999. The Qinghai loan would have been the last project for which China would be eligible to receive assistance from IDA.

Figure 1. Location of Qinghai Province

The Qinghai project would have helped move 58,000 people from six counties in the arid hill country of eastern Qinghai to dry but potentially irrigable areas in Dulan county, Haixi autonomous prefecture, near the center of the province. (See figure 1) It would have funded construction of a new dam, renovation of an existing dam, and construction of irrigation and drainage facilities on 19,200 hectares of previously uncultivated land. It would have provided the settlers with livestock, seeds, and other supplies and given them training on improved agricultural and livestock methods. Basic social services, such as health and education, also would have been provided. The 4,000 people living in the move-in area are mostly nomadic herders. The people in the eastern counties, from which the settlers will come, reportedly have per capita incomes of around $25 to $60 a year. The Bank claims that on-site poverty alleviation efforts in those counties would be difficult, if not impossible, because of inaccessibility, land scarcity and severe environmental degradation in that region.

---

[2] For further information on the World Bank and other MDBs, see: CRS Issue Brief IB96008, *Multilateral Development Banks: Issues for Congress,* by Jonathan E. Sanford.

CONCERNS OF THE CRITICS

Negative Cultural Impact on Tibetans

Critics identified at least four factors as the basis for their opposition to the Qinghai loan. First, many people were concerned that the project would have an undesirable effect on the ethnic make-up of the region. Most of the new settlers would be of non-Tibetan ancestry. Tibetan exile groups argued that the loan would result in "cultural genocide" and that the immigrants would overwhelm the local culture.[3] Many also worried that the influx of new residents would cause the prefecture where the project is sited to lose its designation as a Tibetan-Mongolian autonomous area, with a consequential lose of government posts for minorities and less support for bilingual education and cultural preservation.[4]

Opponents mobilized wide support, including active endorsements by popular figures from the entertainment industry, and they secured thousands of signatures worldwide protesting the project. Human rights campaigners demanded that it be cancelled. Supporters of Tibetan autonomy were particularly vocal in their criticism of the project. John Ackerly, President of the International Campaign for Tibet, claimed that the Bank "has no problem with moving Chinese into Tibet as long as it meets environmental and social requirements." He said the Bank has " a very myopic view of what the requirements are." Alison Reynolds, Director of the Free Tibet Campaign, argued that the international financial institutions "should not finance China's effort to reduce Tibetans to a minority in their own land."[5] Supporters of Tibet feared, she said, that the project would "set the precedent legitimizing Chinese population transfer to Tibet." The Dalai Lama, exiled spiritual head of the Tibetan people, noted that China's actions were putting Tibet's unique culture and the survival of the Tibetans as a distinct people at risk. He said "The present situation inside Tibet is very, very critical," and he added that "time is running out."[6] Ackerly said that "We are discouraged the Bank - would want to have on its records such a repugnant project."[7]

---

[3] See, for example: Sathnam Sanghera. Tibet Report Dispute Throws World Bank into Disarray: Directors' Ruling on Publication has Fuelled Anger Over Loan. *Financial Times,* June 26, 2000, p. 10. See also" World Bank Directors Mull Tibet Resettlement Project. *Agence France Presse International,* June 22, 2000.

[4] See, for instance: Renee Schoof China, World Bank plan to move 57,800 farmers draws criticism; U.S., others say relocation will harm environment, Tibetan, Mongolian culture. *Milwaukee Journal Sentinel,* September 12, 1999, p. 19. Distributed by the Associated Press.

[5] Alison Reynolds, Tibetan Takeover. *The Ecologist,* September 2000, p. 20.

[6] Ackerly and the Dali Lama are both quoted in *Agence France Presse,* note 2.

[7] Quoted in: Internal Report Criticizes World Bank China Project. *Agence France Presse,* June 27, 2000.

In March 2000, Chinese Prime Minister Zhu Rongji said, in his annual policy address, that China's efforts in the West would "strengthen national unity, safeguard social stability and consolidate border defense." A prominent Tibet scholar noted that comments of this sort have alarmed Tibetans. "It seems to signal something Tibetans have dreaded for decades, a real Chinese determination to absorb Tibet," he said. "To Tibetan ears this sounds ominous, perhaps even the onset of a final solution."[8]

Some critics claimed[9] that Qinghai had been created as a separate province from Tibet by the Communists after 1949 in order to reduce the influence of Tibetan culture. Critics of the project noted that the Dalai Lama and former Pachen Lama (the second highest-ranking lama in Tibetan Buddhism) were born in Qinghai province, sometimes leaving an impression that they were born in the new settlement area.[10] They were both actually born in the area from which the settlers will move.[11] Nevertheless, critics believe that these ties of birth underscore important historic and cultural links between Qinghai and the region's broader Tibetan heritage. The *Washington Times* said[12] that the Qinghai project was a "thinly veiled ethnic-cleansing scheme" which sought to "debilitate the Tibetan culture." The *South China Post* indicated[13] that there was some doubt whether the Chinese Government would include, within the settlement costs, the cost of relocating Tibetan monks and their temples from the eastern provinces to the new area. Some officials were reportedly adamant that the cost of relocating religious institutions was the responsibility of the villagers themselves.

---

[8] Damien McElroy. Tibet's culture and vultures clash; Bejing is encouraging thousands of "patriotic settlers" to go west, posing a big threat to an ancient way of life. *The Sunday Telegraph* (London), November 19, 2000, p. 37. The Tibet scholar quoted was Gabriel Lafitte.

[9] See, for example: Jason Burke. World Bank says no to Chinese settlers in Tibet. *The Observer,* London, July 9,2000, p. 26. See also Reynolds, note 5, p. 20

[10] See, for example: David Sanger and Joseph Kahn. World Bank Criticizes Itself Over Chinese Project Near Tibet, *The New York Times,* June 27, 2000, p. A7. See also: Jonathan Peterson. China Pull Its Loan Request from World Bank. *The Oregonian,* Portland, Oregon, July 8, 2000, p. A8. Times-Washington Post Service.

[11] See, for example, Comment and Analysis: A move for the Good of China; the World Bank has been unfairly criticized over the Qinghai resettlement project, says Robert Wade. *Financial Times,* July 4, 2000. Wade is a professor of political economy and development at the London School of Economics and served as consultant to the Inspection Panel in the Qinghai Investigation.

[12] More World, Less Bank. *Washington Times,* July 11, 2000, p. A18.

[13] World Bank Walks Away and Poor Pick Up the Party Bill in Qinghai. *South China Morning Post,* Hong Kong, July 14, 2000, p. 6.

Soil Erosion and Water Quality

Second, some critics worried the project would have negative environmental consequences when it leveled the arid wind-swept land in the area for irrigated agriculture. Many were also concerned about the effect the new dam and irrigation systems might have on water quality.[14] They thought the inflow of 58,000 new settlers and the introduction of large-scale irrigated agriculture would have detrimental effects on the environment.[15] They believe the World Bank should have required the Chinese Government to finance a comprehensive environmental impact assessment before sending the project to the Executive Board for consideration.

Consultation and Voluntary Settlement

Third, critics questioned whether the resettlement planned for the Qinghai project was truly voluntary.[16] The World Bank has a policy against involuntary resettlement. Critics argued that it is difficult to know whether the settlers are willing migrants or whether they were willing to move because they feared government reprisal if they resist government resettlement plans. Likewise, critics say it is hard to know if the current residents really want to convert from a nomadic to a more settled lifestyle. They observed that the Bank's surveys of affected people in both areas were not truly confidential. The also said the Chinese might use prison labor, from a major prison complex located near the settlement area, in project construction.

Transparency and Public Notice

Finally, the critics were concerned about what they believe was a serious lack of transparency on the part of the Bank. They said they first heard of the loan in late April 1999, though it had been under preparation by Bank staff since at least 1997. A summary version of the official document describing the project was posted on the Bank web site in May 1999. A more thorough version was posted

---

[14] See, for example, the following notice distributed by non-governmental organizations(NGOs) concerning a news conference they would hold June 17,1999 across from the World Bank to protest expected cultural and environmental damage. World Bank China Plan Threatens Tibetans, Environment. *PR* Newswire, New York, June 17, 1999

[15] See Schoof note 4 above.

[16] See, for example, *Financial Times,* June 27, 2000, note 3 above.

on June 1, 1999, only a few weeks before the scheduled vote. Many opponents believed that Bank staff worked with the Chinese to delay public notice of the project in order to make their task more difficult.

THE WORLD BANK'S RESPONSE

Negative Cultural Impact on Tibetans

The World Bank said, in its original reply to critics, that the Qinghai project would not have had a negative influence on the Tibetan population.[17] Nobody would be moving into Qinghai from outside the province. The new settlers would be moving 500 kilometers (about 300 miles) to the west from eastern Qinghai. The settlement area was located about 500 kilometers from the nearest border with Xizang province (Tibet). According to Bank figures, some 69% of the 4,000 current residents of the settlement area are of Mongol ancestry, the remainder being Han (26%) and Hui (5%). From the Bank's figures, it appears that no people of Tibetan ancestry reside in the immediate project area. The Bank reports that people of Han ancestry comprise 53% of the population of Dulan county, the larger area where the project would be located, and 57% of Qinghai province as a whole. Tibetans account for 23% and 26%, respectively, of the population. The World Bank anticipated, from its list of applicants, that 42% of the 58,000 new settlers would be Han, 52% Muslim ethnic minorities (mostly Hui), and 6% Tibetan.

As best can be determined, the critics did not dispute the World Bank's statistics. (See below, however, for the Inspection Panel's conclusions.) Heat was added to the controversy during early 1999 when Daja Meston - an American Tibetan trying to make a unauthorized visit to Dulan county in order to investigate conditions on the ground - suffered serious injury to his spine after falling from a fourth-floor window. He was reportedly being held under guard by Chinese security agents.[18]

The Bank reported, in its basic document explaining the Western Poverty Alleviation project (see note 1) that the Chinese government had agreed to several special loan conditions aimed at preserving ethnic diversity in the settlement area.

---

[17] See: World Bank. China Western Poverty Reduction Project; Summary paper. June 2, 1999. Obtained from World Bank web site in 1999. This document seems to be no longer available from the World Bank site.

[18] "Hong Kong Paper criticizes World Bank policy towards China." BBC Monitoring Asia Pacific, London, July 10,2000. Reference to South China Sunday Morning Post, July 9,2000, p. 10.

The Chinese agreed that the prefecture would continue to be designated a Tibetan and Mongolian Autonomous Area.[19] The nomads could continue their preferred livelihood, if they chose, and corridors would be retained so they could move their flocks across the settled area. Minority settlers would be located as intact communities, according to their place of origin, and would be placed near other ethnically compatible national communities. Settlers would have 30 year leases on terms acceptable to the Bank. Education for minority students in primary and junior secondary schools would be in their natal languages. Healthcare and other social services would be provided by ways compatible with ethnic cultural preferences and in appropriate languages. Cultural centers would be established and supported to develop cultural education and entertainment programs. The Bank said it would monitor the pilot program that aimed to develop "best practices" for use in the overall settlement plan.

Soil Erosion and Water Quality

The Bank maintained, in its June 1999 reply to critics, that no comprehensive Environmental Impact Analysis (EIA) of the Qinghai project was needed. The Bank said that the land reclamation and improvement techniques to be used in the project were familiar types which have been widely used (32 times) in other arid regions of China. It said the settlement area is one of the driest in China and the land is of little value for pasture or habitation due to very sparse groundcover. The region is dotted by salt lakes, along with sand dunes and salty marshes. The Bank says the new dam would be located "off river" and would not interrupt the flow of the local river system. The river flows mainly into salty marsh areas downstream. The planned irrigation would reportedly reduce the groundwater level in those areas by about half a meter. The plan required regular surveys to determine whether undesirable conditions might develop in the swampy areas that would need correction.

Voluntary Settlement and Transparency

The Bank claimed that all prospective settlers were volunteers. It noted that it had many times the number of applicants from the eastern Qinghai counties than

[19] On this point, see Memorandum from Ko-Yung Tung, Vice President and General Counsel, World Bank, to Jim MacNeili, Chairman Inspection Panel. China: Credit No. 3255-CHA....Request for Legal Opinion. April 19, 2000. Included as the final appendix to the Inspection Panel Report. See note 27.

can be accommodated in the settlement area. Finally, the Bank claimed, in its original response, that it gave as much formal advance notice for this project as it gave for other projects with similar a similar environmental classification. As will be noted below, the Bank subsequently retracted its argument on the latter point.

ACTION BY THE U.S. CONGRESS

In response to substantial public concern, Congress took a number of steps to express its dissatisfaction with the Qinghai loan. In mid-1999, during their consideration of the FY 2000 appropriations for U.S. payments to the multilateral development banks (MDBs), the Senate cut $8.4 million and the House cut $8 million from the pending appropriation for IDA in order to demonstrate their disapproval of the Bank's action in June 1999 tentatively approving that loan. This was approximately the U.S. share of the IDA funds supporting the project.[20] In September 1999, 35 Members of the House sponsored legislation aimed at withholding U.S. funds from World Bank projects that would harm the environment or the rights of indigenous peoples.[21] Subsequently, in June 2000, 58 Members of Congress reportedly cosigned a letter to the Bank contending that it was trying to prevent the public from knowing the content of the Inspection Panel's report (see below) before the Bank took final action on the Qinghai project.

Bank management subsequently agreed to make the Panel's report public prior to the Board's review of its recommendations. The formal procedures establishing the Inspection Panel require that its reports may not be released before the Executive Board has discussed them and taken final action on their findings. Critics claimed the Bank was suppressing the report in order to minimize its impact, to limit public discussion of the Panel's findings and to lessen the amount of change that might be required in the Qinghai project.[22] Ironically, the

---

[20] The final appropriation for IDA that year was $61 million less than the President's request but greater than the amounts originally approved by the House and Senate. It is impossible to determine what impact the Qinghai loan had on the final tally. See CRS Issue Brief IB96008 for further details.

[21] The Ecosystem and Indigenous Peoples Protection Act (H.R. 2969), introduced by Representative Christopher Cox on September 29, 1999. There were 34 cosponsors, including John Lewis, John Edward Porter, Cynthia McKinney, and Dana Rohrabacher. The House Banking Committee took no action on the bill. See also: Congress threatens to curb funds to World Bank over Qinghai project loan. *South China Morning Post,* Hong Kong, October 3, 1999, p. 6.

[22] See: Sathnara Sanghera. Tibet lobby forces Bank's hand. *Financial Times.* June 22,2000.

Bank seems to have violated its own rules when it acceded to these requests for early release.[23]

In October 2000, Congress adopted language in the fiscal 2001 Foreign Operations Appropriations Act which addressed the issues raised by the Qinghai loan.[24] In Section 801 of the Act, Congress listed several provisions as conditions for U.S. contributions to the World Bank-managed program to forgive debt owed by Heavily Indebted Poor Countries (HIPCs).[25] These included a requirement directing the Secretary of the Treasury to report to Congress on steps the World Bank and IMF are taking towards the adoption of "policies seeking to minimize the number of projects receiving financing that would displace a population involuntarily or be to the detriment of the people or culture of the area into which the displaced population is to be moved."

REPORT OF THE INDEPENDENT INSPECTION PANEL

The independent Inspection Panel is a three-member body[26] that was created by the World Bank Executive Board in 1993 to give private citizens a forum for voicing complaints that they have been or could be injured by a project financed by the Bank. It receives assignments and reports directly to the Executive Board and is independent of Bank management. It has been requested to investigate twelve cases since it came into being in September 1994.

---

[23] On this point, see a letter to the editors (published under the title Managers were indifferent to Qinghai panel's rules) from Daniel D. Bradlow, Professor of Law and Director, International Legal Studies Program, American University. *Financial Times.*, July 7,2000.

[24] P.L. 106-429 (H.R. 4811). The words quoted are found in subsection C(l)(A)(iv).

[25] For an extensive analysis of the HIPC program, see CRS Report RL30214, *Debt Reduction: Initiatives for the Most Heavily Indebted Poor Countries,* by Larry Nowels.

[26] The three members serve multi-year terms. The Panel is currently chaired by Jim McNeill, a Canadian, who was appointed in 1997. He has held high-level positions in several environmental organizations, including director of Environment for the Organization for Economic Cooperation and Development (OECD) and General Secretary of the World Commission on the Environment and Development. Edward Ayensu, a Ghanaian, was appointed to the Panel in 1998. He is a former Senior Advisor to the President of the African Development Bank and Senior Scientist and the Smithsonian Institution; he has also served in several senior posts in Ghanaian and international scientific organizations. Maartje van Putten, from the Netherlands, was appointed in 1999. She was formerly a member of the European Parliament and an active member of its Committee on Development and Cooperation for ten years. She also has an active relationship with several non-governmental organizations (NGOs). For further information, see the Inspection Panel's web site at [http://www.worldbank.org/ inspectionpanel].

The Inspection Panel found that the Bank was in "apparent violation" of its own rules or policies in seven out of the ten issues the complainant had raised.[27] The Panel found that some of the Bank's procedures questioned by critics were in conformity, however, with Bank guidelines. Likewise, it said the Bank's plans for retroactive financing of certain components (1S9)[28] and its plans for construction of a dam in the project area were also compliant with the rules. (95) Many analyses of the Inspection Panel report in the press are either incomplete or partial, sometimes emphasizing subsidiary points rather than core issues. Some seem to be based on sources other than the document itself.

Project Area Defined Too Narrowly

The Panel found that the underlying problem with the Bank's analysis of the Qinghai project was not what was included but what was left out. The Bank's definition of the Qinghai project area was too narrow, the Panel reported. (25/38) It omitted large adjacent areas and nearby villages, including significant numbers of people, who might be affected by the new settlement. (116) The project would double the population of Dulan county and would likely have an impact on more residents than the 4,000 discussed in the report. (77) The report provided no demographic information on the Tibetan and Mongol residents in adjacent by villages or on the broader population clusters in nearby towns. It did not discuss how the social conditions, ethnicity, and economy of Dulan county might be affected by the project. (3;l-3) The Panel also said that the report did not explore the possible impact the project might have on the people left behind in the eastern counties. Social, environmental, and economic conditions are likely to change, the Panel suggested, if the most active and productive residents were moved to the west, (xxiii/85-7)

No Discussion of Alternatives

The Panel found that project plan failed to determine whether there might be ways the people of the eastern counties could be helped *in situ* without resettlement to Dulan county or through resettlement in urban areas, as the

[27] World Bank. The Inspection Panel. Investigation Report; the Qinghai Project. April 28, 2000. Available from the World Bank web site. Follow procedure in note 1, selecting this document from "Inspection Panel Documents."

[28] The numbers in parentheses show where relevant information may be found in the document under discussion.

Chinese 10th five-year plan proposed. (55) It said that the Bank had failed to discuss any alternatives in its project document before concluding that resettlement was the best option. (56) This violated the Bank's guidelines for project preparation, which require a discussion of alternatives other than the activity presented in the project plan. (58)

The Panel noted that nomadic pastoralism traditionally has been the principal economic activity in Qinghai for many years, though it noted major changes have taken place in recent years as the result of government efforts to modernize the local economy and to encourage a more settled lifestyle. It said that "Nomadic pastoralism as practiced on the Tibetan-Qinghai plateau is a unique ecological adaptation." It faulted the Bank for not evaluating the benefits of continuation of that lifestyle compared to participation in irrigated agriculture. (88-9)

Incomplete Environmental Analysis

The Inspection Panel concluded that the Qinghai project should have been categorized as an "A" project for environmental purposes. (72-3) This requires a more detailed environmental impact assessment and earlier public notice. The Panel noted that several components - construction of a dam, a large irrigation area, extensive land reclamation, and resettlement - which it said are usually the kinds of activities that generally require an "A" categorization. (67) The Panel agreed that the plan for construction of the dam complied with Bank rules. (95) It expressed concern, though, that the project document did not say what provisions had been made in its design to deal with seismic activity. The Panel noted that there had been two major earthquakes in Qinghai since 1937. (96) The Panel found, nevertheless, that the Bank had complied with its environmental policy on the safety of dams, one of the items included in the complaint.

The Panel found that the environmental impact analysis in the project documents was inadequate. It did not examine possible effects on the broader region. (77) It did not discuss what the consequences might be, for example, if the new villages in the settlement area become poles for further development hi Dulan county. (83-5) It did not assess possible social and environmental effects on villages in the move-out area. (86-7) Likewise, for the move-in area, the project plan did not explain how the settlers would dispose of their wastes nor did it explore any possible impact on surrounding areas and those downstream. (91) It did not discuss alternatives to irrigation nor did it compare that method of agriculture with other dry-land methods currently used in the settlement area. (56) It did not assess the possible downstream effects of damming the river, including effects on seasonal drainage and on wetlands. These might have negative consequences for nomads and migratory wildlife. (141) It made no separate evaluation of the possible effect of the pesticides that the Chinese government would purchase for the project with its counterpart funds. (97) The project did not document existing environmental baseline conditions (78) The project documents also failed to discuss issues of biodiversity or whether the project might impact areas that were important for rare, vulnerable, or endangered species. It provided no comprehensive list of the flora and fauna living in the area (79/82) and no plan for the conservation of natural habitats (98) These are required by Bank rules. The Panel noted that there had been one report suggesting that increased human habitation in the area might have negative effects on black-necked cranes nesting in saline wetlands down-river from the project site. (99)

Ethnicity, Consultation, and Voluntary Settlement

The Inspection Panel found that the Bank had violated its policies on the treatment of indigenous peoples and involuntary resettlement. The Bank's treatment of ethnic issues was faulty and often failed to meet required procedural deadlines. The Panel reported population figures for the five townships surrounding the project area that were somewhat different from those provided by the Bank. It said the 24,200 people in the expanded area were 49% Han, 24% Mongol, and 12% Tibetan. The remaining 15% were members of the Hui, Sala, and Tu ethnic groups. (44)

The Panel agreed that the inflow of new residents would cause some "diluting" of the current ethnic composition of the project area. In particular, it said, "the closer one gets to the irrigation site, the greater the 'diluting' effects of the in-migration of settlers from elsewhere, especially if one focuses on the Tibetan and Mongol populations for whom the autonomous status of this prefecture was created." (132) The Panel noted that the Tibetan and Mongol share of the population in Dulan county would decrease from 37% before settlement to 21% afterwards. In the townships immediately adjacent to the project, it reported, the Tibetan and Mongol ethnic composition would decline from 60% before settlement to 11% afterwards. In the project site itself with 58,000 new people being added to the existing 4,000 residents, the Tibetan share would almost double (to 6%) while the Mongol share would fall from 70% to 5% of the total. (132) The Panel expressed concerns about the possibility that the Tibetan and Mongol groups might be hurt (through loss of preferences) if China changed the status of the Haixi autonomous prefecture. (132)

The principal focus of the Panel's analysis focused on the lack of any explicit ethnic impact analyses in the project plan. The Bank claimed that, because minority ethnic groups were an integral part of the project, the discussion of their special needs in the project plan was sufficient. (106) The Panel found otherwise. It said a separate Indigenous Peoples Development Plan must be prepared for each of the five minority groups included in the project. (110/130-1) Preservation of their ethnic identity was important, the Panel said, because - even though many (including Tibetans) no longer spoke traditional minority languages or practiced minority religions - membership in a recognized minority allowed them special treatment under Chinese law. This included exemption from the one-child policy and preferential admission to some schools and jobs. (103)

The Panel noted that, during its visits to the move-in area in central Qinghai, a "climate of fear" was palpable, in which many people were clearly afraid to talk about the project - though many who did speak expressed strong opposition, (xix/53) There had not been sufficient consultation, the Panel found, with the nomadic pastoralists. The interviews were not sufficiently confidential to produce valid results. (45) The Bank had interviewed the nomads living in the immediate area, but it did not consult with the 2,400 nomads who move their flocks through the area twice annually. (42-3) Evidently, though the project made the same provisions for both groups, the lack of consultation with the second group meant that their participation did not comply with the rules concerning involuntary resettlement. It said the Bank had also not considered the environmental consequences of routing the migrating flocks through specific channels and crossing points as they traversed the settlement area. (89-90)

In eastern Qinghai, the Panel also found that the consultation process with the potential settlers was similarly flawed. One could not determine, from the interview data, whether people's support for the settlement program was voluntary or coerced. (45) Nevertheless, in terms of the larger issue, the Panel concluded that the prospective emigrants from the eastern counties were probably moving voluntarily rather than through compulsion. Among other things, it noted that the number of applicants far exceeded the available openings in the settlement program. (137-9) It found, however, that insufficient provision would be made for the people left behind and this was a violation of Bank rules on resettlement. (87)

Transparency and Public Notice

Finally, the Inspection Panel agreed with a subsequent admission by Bank management (158) that the Bank had not given the public sufficient timely notice of the project. In particular, project documents had not been submitted to the Bank's InfoShop in a timely manner. (159) If the project had been categorized as an "A" project, a project summary and detailed environmental impact study should have been released six months before the project was sent to the Board of Executive Directors for possible approval. All of these failings were clear violations, the Panel said, of established Bank rules and procedures.

MANAGEMENT'S ALTERNATIVE PROPOSAL

World Bank management acknowledged, in its formal response to the Inspection Panel report, that there had been many deficiencies in the preparation and design of the Qinghai project and its supporting documentation.[29] It agreed that more should have been done to ensure confidentiality in the consultation process, that more could have been done to involve affected people in the project design, that a more thorough environmental analysis would have improved project preparation, that the Bank's documentation should have been better, and that information should have been disclosed more promptly. (2) Management disagreed with the Panel's finding, however, that the Bank had not complied with its own policies and procedures. The source of this disagreement, it said, were differing views as to how the Bank's written guidelines should be interpreted. It noted that there was disagreement, for example, about the steps the Bank needed to take in order to comply with the prohibition against "significant, irreversible sector-wide impacts" or the requirement for "meaningful consultation" or the requirement that the Bank exercise "due diligence" in its design and implementation of projects.[30]

Looking to the future, Management said that the Bank would do an environmental analysis of the project which met the standards for an "A" project, though it said this would not include an investigation of alternatives as recommended by the Panel. It said it would do a literature review and selected site surveys to assess possible difficulties concerning biodiversity, but this would not include studies that were irrelevant to the project design. (4-5) It said it would undertake further consultations with affected people in the area, with special

[29] World Bank. Management Report and Recommendation in Response to the Inspection Panel Investigation Report. June 21,2000. INSP/R202-4/2. This is a lettertothe Executive Board by Bank President James Wolfensohn, along with an 11 page attachment. Also included were a 40 page background paper, and a 26 page paper on Bank environmental and social policies. The report and accompanying documents are available from the World Bank web site. Use the procedure described in note 1 and select "Management Report."

[30] Background paper included with Management Report, p. 7

attention to maintaining the integrity and confidentiality of the process. (3) Management also said that it should do a separate Indigenous Peoples Development plan for the Qinghai project. (3) It argued, however, that a single report for all indigenous groups was more appropriate, since this would allow discussion of cross-cultural or relational issues. (5) The background paper accompanying the Management report included a broader discussion of these points.

On the larger picture, the Bank argued that its staff should not be required to present a formal analysis of alternatives that had been proven unfeasible or unproductive in other similar contexts. (S) Many of the alternative types of projects had been discussed by staff during the preparation process but these details were not included in the report. Management said these alternative approaches had been studied in depth in prior years. It included documentation to this effect as an annex to the background paper accompanying its response to the Inspection Panel's report. Management said it would commission a number of studies to examine particular issues raised in the Panel. These would be less comprehensive, however, than the broad range of issues proposed in the Panel report. The new studies should focus, Management said, on areas or issues that might help the Bank acquire information relevant to the design or implementation of the Qinghai project. (5)

Management said that the work necessary to respond fully to the issues raised by the Inspection Panel's report would cost about $3 million and would require 15 to 18 months. It said the work contemplated by its alternate plan would cost about $2.1 million. It said this would delay implementation of the Qinghai project by only 12 to 15 months. (6) If the Executive Board approved its plan, Management said it would report the results of the subsequent studies and inquiries to the Board and h would proceed with the project without further action by the Board if the results of the additional work proved satisfactory. (4)

DENOUEMENT

After a tense two-day meeting, the World Bank Executive Board decided on July 7, 2000 to put aside the recommendations of Bank management and to require the Chinese government to remedy the concerns identified by the Inspection Panel and to face a second vote before the Qinghai project could be finally approved. The United States, Japan, Germany and the Netherlands reportedly took leading roles in marshaling opposition to the Qinghai loan. Britain supported the loan. The Associated Press quoted a U.S. Treasury source after the vote as saying "The Board could not agree to support these recommendations [by Management] without further Board review and approval after the studies were completed."[31] Another source quoted a senior Treasury official as saying that "We and numerous other shareholders were not prepared to support this project, because we did not believe that it was in compliance with the Bank's own policies." He went on to say that "The Bank needs to prepare specific proposals to give the shareholders a greater sense of confidence that Management has the internal capacity to apply its established internal policies,"[32] U.S. Executive Director Jan Piercy was reportedly more blunt, telling the Board that "It is time for this organization to see the issue for what it is-delivering on its own commitments to credible internal controls and faithful execution of agreed policies and procedures. It is time to take responsibility."[33]

Following the Board's decision, China withdrew its application for the Qinghai portion of the Western Poverty Reduction Project. In a statement quoted on the World Bank's web page, Zhu Xian, China's Executive Director, told the Board that "China accepts no-conditions beyond Management's original recommendations that had been agreed between Management and my authorities."[34] Particularly unacceptable, he said, was the requirement that China come "back to the Board for approval again for a project that was already approved last year." Instead, he reported, "China will therefore turn to its own resources to implement the Qinghai Component of the project, and in its own way."

Zhu said the Bank's compliance policies for the Qinghai loan had been "interpreted by some to an extreme and used for political purposes." The official Chinese press concluded later that the Bank and other countries had "buckled under pressure from the United States and some Tibetan separatists," in furtherance of U. S. foreign policy goals.[35] A spokesman for China's Foreign Ministry denounced, on July 11, the "unreasonable demands" and "obstacles for

---

[31] World Bank Kills China Project Loan. *The Washington Post,* July 8,2000, p. A12.

[32] Joseph Kahn. World Bank Rejects China's Proposal to Settle Farmers. *New York Times,* July 8,2000, p. 3.

[33] Sathnam Sanghera and Stephen Fidler. World Bank chief under fire after Chinese project. *The Financial Times* (London), July 14, 2000, p. 10.

[34] World Bank. China to Implement Qinghai Portion of Western Poverty Reduction Project with its Own Resources. July 7,2000. Press Release 2001/004/EAP. For a copy, follow the procedure in note 1.

[35] Jin Zeqing. Loan rejection reveals US agenda. *China Daily.* July 18, 2000, p. 4. North American edition. The article said that "U.S. officials thought the loans should not come for free; they thought Uncle Sam should get something out of it." The United States hoped, it said, to "force the Chinese government to buy its hard-to-sell values" by attaching additional conditions to the project.

political reasons" which some developed countries had placed against the Qinghai project.[36] He cited the United States and Japan in particular and he said that "China strongly opposes politicization of World Bank activities." The project "fully conforms to the policy and the Articles of Agreement of the World Bank and has been welcomed by the people of the region," he argued. The Foreign Ministry spokesman said that China would go ahead with the project with its own funds and that "any attempt to obstruct the implementation of the project is doomed to failure."

Opponents of the Qinghai project were reportedly jubilant with the result. "This is a major victory," said Alison Reynolds, director of the Free Tibet Campaign in London. "We have stopped China getting an international stamp of approval for its policy of population transfer into Tibet."[37] Joshua Schrei, another opponent of the loan, added that "This is the first time that an international institution has ever stood up to the Chinese government. Maybe now we will find out *if* the Chinese government's bark is worse than their bite."[38]

However, others expressed concern that an absence of World Bank supervision would allow China to implement the resettlement scheme with little regard for the protections for minority culture previously included in the World Bank plan. Kate Saunders of the Tibet Information Network claimed that defeat of the Qinghai loan had sent a signal which might limit future international funding for projects in Tibet. She also worried, however, that "Beijing [would] take a tougher approach towards the project and possibly towards the whole question of development and resettlement in Tibetan areas."[39] Some critics hoped, that the Bank "should use the leverage of those additional millions in loans [for other projects] to persuade China to give up its resettlement scheme."[40] Few believed, though, that the Bank or its major member countries would support such a view.

---

[36] Sathnam Sanghera. BBC Monitoring International Reports: China to Continue Cooperation with World Bank. July 11, 2000. BBC News Service.

[37] Jason Burke. World Bank says no to Chinese settlers in Tibet. *The Observer*, London, July 9,2000, p. 26

[38] Damien McElroy. Tibetans jubilant over loan U-turn on settlers. *The Sunday Telegraph*, London, July 9, 2000, p. 28.

[39] *Ibid.*

[40] Globalizing "the world's roof." *San Francisco Examiner.*, July 9, 2000, p. C-14.

ANALYSIS

How Widespread are the Problems?

The report from the Inspection Panel indicates that the World Bank made a number of important policy and procedural errors during its preparation of the Qinghai project plan. These are serious concerns. They tend to undercut public confidence in the Bank and the integrity of its operations. The Bank Executive Board and Senior Management are likely to analyze whether the Qinghai project is an isolated instance or whether similar deficiencies can be found in other World Bank projects in other countries. Examination of the other two components of the Western Poverty Alleviation project (see below) suggests that the Qinghai project may not be unique. The Board and senior management may act to strengthen their control procedures in order to better assure themselves and the public that the staff complies with the Bank's official policies and procedures.

The Board may also assess whether Bank staff can identify and design projects in a timely and efficient manner while still complying with the many requirements currently on its books. Observers could conclude that the Board and Senior Management have not given the staff enough guidance as to the relative emphasis they should place on the many requirements embodied in Bank rules. Consequently, different project managers may give different emphasis to various rules. One suspects that a detailed examination of many other Bank projects might reveal instances where Bank staff did not comply fully with every procedural or policy rule.

Most people would probably agree that all of the goals embodied in Bank policy - the alleviation of human poverty and the undisturbed preservation of the habitat for rare waterfowl, for example - are not necessarily of equal value. (Nor are they necessarily in conflict). Over the past decades, many goals and priorities have been added to the Bank's rules. On their own terms, these were all found to be desirable. However, no organization can pursue all of its goals simultaneously and with equal vigor. Likewise, from a procedural perspective, it is unclear from prior statements by Bank management what relative emphasis the Bank should give to the preferences of its borrowers and the various policy guidelines (such as environmental or social policy considerations) embodied in the Bank's rules. The latter may not be high priorities to the borrower government.[41] The Executive

[41] Rich quotes a comment made by one senior manager during a 1996 session between Bank President Wolfensohn and 300 top managers in reference to the former's appeal for greater client responsiveness on the part of Bank staff. "We have to make a choice. Either we treat our governments as clients and we behave like merchant banks, in which case we owe it [to

Board might provide some additional guidelines to help the staff weigh and balance more effectively the Bank's many policy and procedural objectives.

The Report in Light of Charges by Critics

The Inspection Panel found that the World Bank had committed serious errors in its preparation of the Qinghai project. However, few seem to be the kinds of errors which correspond to the strongest concerns voiced by the critics in their protests against the Qinghai loan. Some observers suggest that the intensity of the opposition to the Qinghai project does not seem to be explained by the kinds of policy, procedural or technical errors which the Inspection Panel identified. In retrospect, it seems that two more fundamental issues - the Chinese government's relationship with China's ethnic minorities and the Bank's overall relationship with China - were likely major factors amplifying much of the intense public opposition to the Qinghai project. In some ways, the Qinghai project may have been a proxy for larger issues and a forum in where critics could raise issues of broader substantial concern.

Negative Cultural Impact on Tibetans

The report of the Inspection Panel does not seem to support the charge that the Qinghai project would result in "cultural genocide" for the Tibetans and other minority groups living near the project area. The panel said the immigration of new settlers would "dilute" the Mongolian and Tibetan share of the local population. There did not seem to be any indication in the Panel's report, however, that decline in their population share from one-third to one-fifth would lead to the destruction of their ethnic cultures.[42] The Panel's principal concern was whether a decline in the Mongolian and Tibetan share would encourage the Chinese

---

ourselves and our counterparts]...to stop talking about the environment, about women in development, about poverty alleviation, and so on, as priorities...[But ifj the government is not our client... {then] the client is the people of the countries we work with, and the governments are agencies, instruments, with whom we work to meet our clients' needs." In the latter case, the Bank would need to persuade countries to borrow money to meet the needs of the poorer and less influential members of their societies rather than the needs which the governments believe are priority concerns. Bruce Rich. Still waiting; World Bank fails to alleviate poverty. *The Ecologist,* September 2000, p. 8.

[42] As noted before, the Panel found that -except in the immediate project area - the Tibetan and Mongol groups did not comprise a majority of the population. The Panel noted that, in Dulan county, the combined Tibetan-Mongol share of the population would decline from about one-third to about one-fifth of the total. In the immediate project area, a lightly populated area, the Mongol share would decline from about 60% to about 11%.

government someday to terminate the special status for the Mongol and Tibetan Autonomous Area. The question was not an erosion of these groups cultural identity but rather a potential loss of special status.

The Panel found that most of the residents in the immediate project area were Mongol, while few were Tibetan. The Tibetan share of the population in that area would increase after implementation of the project. From the project document and Inspection Panel report, it appears that the various ethnic groups in the area do not live in isolated villages which have little contact with neighboring groups.

The Panel said there were many unanswered questions about the project's larger social impact. It said that the Bank had to prepare a separate Indigenous People's Development Plan (IPDP) for each of the five minority ethnic groups living in the broader project area (instead of one IPDP for all.) These are serious concerns, but - considering that ethnic minorities would constitute the bulk of the new immigrants to the area - they do not seem a strong basis for concluding that the Qinghai project would likely have led to the replacement of the local minority cultures by the nationally predominant Han culture. The Panel said the Bank should have discussed alternatives to resettlement in its project plan. It did not suggest, however, that the concept of resettlement was necessarily flawed.

Possible Negative Cultural Effects in Other Provinces

No questions were raised in this controversy about the possible impact which the other two components (in Gansu province and Inner Mongolia) of the Western Poverty Reduction project might have on the Hui and Mongol minorities in those areas. The point here is not necessarily to further criticize the World Bank but to note that the yardsticks which were used by critics in their evaluation of the Qinghai scheme were evidently not applied to the companion projects in the other two provinces. It appears from the project document[43] that - in terms of possible cultural threats to minorities - there might be reasons there for concern. In the Gansu project area, people of Hui ancestry account for about 7% of the population. In the Inner Mongolia project area, people of Mongol ancestry comprise 14% of the residents. The rest in both areas are Han Chinese. (23) The percentage of Han residents is somewhat higher in each project area than the percentage for each province as a whole. It does not appear, from the project document, that the World Bank has prepared Indigenous Peoples Development Plans for the Hui or Mongol residents of the two project areas nor any for the

---

[43] See note 1.

several other minority groups which comprise a small fraction of the population in the broader zone around each project area.

From the budget statements in the Bank project document, it appears that health facilities are the principal social service provided by the Gansu and Inner Mongolia projects. (82) There seem to be none of the cultural and educational services for minority groups that were included in the Qinghai plan. The villages benefitting from the Gansu and Inner Mongolia projects are very poor and very isolated. The Bank says that 216 kilometers of new road will be built in the two provinces, benefitting 340,000 people. (6) Along with economic development, the new roads will enhance communication between these remote villagers and the outside world. (8) These changes seem likely to raise living standards for the people in the project area. However, one might ask whether increased interaction with the much more numerous Han population of the area will put the cultural integrity of the small Hui and Mongol groups in these areas under possible strain.

Soil Erosion and Water Quality

Likewise, the Inspection Panel did not find that the irrigation and settlement of central Qinghai would cause significant environmental damage. The Panel said the project needed a broader environmental impact study because it might effect areas outside the immediate project zone and -*prima facie* - because it involved the construction of a dam and irrigation works. It did not report, however, that irrigation of the loess plateau in central Qinghai would lead to soil erosion. The Panel did not indicate that it believed the Bank's intended methods for converting the area from arid pasture to irrigated farmland were environmental unsound. In terms of water quality, the Panel said the project plan needed to indicate how the settlers were going to dispose of their wastes. It also said that studies should be done concerning possible negative effects on biodiversity and on rare waterfowl nesting downstream. The Panel did not conclude, however, that the project posed a necessary threat to water quality.

Possible Environmental Effects in Other Provinces

No questions were raised by critics, during the debate about the Qinghai project, about any environmental problems in the other two components of the Western Poverty Reduction project. The Bank did not report that any environmental studies were done for these projects, though it said that standard environmental implementation and monitoring procedures would be employed. The Bank said that no environmental issues were identified in Gansu and Inner Mongolia "because the bulk of the Project activities are expected to produce positive environmental impacts." (23) Assurances of this type are not usually considered to be adequate substitutes for independent environmental impact analysis.

A reading of the project document suggests that issues which were the grounds for serious concern in the Qinghai project were overlooked in the other two areas. Information on all three projects was available to the Executive Board and the public in the same Bank project document.

As in Qinghai, the terrain in Gansu and Inner Mongolia is very arid. The World Bank will finance there some of the same methods for converting the land to irrigation that it would have used in Qinghai. No major new dams or irrigation works are planned, but more new land will be brought under irrigation there than in Qinghai. Likewise, the landscape in Gansu and Inner Mongolia will be transformed through new terracing.[44] The Bank says this will contribute to soil and water conservation. Many new wells will also be dug.[45] The World Bank says the new wells will increase from 25% to 62%[46] the percentage of exploitable groundwater that will be put to use either for irrigation or for providing drinking water to more than 300,000 people living in the two provinces. (6/64)

The new terracing and the increased irrigation and water use contemplated by the Gansu and Inner Mongolia projects may have unwanted environmental effects. The project document does not indicate that any were explored. Likewise, to echo points the Inspection Panel made about the Qinghai project, the Bank did not indicate in its project document what the effects might be - particularly for groundwater - if the areas benefitting from the projects in Gansu and Inner Mongolia become future centers for increased population and growth. It included no discussion of biodiversity. It also included no discussion of alternatives, including ways the goals of the two projects might be achieved without irrigation, terracing, or new wells.

Consultation and Voluntary Settlement

The Inspection Panel agreed with critics that the Bank's consultation with potential settlers and residents in the Qinghai project had not been sufficiently confidential. Hence, it agreed that one could not tell from the results of those interviews whether their involvement in the resettlement scheme is voluntary or not. The Panel found that the Bank had violated its policy against involuntary

---

44 New irrigation in Gansu and Inner Mongolia will total 34,050 hectares, compared with 19,200 hectares in Qinghai. (6/64) Terracing will produce 26,500 hectares of irrigated farmland. (6)

45 The project in Inner Mongolia will sink 11,000 new wells and refurbish over 3,500 existing wells. Some wells will also be dug in Gansu and works for cistern-based irrigation will be constructed.

46 The latter figure was calculated by CRS using data published in the project document.

resettlement by not consulting with the pastoralists who pass through the project area twice annually and by not making adequate provision to help the people who remained behind in the eastern counties. However, the Panel did not support the charge by critics that the people moving from the east to central Qinghai were doing so involuntarily. The Panel decided that they were most likely voluntary migrants.

While the Panel agreed that there should have been better consultation with the residents of the future project area, it did not suggest that the Bank should have cancelled the project if it found that these people did not want 58,000 new neighbors. The Bank's rules do not require that local residents must welcome the new residents before a settlement project may begin. Likewise, the Qinghai project offered the current residents a choice between continued pastoralism or a shift to settled agriculture. This would have likely diminished the number of persons pursuing the traditional lifestyle and it would have lessened the nomads' earlier freedom of movement. It does not appear, however, that the Bank's rules require it to preserve "unique" lifestyles by denying their participants access to new opportunities aimed at reducing their levels of poverty.

Consultation and Voluntary Relocation in Other Provinces

It seems, from the project document, that the methods the Bank used to interview people living in the Gansu and Inner Mongolian project areas were essentially the same as those used in Qinghai. The project document indicates that the Bank consulted with sample villages, particularly minority villages, to help assure that the concerns of the residents were sufficiently integrated into the project plan. It does not appear, however, that all villages were consulted. The projects in Gansu and Inner Mongolia are not resettlement projects. Therefore the rules concerning involuntary resettlement do not apply. In Gansu, however, the project plans to place 65,700 persons who are categorized as surplus rural laborers into alternative forms of non-farm employment. (70) This shift is probably voluntary, considering that employment opportunities in rural Gansu are apparently scarce. Nevertheless, the same questions about confidentiality and individual consent might be raised here as they were raised regarding the project in Qinghai.

Transparency and Public Notice

The Inspection Panel agreed with the critics that the preparation process for the Qinghai project should have been more transparent and the Bank provided inadequate public notice. The Panel also said that, because it believed the project should have been categorized as an "A" project, an environmental impact assessment (EIA) and public notice should have been filed at least six months in advance of its presentation to the Executive Board. The Panel said that a full EIA must be done before the Qinghai project could go forward. It was not clear from the report, however, whether a six-month notification period would be required for public review of the EIA before it could go to the Board.

Issues of public notice were not raised as regards the other two components of the Western Poverty Alleviation project. Because they were all parts of the same project, the same concerns about public notice arise for the Gansu and Inner Mongolian projects as for that in Qinghai. Because no critics suggested that environmental studies should have been prepared for the projects in the other two provinces, the issue about six-months advance notice was not addressed. Nevertheless, examination of the project document suggests that there may be grounds for requiring "A" category environmental treatment there as well. The Gansu and Inner Mongolian projects involve extensive irrigation and land movement for terracing. As noted before, the Inspection Panel said that extensive irrigation and land reclamation were *ipso facto* conditions requiring an "A" classification.

The World Bank did not provide public notice of the Western Poverty Alleviation project through its internet project information system until May 1999. However, the World Bank had published information earlier indicating that it was preparing plans for a settlement project and other activities in Qinghai and the other two provinces of China. The Bank's Monthly Operational Summary (MOS) first listed this project in February 1998. It stated that it would be an environmental category "B" project, Qinghai would be one of the sites, and it would involve (among other things) voluntary resettlement.[47] Later issues of the MOS also mentioned irrigation and land improvement.[48] The MOS is also printed monthly by the United Nations in its publication *Development Business,* which is available to subscribers. Notice of this project ceased to be carried in the MOS in May 1999 as the project information documents (PID) were being prepared for publication on the World Bank web site. The World Bank may not have been calling attention to its plans for a Qinghai loan, but the MOS did give public notice nearly eighteen months before the project was presented to the Bank's Executive Board.

The terse language in the MOS did not provide sufficient detail for any analysis of the merits of the Qinghai project. It does not meet the standards for

---

[47] World Bank.*Monthly Operational* Summary, reprinted in *Development Business*. February 1998, pp. 27-8.

[48] For example, the *Monthly Operational Summary* for December 1998, p. 24.

public disclosure embodied in the Bank's current transparency regime. However, it could have been a basis for pointed inquiries to the Bank if it had come to the attention of the U.S. Treasury, the U.S. Executive Director at the World Bank, or outside observers such as the non-governmental organizations concerned about Tibet. Many of these have access or receive monthly copies of the MOS from the Bank. The evident fact that this notice was missed, by the parties who later expressed deep concern, suggests that outside observers may be depending too much on the new electronic notification procedures to the detriment of alternative sources of information which they would have used in earlier days.

Qinghai and Tibet

Many critics of the World Bank loan tended to equate Qinghai province with Tibet. They say the proposed project in Qinghai would have helped the Chinese separate Qinghai from Tibet and would help undercut Tibet's claims to autonomy.

The historical record is controversial on this point. Tibetans have long considered Qinghai to be part of their national territory, along with parts of Gansu, Yunnan, and Sichuan provinces, though many people of other nationalities have lived there for many years. The legal situation is a tangle of conflicting claims. During the nineteenth century, Britain sought to guarantee a separate status for Tibet, in treaties it signed with the Chinese Empire. The Empire made a number of assurances at that time. Later, the Imperial Government and its successors issued contrary statements and took contrary actions which treated Tibet as a portion of China. During periods of national weakness, the Chinese central government has exercised little control over Tibet and other peripheral or ethnic regions. At other times, when the capacity of the central government was greater, it tried to exercise what it considered to be its sovereign authority over Tibet and other similar areas. The international legal status of Tibet, the earlier treaties, and subsequent official statements and actions by successive Chinese Governments is a matter of dispute. Though many in Congress and the Administration have criticized the Chinese Government's current policies towards Tibet, the U.S. Government has never recognized Tibet as being independent from China.[49]

[49] In the daily press briefing of October 8, 1987, responding to a question concerning what year the United States formally recognized Tibet as part of China, the State Department's Public Affairs office issued the following statement; 'We have never recognized Tibet as a sovereign state independent of China. We first made the statement that we considered Tibet to be a part of China in 1978; however, our earlier formulations were not inconsistent with that statement, and we have never challenged China's claim. No third country recognizes Tibet as a state

Tibetans claim that their historic relationship with China was never one of political subservience, that Tibet through history has enjoyed a unique civilization and identity, and that Tibet functioned as an independent country for all practical purposes until 1950. The Chinese claim that historically Tibet had a subservient feudal relationship with the Chinese sovereign, that China actively governed the province from time to time, and that the modern process of national integration - which. includes the extension of Chinese government control to Tibet - is an absolute right of sovereignty.

It is clear that the present boundaries of Qinghai came into being well before the Communists won the civil war in 1949 or before Chinese troops entered Tibet in 1951. Reference was made on this point to maps currently held by the Library of Congress Geography and Map Division. Some European maps published before 1911 show Tibet as an area outside the Chinese empire. Others recognize some Chinese suzerainty but treat everything south and east of Koko Nor (a major lake in what is now northeastern Qinghai) as part of Tibet. No official Chinese maps from the period have been found. However, a map of China (in Chinese) prepared in 1875 for the Japanese Army General Staff shows separate provinces in the area where Qinghai and Xizang (Tibet) are located today. This may reflect the official Chinese view. No alternative maps from Tibet are available.[50]

UNDERLYING ISSUES

There appear to be few compelling technical, procedural, or operational issues which explain why - compared to the other two components of the larger project, for instance - the Qinghai project became the focus of sustained international public controversy. The Independent Inspection Panel raised serious questions whether the Bank had complied with its policies and procedures in this case, but the findings of the Panel do not seem to bolster the critics' strongest arguments against the Qinghai project. It appears that all the remedial steps the Panel

independent of China." The latter includes Britain, whose treaties with Imperial China are used by some as the basis for arguments supporting Tibetan independence.

[50] Some Western maps in the 1920s continued to define Tibet in broad terms. However, Chinese-language maps published in Shanghai during the 1920s and 1930s show a separate province with boundaries similar to those of modern Qinghai. A map published for the U. S. Department of Commerce, by Rand-McNally in 1926, shows a Chinese political subdivision named "Kokonor SAD" in the area now called Qinghai. The London Geographic Institute, in an undated map evidently prepared before World War Two, also shows Tibet and Kokonor (Qinghai) to be separate provinces.

recommended could have been done without necessarily prejudicing the project's future prospects for implementation.

China and its Ethnic Minorities

The Qinghai loan raised to international view the perennial question of how the central government of China should relate to the country's ethnic minorities. As noted before, the Chinese government has sought to exercise its claims of sovereignty over the peripheral parts of China whenever it had the capacity to do so. It has also looked favorably upon (and sometimes helped) the westward flow of people from the heavily populated areas of China.

The experience of the Hui people in Gansu province, north and northeast of Qinghai, is a case in point. After defeating a major rebellion by the Hui in 1877, the government of China increasingly tightened its control over the area.[51] The flow of people from the eastern provinces increased substantially. The World Bank reported, in its project document, that Han Chinese now make up 88% of the population in the province. Increasingly, during the past century, the Chinese government has sought to integrate the Hui and other minority groups into the national culture.[52] This often has had the effect of strengthening the self-identity of minority groups.[53]

The Chinese government currently has underway a campaign, under the slogan "Develop the West" aimed at promoting rapid economic growth in several western provinces. These include Tibet, Qinghai, Ningxia, Gansu, Sichuan, Yunnan, Guizhou, and Shaanxi provinces. For the most part, these are minority areas. They comprise 56% of China's total land area but only 23% of its

[51] The Hui are the largest Chinese Muslim group and the second largest minority ethnic group. The Chinese government only recognized them officially as a separate ethnic group in 1950, by which time a substantial amount of migration into the area had occurred.

[52] One historian concluded that the "aggressive Hanification [Sinification] of Hui territory" during the period 1895-1935 showed the Chinese "imperative for domination of the frontier." Increasingly, he says, concepts such as sovereign rights, national defense, and stable borders '"have begun to eliminate the old vague distinctions between the central kingdom and the various barbarians." Increasingly, he reports, the driving concept is one seeking "a coherent national identity, one which must by sheer force of numbers be a *Han* identity. Jonathan Lipman, *The Border World of Gansu, 1895-2935,* quoted in Dru Gladney, *Muslim Chinese: Ethnic Nationalism in the People's Republic,* p. 318. Emphasis in the original.

[53] Gladney notes *(Ibid.)* that, in many ways, China's ethnic groups have become stronger and more assertive as their interaction with the main body of China's population has increased. Often, increased contact has not led to Sinicization, he says, but rather to increased solidarity on the part of the members of an ethnic group and a greater sense of ethnic identity. He also notes that the concept "Ban" should not be equated with the term "Chinese," as many ethnic groups comprise the main body of China's population.

population. The government says it wants to counter the growing income disparities between the eastern seaboard provinces and those inland. Some 90% of the people in China with incomes below the poverty line ($100 a year) live in the western region. Tibet has one of the higher income levels among this group.[54]

In the past half-dozen years, the World Bank has financed ten agricultural development and poverty-alleviation projects in areas of China having substantial minority populations.[55] On March 17,2000, the World Bank's vice president for the East Asia and Pacific region, Jemal-ud-din Kassum, reportedly announced that the Bank would help support the government's plans for development of the west. He pledged that the Bank would lend at least $1 billion to China for major projects in that part of the country.[56] The Chinese government has announced a $500 billion development program for the region, including an initial ten projects (mostly infrastructure).[57] The government reportedly expects that the west will provide China with over half its electricity and 60% of the raw materials needed by the eastern provinces.[58] In August 2000, China signed an agreement with foreign companies creating the International Alliance on Developing Western China.[59]

Since 1997, President Jiang Zemin has spoken frequently of the need for development in the western region. According to Chinese sources, he has stressed the importance of halting soil erosion, turning fragile farmland into forests, and improving the ecological environment in the region. In November 1999, President Jiang and Premier Zhu Rongji told a national economic conference that development of the west is very important for stimulating domestic demand, promoting economic growth national unity, social stability and solid frontier defense.[60] Chen Dongshen, a member of the cabinet appointed team preparing the

---

[54] See Damien McElroy. China's Promise to Win the West. *Scotland on Sunday* (Edinburgh), first edition, August 27,2000, p. B4.

[55] These include the Western Poverty Reduction Project discussed in this report, plus two in the Tarim Basin, two for rehabilitation of the loess plateau watershed, and one each in the Qiaba mountains, the Gansu-Hexi corridor, Shanxi province, and southwest provinces including Yunnan and Guizhou. World Bank Annual Reports, various years.

[56] Chronology: Government Efforts in Developing Western Area in 2000. Xinhua News Agency-Ceis. October 19, 2000.

[57] See McElroy, note 54 .

[58] Background: Development of Western China. Xinhua News Agency-Ceis. October 19, 2000. Other Chinese news sources report that Chinese scientists believe that, despite previous thought to the contrary, the western provinces have abundant reserves of oil and natural gas. One estimate suggested that at least 13 billion tons of oil and natural gas are buried in die northwest region of China. Scientists Believe Oil Plentiful in West China. Xinhua News Agency-Ceis. October 9, 2000.

[59] International Alliance on Development of Western China Established in Beijing. BBC Monitoring Asia Pacific-Political (London). August 8,2000.

[60] See: Background, note 58.

master plan for the program, explained the purposes of the program somewhat differently. He reportedly said that the plan would "smash our enemies who want to use poverty and the contradictions between races to create a Kosovo-style crisis in Asia."[61]

Tibetan National Concerns

The Qinghai loan helped the Tibetan advocacy community publicize their concerns. The project was located in a province adjacent to Tibet, in an area the Tibetans considered to be historically "theirs," and it involved Tibetan people. Qinghai was the locus of the loan, but the issues which the Tibetan critics raised mainly had to do with objectionable Chinese activities in Tibet. In effect, the Qinghai loan offered the Tibetan community an opportunity to promote a kind of international referendum on the Chinese government's policies and practices in Tibet.

Chinese activities in Tibet have been the focus of considerable international attention for many years.[62] The Dali Lama, on behalf of Tibet, reportedly has sought to negotiate with the Chinese some form of autonomy within a larger Chinese framework. In recent years, the Chinese government has been unwilling to hold such talks. Many Tibetans fear that time may be running out for the cause of Tibetan independence, given the influx of non-Tibetan residents and the passage of time. Estimates as to the number of non-Tibetan immigrants range from a few hundred thousand to several million. In addition, many Tibetans believe that the Chinese government is laying the groundwork for controlling the selection of the next Dali Lama, after the current incumbent dies. Several generations of young Tibetans have been exposed to the broader currents of Chinese society and may now identify as much with China as they do with Tibet.

Few people outside the Bank and the Chinese government knew in early 1999 what the project intended to do in central Qinghai. The area was closed to outside visitation, communications with local residents were tenuous, and the Bank was not very forthcoming about its plans for the area. The critics believed they had good reasons to doubt the intentions of the Chinese government, based on their experiences in Tibet, the Three Gorges dam, and other matters. Hence, in the absence of knowledge drawn from inspections on the ground, they marshaled the best arguments available. The Bank and the Chinese government may have done

---

[61] See McElroy, note 54.

[62] For a more complete discussion of this issue, see CRS Report RS20395, *Tibet and China: Current Issues and Implications for U.S. Policy.*, by Kerry B. Dumbaugh.

themselves a disservice by restricting access to the area and to information about the upcoming project. On the other hand, the Chinese may have been sensitive to issues involving Tibet because of past controversies. Perhaps they thought they might have had a better chance of success if they broached news of the project later, rather than earlier, in the preparation process.

The World Bank and China

Another set of factors strengthening the intensity of the protest against the Qinghai loan involves the uncertainties which surround China's future relationship with its neighbors and with the United States. Some observers believe that China is an emerging peer competitor of the United States. In this light, they question whether it is prudent for the United States and others to help strengthen China's productive capacity through assistance programs such as those funded by the multilateral banks. They believe that future authoritarian governments will use the increased capacity of the Chinese economy to support a more assertive foreign policy.

Other observers agree that there are strains in current U.S.-China relations. However, they say it is not inevitable that China will become a foreign policy opponent of the United States in future years. Treating China as an opponent now will be the best way of assuring that it will be an opponent later, they argue, after its economic and military capacity have increased. They believe a more engaged and less confrontational approach to China might produce more desirable results in future years. Over time, they predict, the underlying structure of China's social system and economy will change, as diversity and market economic principles become more pervasive. This would have a positive effect on the evolution of the Chinese political system. They say that MDB assistance can be an important part of this process. The principles embodied in MDB projects can help open up the Chinese system, they argue, and help lay the foundation for a more positive future.

Successive U.S. Administrations have pursued, with broad international support, a policy of engagement with China which aims to strengthen relations, deepen economic ties, and encourage the growth of constructive links to the outside world.[63] In 1999, Congress put U.S. trade relations with China on a more

[63] For a more thorough analysis, see CRS Issue Brief IB98018, *China-U.S. Relations*, by Kerry Dumbaugh. See also CRS Report 98-485, *China: Possible Missile Technology Transfer from U.S. Satellite Export Policy}- Background and Chronology.*, by Shirley A. Kan.

stable basis through passage of legislation according China permanent normal trade relations (PNTR).[64] However, the United States and China also have major differences. The United States asserts that it has major interests in Asia, for example, while China sees itself as the major country in the region and believes the United States should have a much more limited role. The United States is concerned, among other things, about human rights conditions in China, possible espionage and electoral violations, actions facilitating the proliferation of weapons of mass destruction, and the peaceful settlement of the Taiwan issue. China has criticized the United States in recent official statements and declared that "new negative developments in [China's] security situation" were the result of U.S. actions.

During much of the past decade, China has been the largest single borrower from the World Bank (and from the ADB as well). Since it began lending in 1985, the World Bank has provided assistance to China from both its principal loan windows. As noted before, the International Bank for Reconstruction and Development (IBRD) lends at near- market rates using money borrowed on commercial terms in world capital markets. The International Development Association (IDA) lends at highly conditional rates using money contributed by the United States and other major countries. By mutual agreement between China and the World Bank - and at the strong urging of the United States - 1999 was the last year in which China was eligible for IDA loans.

Figure 2 shows the amount the World Bank has lent to China annually through the IBRD and EDA. In recent years, the World Bank has lent an increasing share of its assistance to China on the harder IBRD terms. In addition, the amount lent has declined substantially in recent years from the peaks set in the mid-1990s. The IBRD and IDA have financed different types of activities. Figure 3 and Table 1 show the relative amounts the IBRD and IDA have lent for projects in different sectors. The IBRD lent some 74% of its funds (over $17 billion) for the construction of infrastructure and industrial projects. (Most of the latter were agro-industry.) The IBRD lent only about 18% of its funds for social programs and agricultural projects aimed at the alleviation of poverty. IDA, by contrast, lent over 76% of its resources in China (about $7 billion) for the latter types of activities and only 11% for infrastructure and industry (most of this in very poor areas.)

[64] See CRS Issue Brief IB91121, *China-U.S. Trade Issues*, by Wayne M. Morrison.

Figure 2. World Bank Loans to China, Annual Amounts
(Millions of U.S. Dollars)

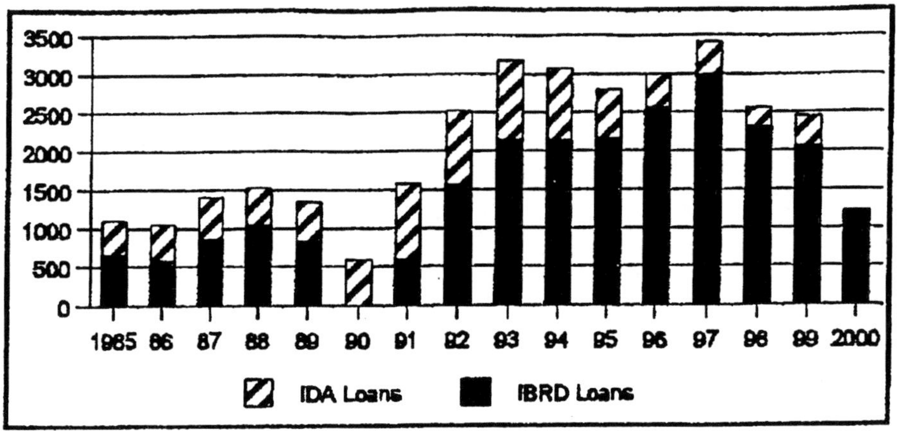

Figure 3. World Bank Loans to China, Type (1985-2000; Millions of U.S. Dollars)

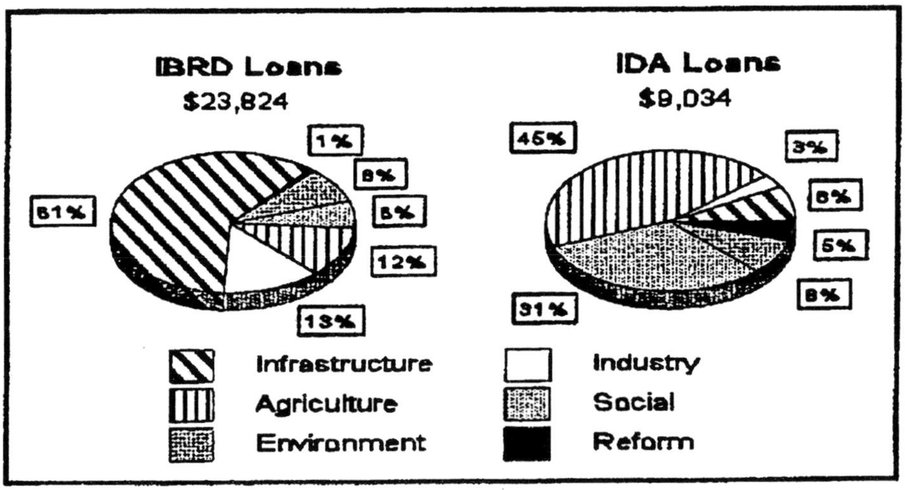

Table 1. World Bank Lending to China, Sector Amounts
(IBRD and n)A, Millions of U.S. Dollars)[65]

	IBRD Amount	IDA Amount
Infrastructure	$14,421	$738
Industry	$3,063	$276
Agriculture	$2,800	$4,051
Social	$1,453	$2,835
Environment	$1,904	$725
Reform	$183	$410

With the termination of IDA assistance to China, most World Bank assistance will likely go for infrastructure and industrial projects. The share aimed at the direct alleviation of poverty will likely decline. Two questions arise. First, will China be willing to borrow substantial amounts on the harder IBRD terms to fond social and rural poverty projects? The Qinghai project and its sister projects in Gansu and Inner Mongolia were financed with a blend of IBRD and IDA resources. In 1999 and 2000, agriculture (mainly for poverty alleviation) has comprised one-third to one-half of IBRD lending in China. Whether this shows a trend or whether it is a short-term phenomenon is not evident at this point.

Second, will the Bank's support for infrastructure and industry promote broad-based reform in China's legal, regulatory, and economic procedures? Most analysts believe that a market economy cannot function well without an effective legal system based on the rule of law, good governance, and effective (but impartial) regulatory procedures (such as bank supervision and oversight of capital and financial markets.) Support for these principles is implicit (and sometimes explicit) in many MDB loans. However, MDB loans comprise but a small portion of China's total foreign borrowing and its capital inflow. Analysts

[65] Source for Figures 2 and 3 and Table 1: World Bank Annual Reports, 1985-2000. The infrastructure category includes transportation, telecommunications, and electric power. The industry category includes agro-industry and agro-commercial activities. The social category includes health, education, water and sewerage, and post-disaster reconstruction. Agriculture includes mainly rural poverty alleviation programs, irrigation, and maintenance of dikes. Environment includes both preservation and reduction of emissions. Reform includes financial and economic policy reform as well as the reform of labor markets.

disagree whether the conditions associated with MDB loans can have a broad and significant effect on social and economic trends in China as a whole.

The Inspection Panel and the critics of the Qinghai loan have raised a third important question. This asks whether World Bank management can implement its programs in China in accordance with Bank rules and whether the government of China will comply with Bank rules and the conditions on Bank loans. Bank management originally claimed, in its defense of the Qinghai loan, that "in China things are done differently" and the rules and procedures applicable in other regions can often not be implemented there. The Inspection Panel disagreed quite strongly with this assertion. Bank management may be correct that the Bank needs to be flexible in its operations in China. The Chinese government may be willing to take suggestions but it apparently unwilling to be seen as acquiescing to pressure or MDB conditionally. The United States and most other major countries seem to want the Bank to continue its engagement with that country. Nevertheless, Bank management may decide to take steps which assure the Bank's member countries and the public that, in being flexible, the Bank is not failing to implement the basic rules and requirements that many believe are the hallmarks of effective MDB loans.

BIBLIOGRAPHY

A case for aid: building a consensus for development assistance.
Published/Created: Washington, D.C.: World Bank, c2002.
Related Authors: Wolfensohn, James D. United Nations International Conference on Financing for Development (2002: Monterrey, Mexico)
Description: ix, 215 p.: ill.; 23 cm.
ISBN: 0821351621 (pbk.)
Notes: "Includes 'A partnership for development and peace' by James D. Wolfensohn." "... a selection of readings related to the United Nations International Conference on Financing for Development, which was held in Monterrey, Mexico, March 18-22-2002."--p. v. Includes bibliographical references (p. 177-183).
Subjects: United Nations--Economic assistance--Decision making. Consensus (Social sciences)--Developing countries.
LC Classification: HC60 .C29667 2002
Dewey Class No.: 338.91/09172/4 21

Advancing gender equality: World Bank action since Beijing /[Karen Mason ... [et al].
Published/Created: Washington, D.C.: World Bank, 2000.
Related Authors: Mason, Karen Oppenheim. World Bank.
Description: viii, 36 p.: ill.; 24 cm.
Cancel/Invalid LCCN: 00709502
Notes: Includes bibliographical references (p. 34-36).
Subjects: World Bank. Women's rights. Women in development.
LC Classification: HQ1236 .A39 2000

Advancing social development: a World Bank contribution to the social summit.
Published/Created: Washington, D.C.: World Bank, [1995]
Related Authors: World Bank.
Description: xii, 60 p.; 24 cm.
ISBN: 0821332082

Notes: "March 1995"--T.p. verso. Includes bibliographical references (p. 55-60).
Subjects: World Bank. Human capital. Economic development--Social aspects. Social planning.
LC Classification: HD4904.7 .A34 1995

Advancing sustainable development: the World Bank and Agenda 21.
Published/Created: Washington, DC: World Bank, 1997.
Related Authors: World Bank.
Description: x, 80 p.; 27 cm.
ISBN: 0821339745
Subjects: World Bank. Sustainable development. Economic development--Environmental aspects. Environmental policy--International cooperation.
Series: Environmentally sustainable development studies and monographs series; no. 19
LC Classification: HC79.E5 A354 1997
Dewey Class No.: 363.7 21

Anderson, Jock R., 1941-
The World Bank, the grant program, and the CGIAR: a retrospective review / Jock R. Anderson, Dana G. Dalrymple.
Published/Created: Washington, DC: World Bank, 1999.
Projected Pub. Date: 9909
Related Authors: Dalrymple, Dana G. World Bank. Operations Evaluation Dept.
Description: p. cm.
ISBN: 0821345842
Notes: At head of title: World Bank Operations Evaluation Department. Includes bibliographical references.
Subjects: Consultative Group on International Agricultural Research. World Bank. Agriculture--Research--International cooperation.
LC Classification: S540.8.C66 A63 1999
Dewey Class No.: 630/.72 21

Arneberg, Marie W.
Theory and practice in the World Bank and IMF economic policy models: case study Mozambique / Marie W. Arneberg.
Published/Created: Oslo: Statistisk sentralbyrå, 1996.
Description: 28 p.: ill.; 29 cm.
ISBN: 8253742967
Notes: Includes bibliographical references (p. 24)
Subjects: International Monetary Fund. World Bank. Mozambique--Economic policy.
Series: Rapporter (Norway. Statistisk sentralbyrå); 96/13.
Variant Series: Rapporter, 0806-2056 = Reports; 96/13
LC Classification: HC890 .A76 1996

Assessing development effectiveness: evaluation in the World Bank and the International Finance Corporation / World Bank Operations Evaluation Department.
Published/Created: Washington, D.C.: World Bank, 1998.
Related Authors: World Bank.
Description: vi, 79 p.: ill.; 26 cm.
Notes: Includes bibliographical references.
Subjects: World Bank. International Finance Corporation. Economic development projects--Evaluation.
LC Classification: HC79.E44 A88 1998
Dewey Class No.: 332.1/532 21

Baneth, Jean, 1936-
Selecting development projects for the World Bank / Jean Baneth.
Published/Created: Washington, D.C.: World Bank, c1996.
Description: xv, 75 p.: ill.; 28 cm.
ISBN: 0821336258
Notes: Includes bibliographical references (p. 75).
Subjects: World Bank. Economic development projects--Evaluation. Economic development projects--Finance.
Series: World Bank discussion papers, 0259-210X; 322
LC Classification: HG3881.5.W57 B364 1996
Dewey Class No.: 332.1/532 20

Barbu, Alain, 1949-
Information infrastructure: the World Bank Group's experience: a joint Operations Evaluation Department, Operations Evaluation Group review / Alain Barbu, Rafael Dominguez, William Melody.
Published/Created: Washington, D.C.: Internatonal Finance Corp.: World Bank, 2001.
Related Authors: Dominguez, Rafael. Melody, William H. World Bank. Operations Evaluation Dept.
Description: xxvii, 54 p.: ill.; 28 cm.
ISBN: 0821349694
Notes: Bibliographic references (p. 53-54).
Subjects: Information technology--Telecommunication--Developing countries.
LC Classification: HC59.72.I55 B37 2001
Dewey Class No.: 384/.09172/4 21

Benoit, Philippe.
Project finance at the World Bank: an overview of policies and instruments / Philippe Benoit.
Published/Created: Washington, D.C.: The World Bank, c1996.
Description: xiii, 110 p.: ill.; 27 cm.
ISBN: 0821335219

Notes: Includes bibliographical references (p. 109-110).
Subjects: World Bank. International finance. Economic development projects.
Series: World Bank technical paper, 0253-7494; no. 312
LC Classification: HG3881.5.W57 B46 1996
Dewey Class No.: 332.1/532 20

Bond, Patrick.
Against global apartheid: South Africa meets the World Bank, IMF, and international finance / Patrick Bond.
Published/Created: New York: Zed Books, 2003.
Projected Pub. Date: 0309
Description: p. cm.
ISBN: 1842773925 (cased) 1842773933 (limp)
Notes: Includes bibliographical references and index.
Subjects: World Bank. International Monetary Fund. Apartheid. Globalization. International finance. South Africa--Foreign economic relations.
LC Classification: HF1613.4 .B66 2003
Dewey Class No.: 337.68 21

Bond, Patrick.
Against global apartheid: South Africa meets the World Bank, IMF, and international finance / Patrick Bond.
Published/Created: Cape Town: University of Cape Town Press, 2001.
Description: xxiv, 302 p.: ill.; 21 cm.
ISBN: 1919713565
Notes: Includes bibliographical references and index.
Subjects: World Bank. International Monetary Fund. Apartheid. Globalization. International finance. South Africa--Foreign economic relations.
LC Classification: HF1613.4

Brydon, Lynne.
Adjusting society: the World Bank, the IMF, and Ghana / Lynne Brydon and Karen Legge.
Published/Created: London; New York: Tauris Academic Studies; New York: In the United States of America and Canada distributed by St. Martin's Press, 1996.
Related Authors: Legge, Karen.
Description: x, 222 p.: maps; 23 cm.
ISBN: 1860640001
Notes: Includes bibliographical references (p. 207-215) and index.
Subjects: World Bank. International Monetary Fund. Structural adjustment (Economic policy)--Ghana--Economic conditions--1957-1979 & 1979-
Series: International library of African studies; v. 5.
Variant Series: International library of African studies; 5
LC Classification: HC1060 .B79 1996

Buvini´c, Mayra.
Investing in women: progress and prospects for the World Bank / Mayra Buvini´c, Catherine Gwin, and Lisa M. Bates.
Published/Created: Washington, D.C.: Published by the Overseas Development Council in cooperation with the International Center for Research on Women; Baltimore, MD: Distributed by the Johns Hopkins University Press, c1996.
Related Authors: Gwin, Catherine. Bates, Lisa M.
Description: ix, 115 p.; 23 cm.
ISBN: 1565170180 (pbk.: alk. paper)
Notes: Includes bibliographical references (p. 80-84).
Subjects: World Bank. Women in development--Developing countries. Women--Developing countries--Economic conditions. Women--Developing countries--Social conditions.
Series: Policy essay; no. 19
LC Classification: HQ1240.5.D44 B88 1996
Dewey Class No.: 338.9/0083 20

Chossudovsky, Michel.
The globalisation of poverty: impacts of IMF and World Bank reforms / Michel Chossudovsky.
Published/Created: Penang, Malaysia: Third World Network, c1997.
Description: 280 p.: ill.; 22 cm.
ISBN: 9839747231
Notes: Includes bibliographical references (p. [265]-272) and index.
Subjects: International Monetary Fund. World Bank. Poverty. International finance.
LC Classification: HC79.P6 C48 1997
Dewey Class No.: 332.1/52 21

Civil service reform: strengthening World Bank and IMF collaboration.
Published/Created: Washington, D.C.: The World Bank, c2002.
Related Authors: World Bank. International Monetary Fund.
Description: xii, 84 p.: ill.; 23 cm.
ISBN: 0821350951
Notes: Includes bibliographical references (p. 78-80) and index.
Subjects: International Monetary Fund. World Bank. International finance. Development banks.
Series: Directions in development (Washington, D.C.)
Variant Series: Directions in development
LC Classification: HG3881.5.W57 C478 2002
Dewey Class No.: 351 21

Cling, Jean-Pierre.
New international poverty reduction strategies / Jean-Pierre Cling, Mireille Razafindrakoto & Francois Roubaud.

Published/Created: London; New York: Routledge, 2003.
Projected Pub. Date: 0305
Related Authors: Razafindrakoto, Mireille. Roubaud, François.
Description: p. cm.
ISBN: 0415307007
Notes: Includes bibliographical references and index.
Subjects: World Bank. Economic assistance--Case studies. Poverty--Case studies.
Series: Routledge studies in development economics; 35
LC Classification: HC60 .C526 2003
Dewey Class No.: 339.4/6 21

Cobb, John B.
The earthist challenge to economism: a theological critique of the World Bank / John B. Cobb, Jr.
Published/Created: New York, N.Y.: St. Martin's Press, 1999.
Description: ix, 192 p.; 23 cm.
ISBN: 0312218389 (recycled paper)
Notes: Includes bibliographical references and index.
Subjects: World Bank. Economics--Religious aspects--Christianity. Economic man. Sustainable development. Environmental degradation.
LC Classification: HG3881.5.W57 C63 1999
Dewey Class No.: 332.1/532 21

Cultural heritage and development: a framework for action in the Middle East and North Africa / The World Bank.
Published/Created: Washington, D.C.: World Bank, c2001.
Related Authors: World Bank.
Description: x, 102 p.: col. ill., col. maps; 26 cm.
ISBN: 0821349384 (pbk.)
Notes: Includes bibliographical references (p. [91]-95). Includes illustration credits (p. [101]-102).
Subjects: World Bank. Cultural property--Protection--Middle East. Cultural property--Protection--Africa, North. Economic development--Social aspects--Middle East. Economic development--Social aspects--Africa, North.
Series: Orientations in development.
Variant Series: Orientations in development series
LC Classification: DS57 .C82 2001
Dewey Class No.: 363.6/9/0956 21

Datta Mitra, Jayati.
Fiscal management in adjustment lending / Jayati Datta-Mitra.
Published/Created: Washington, D.C.: World Bank, 1997.
Related Authors: World Bank.
Description: xviii, 179 p.: ill.; 28 cm.
ISBN: 0821339656(pbk.)

Notes: Includes bibliographical references.
Subjects: World Bank. Fiscal policy--Developing countries. Loans, Foreign--Developing countries. Budget deficits--Developing countries. Structural adjustment (Economic policy)--Developing countries.
Series: A World Bank operations evaluation study, 1011-0984
LC Classification: HJ1620 .D377 1997
Dewey Class No.: 332.1/532 21

Dayton, Julia, 1967-
World Bank HIV/AIDS interventions: ex-ante and ex-post evaluation / Julia Dayton.
Published/Created: Washington, D.C.: World Bank, c1998.
Description: v, 35 p.: ill.; 28 cm.
ISBN: 0821342517
Notes: Includes bibliographical references (p. 35).
Subjects: World Bank. AIDS (Disease)--Prevention--Economic aspects.
Series: World Bank discussion papers; 389.
Variant Series: World Bank discussion paper; no. 389
LC Classification: RA644.A25 D39 1998
Dewey Class No.: 362.1/969792 21

Democratizing the global economy: the battle against the Work Bank and the IMF / edited by Kevin Danaher.
Published/Created: Monroe, ME: Common Courage Press, 2000.
Projected Pub. Date: 0012
Related Authors: Danaher, Kevin, 1950-
Description: p. cm.
ISBN: 1567512097 (cloth) 1567512089 (pbk.)
Notes: Includes index.
Subjects: World Bank. International Monetary Fund. International economic relations. Structural adjustment (Economic policy) Economic assistance--Developing countries. Democracy.
LC Classification: HF1359 .D46 2000
Dewey Class No.: 332.1/52 21

Development and human rights: the role of the World Bank.
Published/Created: Washington, DC: World Bank, 1998.
Projected Pub. Date: 9810
Related Authors: World Bank.
Description: p. cm.
ISBN: 0821343408
Subjects: Human rights--Developing countries. Economic development.
LC Classification: JC599.D44 W67 1998
Dewey Class No.: 332.1/532 21

Disinvesting in health: the World Bank's prescriptions for health / editor, Mohan Rao.
Published/Created: Thousand Oaks, CA: Sage Publications, 1999.
Related Authors: Rao, Mohan, 1953- World Bank.
Description: 238 p.: ill.; 22 cm.
ISBN: 0761993479 (cl.) 0761993487 (pa.)
Notes: Includes bibliographical references and index.
Subjects: World Bank. Medical policy--India--Congresses. Medical care--India--Finance--Congresses. Medical assistance--India--Congresses.
LC Classification: RA395.I5 D57 1999
Dewey Class No.: 362.1/0954 21

Economic analysis of World Bank education projects and project outcomes [electronic resource] / Ayesha Vawda ... [et al.].
Published/Created: Washington, DC: World Bank, Human Development Network, Education Team, and East Asia and Pacific Region, Human Development Sector Unit, [2001]
Related Authors: Vawda, Ayesha. World Bank. Human Development Network. Education Team. World Bank. East Asia and Pacific Regional Office. Human Development Sector Unit.
Summary: Outcomes on World Bank education projects are better when the quality of project appraisal is good.
Additional Form Avail.: Also available in print.
Subjects: World Bank. Vocational education--Finance--Evaluation.
Series: Policy research working papers; 2564.
Variant Series: Policy research working paper; 2564
LC Classification: HG3881.5.W57

Eriksson, John R. (John Rudolph), 1935-
The drive to partnership: aid coordination and the World Bank / John Eriksson.
Published/Created: Washington, D.C.: World Bank, 2001.
Description: xxxii, 78 p.: ill.; 28 cm.
ISBN: 0821349406
Notes: At head of title: World Bank Operations Evaluation Department, OED. Includes bibliographical references (p.73-78).
Subjects: World Bank. Economic assistance--International cooperation.
LC Classification: HC60 .E67 2001
Dewey Class No.: 332.1/532 21

Evans, Alison.
Poverty reduction in the 1990s: an evaluation of strategy and performance / Alison Evans.
Published/Created: Washington, D.C.: World Bank, 2000.
Description: xxiv, 61 p.: ill.; 28 cm.
ISBN: 0821348205 (pbk.)
Notes: At head of title: "World Bank Operations Evaluation Department."

Includes bibliographical references (p. 57-60).
Subjects: World Bank. Economic assistance--Developing countries--Evaluation. Poverty--Developing countries.
LC Classification: HC60 .E834 2000
Dewey Class No.: 338.9/009172/6 21

Faith in development: partnership between the World Bank and the churches of Africa / edited by Deryke Belshaw, Robert Calderisi, Chris Sugden; foreword by James D. Wolfensohn and George Carey.
Published/Created: Washington, DC: World Bank, c2001.
Related Authors: Belshaw, D. G. R. Calderisi, Robert. Sugden, Chris, 1948-
Description: x, 246 p.; 23 cm.
ISBN: 0821348485
Notes: Papers presented at a conference held in Mar. 2000 in Nairobi, Kenya. Includes bibliographical references.
Subjects: World Bank. Economic assistance--Moral and ethical aspects--Africa Congresses. Economic development--Religious aspects--Christianity Congresses.
LC Classification: HC800 .F34 2001
Dewey Class No.: 338.91/096 21

Fallon, Peter, 1946-
Child labor: issues and directions for the World Bank / Peter Fallon and Zafiris Tzannatos.
Published/Created: Washington, D.C.: Social Protection, Human Development Network, World Bank, c1998.
Related Authors: Tzannatos, Zafiris, 1953-
Description: viii, 22 p.: ill.; 23 cm.
ISBN: 0821341839
Notes: Includes bibliographical references (p. 22).
Subjects: World Bank. Child labor. Child welfare.
LC Classification: HD6231 .F35 1998
Dewey Class No.: 331.3/1 21

Financial management and disbursement in World Bank financed projects [computer file]: self-learning program.
Edition Information: Version 1.0.
Published/Created: [Washington, D.C.]: World Bank, [2000].
Related Authors: World Bank.
Description: 1 computer optical disc; 4 3/4 in. + 1 user guide.
ISBN: 0821346652
Computer File Info.: Computer data and program.
Summary: Covers the World Bank's project financial management and disbursement policies, guidelines, and requirements. Features graphics and sound.
Notes: Title from disc label. System requirements: PC; 12MB RAM; Windows 95 or higher; SVGA graphics display (640 x 480 resolution with 256 colors); double-

speed CD-ROM drive; sound card with speakers or headphones.
Subjects: World Bank. Economic development projects--Finance.
LC Classification: HG3881.5.W57
Dewey Class No.: 658.15 13

Fuel for change: World Bank energy policy - rhetoric and reality / edited by Ian Tellam.
Variant Fuel for change: World Bank energy policy - rhetoric vs reality
Published/Created: London; New York: Zed Books, c2000.
Related Authors: Tellam, Ian.
Description: xvi, 208 p.; 23 cm.
ISBN: 185649781X (cased) 1856497828 (limp)
Notes: Includes bibliographical references (p. [201]) and index.
Subjects: World Bank. Energy development--Developing countries--Finance--Case studies. Energy development--Europe, Eastern--Finance--Case studies. Renewable energy sources--Developing countries. Renewable energy sources--Europe, Eastern.
LC Classification: HD9502.D442 F83 2000
Dewey Class No.: 333.79 21

Gilbert, Roy.
Improving the lives of the poor by investing in cities: a performance update / Roy Gilbert.
Published/Created: Washington, DC: World Bank, 2003.
Projected Pub. Date: 0307
Description: p. cm.
ISBN: 0821355406
Notes: Includes bibliographical references.
Subjects: World Bank. Community development, Urban--Developing countries Evaluation. Economic assistance--Developing countries--Evaluation.
Series: World Bank operations evaluation study.
Variant Series: Operations evaluation studies
LC Classification: HN981.C6 G55 2003
Dewey Class No.: 307.1/416/091724 21

Global development fifty years after Bretton Woods: essays in honour of Gerald K. Helleiner / edited by Roy Culpeper, Albert Berry, and Frances Stewart.
Published/Created: New York: St. Martin's Press, 1996.
Related Authors: Helleiner, Gerald K. Culpeper, Roy, 1947- Berry, Albert. Stewart, Frances.
Description: xiii, 381 p.: ill.; 23 cm.
ISBN: 0312162820 (cloth) 0312162839 (pbk.)
Notes: "Gerald K. Helleiner's publications": p. 356-375. Includes bibliographical references and index.
Subjects: Helleiner, Gerald K. World Bank. International Monetary Fund.

International finance. International economic relations.
LC Classification: HG3881 .G5727 1997
Dewey Class No.: 337 20

Harriss, John.
Depoliticizing development: the World Bank and social capital / John Harriss.
Published/Created: London: Anthem Press, 2002.
Description: 149 p.; 25 cm.
ISBN: 1843310481 184331049X (pbk.)
Notes: Includes bibliographical references (p. [137]-143) and index.
Subjects: World Bank. Infrastructure (Economics)
LC Classification: HC79.C3 H367 2002
Dewey Class No.: 363 21

Harriss, John.
Depoliticizing development: the World Bank and social capital / John Harriss.
Published/Created: New Delhi: Leftword Books, 2001.
Description: 145 p.; 22 cm.
ISBN: 8187496169
Notes: Includes bibliographical references (p. [126]-132) and index.
Subjects: World Bank. Infrastructure (Economics)
LC Classification: HC79.C3 H367 2001
Dewey Class No.: 363 21

Helping countries combat curruption: progress at the World Bank since 1997.
Published/Created: Washington, D.C.: World Bank, 2000.
Related Authors: World Bank. Poverty Reduction and Economic Management. World Bank. Operational Core Services Network.
Description: vi, 109 p.: ill.; 24 cm.
Notes: "June 2000." "This report was produced as a joint effort of the Poverty Reduction and Economic Management (PREM) Network and the Operational Core Services (OCS) Network at the World Bank"--P. iii. Includes bibliographical references (p. 51-52).
Subjects: World Bank. International finance--Corrupt practices. Corruption--Prevention. Political corruption--Prevention.
LC Classification: HG3881.5.W57 H54 2000

Heneveld, Ward.
Schools count: World Bank project designs and the quality of primary education in sub-Saharan Africa / Ward Heneveld and Helen Craig.
Published/Created: Washington, D.C.: World Bank, c1996.
Related Authors: Craig, Helen, 1959- World Bank.
Description: xvii, 127 p.: ill.; 28 cm.
ISBN: 0821334603
Notes: Includes bibliographical references (p. 113-127).

Subjects: World Bank. Education, Elementary--Africa, Sub-Saharan. Educational assistance--Africa, Sub-Saharan. Educational evaluation--Africa, Sub-Saharan. Educational surveys--Africa, Sub-Saharan.
Series: World Bank technical paper; no. 303. World Bank technical paper. Africa Technical Department series.
Variant Series: World Bank technical paper, 0253-7494; 303. Africa Technical series
LC Classification: LA1502 .H45 1995
Dewey Class No.: 372.967 20

Huizinga, Harry.
Are there synergies between World Bank partial credit guarantees and private lending? / Harry Huizinga.
Published/Created: Washington, DC: World Bank, Development Research Group, [1997]
Related Authors: World Bank. Development Research Group.
Description: 15 p.; 28 cm.
Notes: "August 1997"--Cover. Includes bibliographical references (p. 14).
Subjects: World Bank. International economic integration. Loans
Series: Policy research working papers; 1802.
Variant Series: Policy research working paper; 1802
LC Classification: HG3881.5.W57 P63 no. 1802

Huther, Jeff, 1960-
Anti-corruption policies and programs [electronic resource]: a framework for evaluation / Jeff Huther and Anwar Shah.
Published/Created: Washington, DC: World Bank, Operations Evaluation Department, Country Evaluation and Regional Relations Division, [2000]
Related Authors: Shah, Anwar. World Bank. Country Evaluation and Regional Relations Division.
Summary: In a largely corruption-free environment, anti-corruption agencies, ethics offices, and ombudsman strengthen the standards of accountability. In countries with endemic corruption, however, the same institutions function in form but not in substance; under a best-case scenario such institutions might be helpful, but the more likely outcome is that they help to preserve social injustice.
Notes: Title from title screen as viewed on Oct. 01, 2002. "December 2000"--Cover. Includes bibliographical references (p. 14-17). Mode of access: World Wide Web.
Additional Form Avail.: Also available in print.
Subjects: World Bank. Economic development projects. Political corruption--Bribery--Public administration--Corrupt practices--Prevention. Political ethics.
Series: Policy research working papers; 2501.
Variant Series: Policy research working paper; 2501
LC Classification: HG3881.5.W57

IDA in action 1993-1996: the pursuit of sustained poverty reduction: summary.
Variant International Development Association in action 1993-1996
Published/Created: Washington, D.C.: World Bank, c1997.
Related Authors: World Bank.
Description: iv, 29 p.: ill., 1 col. map.; 28 cm.
ISBN: 082133963X
Notes: Includes bibliographical references (p. 26).
Subjects: World Bank. International Development Association. Economic assistance--Developing countries. Poverty--Developing countries.
LC Classification: HG3881.5.W57 I33 1997

IMF and World Bank sponsored structural adjustment programs in Africa: Ghana's experience, 1983-1999 / edited by Kwadwo Konadu-Agyemang.
Published/Created: Burlington, VT: Ashgate, 2001.
Related Authors: Konadu-Agyemang, Kwadwo.
Description: xii, 444 p.: ill.; 23 cm.
ISBN: 0754613968
Notes: Includes bibliographical references and index.
Subjects: International Monetary Fund. World Bank. Structural adjustment (Economic policy)--Ghana. Ghana--Economic conditions--1979-
Series: University of North London voices in development management.
Variant Series: Voices in development management
LC Classification: HC1060 .I45 2001

Intellectual property rights in agriculture: the World Bank's role in assisting borrower and member countries / Uma Lele, William Lesser, Gesa Horstkotte-Wesseler, editors.
Published/Created: Washington, D.C.: World Bank, c2000 (1999 printing)
Related Authors: Lele, Uma J. Lesser, William. Horstkotte-Wesseler, Gesa, 1965-
Description: x, 87 p.; 28 cm.
ISBN: 082134496X
Notes: Includes bibliographical references.
Subjects: World Bank. Intellectual property--Developing countries. Agriculture--Research--Law and legislation--Developing countries.
Series: Environmentally and socially sustainable development. Rural development
LC Classification: K1401 .I567 2000
Dewey Class No.: 630/.7/2 21

January, Brendan, 1972-
Globalize it!: the stories of the IMF, the World Bank, the WTO, and those who protest / Brendan January.
Published/Created: Brookfield, Conn.: Twenty-First Century Books, c2003.
Projected Pub. Date: 0310
Description: v. cm.

ISBN: 0761324178 (lib. bdg.)
Contents: The battle of Seattle -- A world order: the foundations of globalization -- I don't want to be like Mike -- Globalization is good for the globe -- Killing the world to save it? -- Whose culture? -- Protest -- The IMF faces a meltdown: economic crisis in Mexico, Russia, and Asia -- Mistakes and resolve -- A new world.
Notes: Includes bibliographical references and index.
Subjects: World Bank. International Monetary Fund. World Trade Organization. World Bank. International Monetary Fund. World Trade Organization. International economic integration--Juvenile literature. Globalization--Juvenile literature. Free trade--Juvenile literature. International business enterprises--Juvenile literature. International finance--Juvenile literature. Equality--Juvenile literature. Globalization. Free trade. International business enterprises. International finance.
LC Classification: HF1418.5 .J363 2003
Dewey Class No.: 337 21

Khan, Shahrukh Rafi.
Do IMF & World Bank policies work? / by Shahrukh Rafi Khan.
Published/Created: [Islamabad]: SDPI, 1997.
Description: xix, 206 p.; 21 cm.
Notes: Cover title. Includes bibliographical references.
Subjects: International Monetary Fund. World Bank. Banks and banking, International.
Series: SDPI monograph series; # 6
LC Classification: HG3881.5.I58 K53 1997

Khan, Shahrukh Rafi.
Do World Bank and IMF policies work? / Shahrukh Rafi Khan.
Published/Created: New York, N.Y.: St. Martin's Press, 1999.
Description: x, 197 p.; 23 cm.
ISBN: 0312217048 (cloth)
Notes: Includes bibliographical references and index.
Subjects: World Bank. International Monetary Fund. Banks and banking, International.
LC Classification: HG3881.5.W57 K48 1999
Dewey Class No.: 332.1/5 21

King, Kenneth.
Knowledge for development?: comparing British, Japanese, Swedish and World Bank aid / Kenneth King and Simon McGrath.
Published/Created: New York: Zed Books, 2003.
Projected Pub. Date: 0309
Related Authors: McGrath, Simon A.
Description: p. cm.

ISBN: 1842773240 (cased) 1842773259 (limp)
Notes: Includes bibliographical references and index.
Subjects: Great Britain. Dept. for International Development. Kokusai Ky¯oryoku Jigy¯odan. Sweden. Enheten för internationellt utvecklingssamarbete. World Bank. Economic assistance. Economic assistance, British. Economic assistance, Japanese. Economic assistance, Swedish. Developing countries--Economic conditions.
LC Classification: HC60 .K465 2003
Dewey Class No.: 338.91/09172/4 21

Kirmani, Syed S., 1921-
Fostering riparian cooperation in international river basins: the World Bank at its best in development diplomacy / Syed Kirmani, Guy Le Moigne.
Published/Created: Washington, D.C.: World Bank, 1997.
Related Authors: Le Moigne, Guy J.-M., 1932-
Description: vii, 19 p.: maps; 28 cm.
ISBN: 0821337327
Notes: Includes bibliographical references (p. 18-19).
Subjects: World Bank. International relations. Economic development. Watersheds--Economic aspects. Aral Sea Watershed (Uzbekistan and Kazakstan)--Economic aspects. Indus River Watershed--Economic aspects. Mekong River Watershed--Economic aspects.
Series: World Bank technical paper, 0253-7494; no. 335
LC Classification: JX1395 .K528 1997
Dewey Class No.: 332.1/532 20

Kurian, Priya A.
Engendering the environment?: gender in the World Bank's environmental policies / Priya A. Kurian.
Published/Created: Aldershot Burlington, VT: Ashgate, c2000.
Description: xi, 269 p.; 23 cm.
ISBN: 0754611302
Notes: Includes bibliographical references (p. 234-259) and index.
Subjects: World Bank. Women in economic development. Rural development--Environmental aspects. Economic development--Environmental aspects. Environmental impact analysis.
LC Classification: HQ1240 .K87 2000
National Bib. No.: GBA0-Z9384

Lawyers Committee for Human Rights (U.S.)
Halfway to reform: the World Bank and the Venezuelan justice system / a joint report by the Lawyers Committee for Human Rights and the Venezuelan Program for Human Rights Education and Action.
Published/Created: New York: Lawyers Committee for Human Rights, c1996.
Related Authors: Programa Venezolano de Educación-Acción en Derechos

Humanos.
Description: ii, 149 p.; 23 cm.
ISBN: 0934143862
Notes: "August 1996." Includes bibliographical references.
Subjects: World Bank. Justice, Administration of--Venezuela. Law reform--Venezuela. Judicial corruption--Venezuela.
LC Classification: KHW2501 .L38 1996
Dewey Class No.: 347.87 21

Liebenthal, Andrés, 1947-
Promoting environmental sustainability in development: an evaluation of the World Bank's performance / Andr'es Liebenthal.
Edition Information: 1st ed.
Published/Created: Washington, D.C.: World Bank, 2002.
Related Authors: World Bank. Operations Evaluation Dept.
Description: xxiii, 51 p.: ill.; 28 cm.
ISBN: 0821350536
Notes: Includes bibliographical references (p. 49-51). Summaries in English, French and Spanish.
Additional Form Avail.: Also available on the World Wide Web.
Subjects: World Bank--Developing countries. World Bank. Operations Evaluation Dept. World Bank. Sustainable development--Developing countries. Environmental policy--Developing countries.
LC Classification: HC59.E5 L537 2002
Dewey Class No.: 338.9/27/091724 21

Marquette, Heather, 1972-
Corruption, politics and development: the role of the World Bank / Heather Marquette.
Published/Created: New York, N.Y.: Palgrave Macmillan, 2003.
Projected Pub. Date: 0309
Description: p. cm.
ISBN: 0333999312 (cloth)
Notes: Includes bibliographical references and index.
Subjects: World Bank. International finance--Corrupt practices. Corruption--Prevention. Political corruption--Prevention.
LC Classification: HG3881.5.W57 M27 2003
Dewey Class No.: 364.16/8 21

Mathieu, N.
Industrial restructuring: World Bank experience, future challenges / Nicolas Mathieu.
Published/Created: Washington, D.C.: World Bank, c1996.
Description: xvi, 126 p.: ill.; 27 cm.
ISBN: 0821336142

Notes: Includes bibliographical references (p. 117-118).
Subjects: World Bank. Corporate reorganizations--Case studies. Privatization--Case studies. Industrial policy--Case studies.
Series: A World Bank operations evaluation study, ISSN 1011-0984
LC Classification: HD2746.5 .M33 1996
Dewey Class No.: 338.91 20

Meerman, Jacob, 1931-
Reforming agriculture: the World Bank goes to market / Jacob P. Meerman.
Published/Created: Washington, D.C.: World Bank, 1997.
Related Authors: World Bank. Operations Evaluation Dept.
Description: xv, 162 p.; 28 cm.
ISBN: 0821339095(pbk.)
Notes: Prepared by the Operations Evaluation Dept. Includes bibliographical references.
Subjects: World Bank. Agricultural development projects--Developing countries Evaluation. Agriculture and state--Developing countries.
Series: A World Bank operations evaluation study
LC Classification: HD1431 .M44 1997
Dewey Class No.: 338.1/8 21

Miller-Adams, Michelle, 1959-
The World Bank: new agendas in a changing world / Michelle Miller-Adams.
Published/Created: London; New York: Routledge, c1999.
Description: xii, 176 p. : ill.; 23 cm.
ISBN: 0415193532
Notes: Includes bibliographical references (p. [160]-169) and index.
Series: Routledge studies in development economics
LC Classification: HG3881.5.W57 M55 1999
Dewey Class No.: 332.1/532 21

Nelson, Joan M.
Reforming health and education: the World Bank, the IDB, and complex institutional change / Joan M. Nelson.
Published/Created: Washington, DC: Overseas Development Council; Baltimore, MD: Distributed by the Johns Hopkins University Press, c1999.
Description: xviii, 103 p.; 23 cm.
ISBN: 156517030X (pbk.)
Notes: Includes bibliographical references.
Subjects: World Bank. Inter-American Development Bank. Medical policy. Education and state.
Series: Policy essay; no. 26
LC Classification: HG3881.5.W57 N447 1999
Dewey Class No.: 362.1/0425 21

Nigerian agriculture and the World Bank: a partnership for development / edited by Gbenga Okeowo.
Published/Created: Ilorin, Kwara State, Nigeria: Agricultural and Rural Management Training Institute, c1998.
Related Authors: Okeowo, Gbenga. Agricultural and Rural Management Training Institute (Ilorin, Nigeria)
Description: 38, 9 p.: ill. (some col.); 27 cm.
ISBN: 9782399035
Notes: Includes bibliographical references (p. 16-17).
Subjects: World Bank. Agricultural credit--Nigeria. Agriculture--Nigeria--Finance.
LC Classification: HD1440.N6 N53 1998
Dewey Class No.: 332.7/1/09669 21

Onorato, William T. (William Torrens)
World Bank group assistance for minerals sector development and reform in member countries / William T. Onorato, Peter Fox, John E. Strongman.
Published/Created: Washington, D.C.: World Bank, c1998.
Related Authors: Fox, Peter. Strongman, John, 1947-
Description: viii, 35 p.; 27 cm.
ISBN: 0821342037
Notes: Includes bibliographical references.
Subjects: World Bank. Mineral industries--Developing countries--Finance.
Series: World Bank technical paper, 0253-7494; no. 405
LC Classification: HD9506.D452 O56 1998
Dewey Class No.: 338.2/324/091724 21

Participation in practice: the experience of the World Bank and other stakeholders / edited by Jennifer Rietbergen-McCracken.
Published/Created: Washington, D.C.: World Bank, c1996.
Related Authors: Rietbergen-McCracken, Jennifer, 1962- World Bank.
Description: xi, 97 p.; 28 cm.
ISBN: 0821336843
Notes: Includes bibliographical references.
Subjects: World Bank. Economic development projects--Citizen participation--Case studies.
Series: World Bank discussion papers; 333.
Variant Series: World Bank discussion paper, 0259-210X; no. 333
LC Classification: HG3881.5.W57 P363 1996
Dewey Class No.: 332.1/532 20

Partnerships for development / The World Bank.
Published/Created: Worthing: published by the Creative Communications Group for the World Bank, 2001.
Related Authors: World Bank.

Description: 206 p.: ill. (some col.), maps; 30 cm.
Subjects: World Bank. Sustainable development.
LC Classification: HG3881.5.W57 P365 2001
Dewey Class No.: 332.1/532 21

Pitman, George Keith, 1945-
Bridging troubled waters: assessing the World Bank water resources strategy / George Keith Pitman.
Published/Created: Washington, DC. World Bank, 2002.
Related Authors: World Bank. Operations Evaluation Dept.
Description: xxviii, 116 p.: ill.; 28 cm.
ISBN: 0821351400 (pbk.)
Notes: At head of title: World Bank Operations Evaluation Department, OED. Includes bibliographical references (p. 109-116). Summaries in French and Spanish.
Subjects: World Bank. Water resources development--Economic aspects--Developing countries--Economic assistance--Developing countries--Evaluation.
Series: World Bank operations evaluation study.
Variant Series: Study series
LC Classification: HD1702 .P57 2002
Dewey Class No.: 333.91/009172/4 21

Population and the World Bank: adapting to change.
Edition Information: Rev. ed.
Published/Created: Washington, D.C.: World Bank, c2000.
Related Authors: World Bank.
Description: 47 p.; 28 cm.
ISBN: 0821346636
Notes: Includes bibliographical references.
Subjects: World Bank. Population. Population policy.
Series: Health, nutrition, and population series
LC Classification: HB849.4 .P673 2000
Dewey Class No.: 304.6 21

Population and the World Bank: adapting to change.
Published/Created: Washington, D.C.: World Bank, 1999.
Related Authors: World Bank.
Description: 45 p.: ill., col. map; 28 cm.
ISBN: 0821344404
Notes: Includes bibliographical references.
Subjects: World Bank. Population. Population policy.
Series: Health, nutrition, and population series
LC Classification: HB849.4 .P673 1999
Dewey Class No.: 304.6 21

Post-conflict reconstruction: the role of the World Bank.
Published/Created: Washington, D.C.: World Bank, c1998.
Related Authors: World Bank.
Description: x, 69 p.; 23cm.
ISBN: 0821342150
Notes: Includes bibliographical references (p. 69).
Subjects: World Bank. Economic assistance--Developing countries.
LC Classification: HG3881.5.W57 P67 1998
Dewey Class No.: 658.1/532 21

Pouliquen, Louis Y.
Rural infrastructure from a World Bank perspective: a knowledge management framework / Louis Y. Pouliquen.
Published/Created: Washington, D.C.: World Bank, c1999.
Description: vi, 58 p.: ill.; 28 cm.
ISBN: 0821343092
Notes: Includes bibliographical references.
Subjects: World Bank. Rural development--Finance. Rural development projects--Finance. Infrastructure (Economics)--Finance.
Series: Environmentally and socially sustainable development series. Rural development.
Variant Series: Environmentally and socially sustainable development. Rural development
LC Classification: HG3881.5.W57 P68 1999
Dewey Class No.: 362.1/532 21

Poverty reduction and the World Bank: progress in fiscal 1996 and 1997.
Published/Created: Washington, D.C.: World Bank, c1997.
Related Authors: World Bank.
Description: x, 182 p.; 28 cm.
ISBN: 0821338013
Notes: Updates the report for fiscal 1995, Poverty reduction and the World Bank: progress and challenges for the 1990s (p. vii). Includes bibliographical references (p. 182).
Subjects: World Bank. Economic assistance--Developing countries. Poverty--Developing countries.
LC Classification: HC60 .P667 1997

Poverty reduction and the World Bank: progress in fiscal 1998.
Published/Created: Washington, D.C.: World Bank, c1999.
Related Authors: World Bank.
Description: ix, 117 p.: ill.; 28 cm.
ISBN: 082134384X (pbk.)
Notes: Includes bibliographical references (p. 115-117).
Subjects: World Bank. Economic assistance--Developing countries. Poverty--

Developing countries.
LC Classification: HC60 .P668 1999
Dewey Class No.: 332.1/532 21

Poverty reduction and the World Bank: progress in fiscal 1999.
Published/Created: Washington, D.C.: World Bank, c2000.
Related Authors: World Bank.
Description: viii, 167 p. 27 cm.
ISBN: 0821347071
Notes: Includes bibliographical references (p. 165-167).
Subjects: World Bank. Economic assistance--Developing countries. Poverty--Developing countries.
LC Classification: HC60 .P668 2000
Dewey Class No.: 332.1/532 21

Poverty reduction and the World Bank: progress in operationalizing the WDR 2000/2001.
Published/Created: Washington, D.C.: World Bank, 2002.
Related Authors: World Bank.
Description: vii, 75 p.: ill.; 28 cm.
ISBN: 0821350978
Notes: Includes bibliographical references.
Subjects: World Bank. Economic assistance--Developing countries. Poverty--Developing countries.
LC Classification: HC60 .P669 2002
Dewey Class No.: 339.4/6/091724 21

Pritchett, Lant.
Quantifying vulnerability to poverty: a proposed measure, with application to Indonesia / Lant Pritchett, Asep Suryahadi, Sudarno Sumarto.
Published/Created: [Jakarta: Social Monitoring & Early Response Unit, 2000]
Related Authors: Suryahadi, Asep. Sumarto, Sudarno.
Description: 22 leaves; 30 cm.
Notes: Cover title. "January 2000." Includes bibliographical references (leaves 20-21).
Subjects: World Bank. Poverty--Indonesia--Econometric models. Poor--Indonesia--Econometric models. Income--Indonesia--Econometric models. Consumption (Economics)--Indonesia--Econometric models.
Series: SMERU working paper
LC Classification: HG3881.5.W57 P738 2000

Rahman, Mir Obaidur.
Limiting the role of state: prescription of the World Bank and the Bangladesh economy / Mir Obaidur Rahman.
Published/Created: Dhaka: Bangladesh Public Administration Training Center,

1999.
Related Authors: Bangladesh Public Administration Training Centre.
Description: 76 p.; 24 cm.
Notes: Includes bibliographical references (p. 74).
Subjects: World Bank. Bangladesh--Economic policy.
LC Classification: HC440.8 .R3416 1999
Dewey Class No.: 338.95492 21

Shihata, Ibrahim F. I., 1937-
Complementary reform: essays on legal, judicial, and other institutional reforms supported by the World Bank / Ibrahim F.I. Shihata.
Published/Created: The Hague; Boston: Kluwer Law International, c1997.
Description: xiv, 238 p.; 23 cm.
ISBN: 9041106146
Notes: Includes bibliographical references.
Subjects: World Bank. World Bank Group. Law reform. Justice, Administration of.
LC Classification: K4451. S

Sirisena, Minipura.
World Bank and neocolonialism: a socio-economic, philosophical, and political analysis / M. Sirisena.
Published/Created: Pannipitiya: Stamford Lake Publication, 2001.
Description: 127, [1] p.; 22 cm.
ISBN: 9558156787
Notes: Includes bibliographical references (p. [128]).
Subjects: World Bank. World politics--21st century.
LC Classification: HG3881.5.W57 S57 2001

Social funds and reaching the poor: experiences and future directions: proceedings from an international workshop organized by the World Bank ... [et al.] / edited by Anthony G. Bigio.
Published/Created: Washington, D.C.: World Bank, c1998.
Related Authors: Bigio, Anthony G. World Bank. International Workshop on Social Funds (1997: Washington, D.C.)
Description: vii, 247 p.; 28 cm.
ISBN: 0821342096
Notes: Papers presented at the International Workshop on Social Funds, May 27-30, 1997, Washington, D.C.
Subjects: World Bank. Economic development projects--Citizen participation Congresses. Community development--Congresses. Social funds.
Series: EDI learning resources series
LC Classification: HD75.8 .S66 1998
Dewey Class No.: 338.9/22 21

Sosale, Shobhana, 1963-
Trends in private sector development in World Bank education projects [electronic resource] / by Shobhana Sosale.
Published/Created: Washington, DC: World Bank, Human Development Network, Education Team, [2000]
Related Authors: World Bank. Human Development Network. Education Team.
Summary: The principle underlying trends in Bank education projects is that strengthening the private sector's role in noncompulsory education over time will release public resources for the compulsory (primary) level. The public and private sectors have complementary roles to play.
Notes: Title from title screen as viewed on Oct. 08, 2002. "September 2000"--Cover. Includes bibliographical references (p. 44-49). Mode of access: World Wide Web.
Additional Form Avail.: Also available in print.
Subjects: World Bank. Education, Preschool--Finance. Education, Preschool--Parent participation. Private schools--Finance. Educational assistance.
Series: Policy research working papers; 2452.
Variant Series: Policy research working paper; 2452
LC Classification: HG3881.5.W57

The Bretton Woods-GATT system: retrospect and prospect after fifty years / Orin Kirshner, editor; contributors, Edward M. Bernstein ... [et al.].
Published/Created: Armonk, NY: M. E. Sharpe, c1996.
Related Authors: Kirshner, Orin, 1961- Bernstein, Edward M. (Edward Morris), 1904- Institute for Agriculture and Trade Policy.
Description: xiii, 321 p.; 24 cm.
ISBN: 1563246295 (alk. paper) 1563246309 (pbk.: alk. paper)
Notes: Consists of over twenty papers produced for the Bretton Woods revisited conference, which was convened by the Institute for Agriculture and Trade Policy held in Bretton Woods, N.H., October 15-17, 1994. Includes bibliographical references and index.
Subjects: General Agreement on Tariffs and Trade (Organization) International Monetary Fund. World Bank. United Nations Monetary and Financial Conference (1944: Bretton Woods, N.H.) International finance. Free trade.
LC Classification: HG205 .B74 1996
Dewey Class No.: 332/.042 20

The evolving role of the World Bank: helping meet the challenge of development / editor, K. Sarwar Lateef.
Published/Created: Washington, DC: World Bank, c1995.
Related Authors: Lateef, K. Sarwar.
Description: vii, 230 p.: ill.; 28 cm.
ISBN: 0821332341
Contents: The first half century: an overview / K. Sarwar Lateef -- From reconstruction to development in Europe and Japan / Caroline Doggart -- The

food crisis in South Asia: the case of India / Uma Lele and Balu Bumb -- The Latin American debt crisis / Sebastian Edwards -- The transition in Central and Eastern Europe and the former Soviet Union / Kemal Dervis, Marcelo Selowsky, and Christine Wallich -- The East Asian economic miracle / Vinod Thomas and Peter Stephens -- The challenge of Africa / Ishrat Husain -- Mobilizing private savings for development: IBRD and the capital markets / Kenneth G. Lay.
Notes: Includes bibliographical references.
Subjects: World Bank. Economic assistance. Economic development. Economic history--1945-
LC Classification: HG3881.5.W57 E964 1995
Dewey Class No.: 332.1/532 20

The right conditions: the World Bank, structural adjustment, and forest policy reform / Frances J. Seymour ... [et al.; Carollyne Hutter, editor].
Published/Created: Washington, D.C.: World Resources Institute, c2000.
Related Authors: Seymour, Frances J. Hutter, Carollyne.
Description: vii, 155 p.: ill., maps; 26 cm.
ISBN: 1569734240 (alk. paper)
Notes: Includes bibliographical references.
Subjects: World Bank. Forest policy--Developing countries. Structural adjustment (Economic policy)--Developing countries.
LC Classification: SD669.5 .R54 2000
Dewey Class No.: 333.75/09172/4 21

The struggle for accountability: the World Bank, NGOs, and grassroots movements / edited by Jonathan A. Fox and L. David Brown.
Published/Created: Cambridge, Mass.: MIT Press, c1998.
Related Authors: Fox, Jonathan A. Brown, L. David (L. Dave)
Description: xi, 570 p.: ill.; 24 cm.
ISBN: 0262061996 (hc: alk. paper) 0262561174 (pbk.: alk. paper)
Notes: Includes bibliographical references and index.
Subjects: World Bank. Economic development--Environmental aspects--Developing countries. Political participation. Non-governmental organizations. Social movements--Developing countries.
Series: Global environmental accords.
Variant Series: Global environmental accord
LC Classification: HD75.6 .S77 1998
Dewey Class No.: 332.1/532 21

The World Bank and poverty in Africa: a critical assessment of the Bank's operational strategies for poverty reduction / Elling N. Tjonneland, project leader; Henrik Harboe ... [et al.].
Published/Created: Oslo: Royal Ministry of Foreign Affairs, 1998.
Related Authors: Tjønneland, Elling Njål, 1918- Chr. Michelsens institutt.
Description: 92 p.; 30 cm.

Notes: "Submitted to the Royal Norwegian Ministry of Foreign Affairs by the Chr. Michelsens Institute."
Subjects: World Bank. Economic assistance--Africa, Sub-Saharan. Poverty--Africa, Sub-Saharan.
Series: Evaluation report (Oslo, Norway); 98.7.
Variant Series: UD evaluation report; 7.98
LC Classification: HC800 .W69 1998

The World Bank forest strategy: striking the right balance / Uma Lele ... [et al.].
Published/Created: Washington, D.C.: World Bank, 2000.
Related Authors: Lele, Uma J.
Description: xxxii, 153 p.: ill.; 28 cm.
ISBN: 0821348418 (alk. paper)
Notes: Includes bibliographical references (p. 145-150).
Subjects: World Bank. Forests and forestry--Economic aspects. Forest policy.
Series: World Bank operations evaluation study.
Variant Series: Study series
LC Classification: SD393 .W65 2000
Dewey Class No.: 333.75 21

The World Bank participation sourcebook.
Published/Created: Washington, D.C.: World Bank, c1996.
Related Authors: World Bank. World Bank. Environmentally Sustainable Development.
Description: xvi, 259 p.: ill., map; 28 cm.
ISBN: 0821335588
Notes: "Environmentally Sustainable Development." Includes bibliographical references and index.
Subjects: World Bank. Economic development projects--Case studies--Handbooks, manuals, etc. Economic development projects--Citizen participation--Case studies--Handbooks, manuals, etc. Community development--Case studies--Handbooks, manuals, etc.
LC Classification: HG3881.5.W57 W692 1996
Dewey Class No.: 338.9 20

The World Bank policy on disclosure of information, 2002.
Published/Created: Washington, D.C.: World Bank, 2002.
Related Authors: World Bank.
Description: vi, 30 p.; 23 cm.
ISBN: 0821352164
Subjects: World Bank. Disclosure of information.
LC Classification: HG3881.5.W57 W694 2002
Dewey Class No.: 332.1/532/0684 21

The World Bank: lending on a global scale / edited by Jo Marie Griesgraber and Bernhard G. Gunter.
Published/Created: London; Chicago, Il.: Pluto Press, with Center of Concern, Washington, DC, 1996.
Related Authors: Griesgraber, Jo Marie. Gunter, Bernhard G., 1964- Center of Concern (Washington, D.C.)
Description: xix, 240 p.; 22 cm.
ISBN: 0745310508 (hc)
Notes: Includes bibliographical references (p. 209-223) and index.
Subjects: World Bank. International finance--History. Economic development--History.
Series: Rethinking Bretton Woods; v. 3
LC Classification: HG3881 .R418 1995 vol. 3 HG3881.5.W57
Dewey Class No.: 332/.042 s 332.1/532 20

The World Bank: partnerships for development.
Published/Created: [Worthing, West Sussex, UK]: Creative Communications Group, c2000.
Description: 209 p.: ill.; 30 cm.
Notes: "World Bank 2000"--Cover.
Subjects: World Bank. Economic assistance.
LC Classification: HC60 .W667 2000
Dewey Class No.: 338.91 21

The World Bank: structure and policies / edited by Christopher L. Gilbert and David Vines.
Published/Created: Cambridge; New York: Cambridge University Press, 2000.
Related Authors: Gilbert, C. L. Vines, David.
Description: xxiv, 335 p.: ill.; 24 cm.
ISBN: 0521790956
Notes: Includes bibliographical references and index.
Subjects: World Bank.
Series: Global economic institutions; 3
LC Classification: HG3881.5.W57 W6943 2000
Dewey Class No.: 332.1/532 21

The World Bank's experience with post-conflict reconstruction / Alcira Kreimer ... [et al.].
Published/Created: Washington, D.C.: World Bank, 1998.
Related Authors: Kreimer, Alcira. World Bank. Operations Evaluation Dept.
Description: xix, 96 p.: ill.; 28 cm.
ISBN: 0821342908
Notes: At head of title: World Bank Operations Evaluation Department, OED. "ISSN 1011-6984"--Verso t.p. Includes bibliographical references (p. 53-55).
Subjects: World Bank. Economic assistance--Evaluation.

Series: OED study series
LC Classification: HG3881.5.W57 W6949 1998
Dewey Class No.: 332.1/532 21

United States. Congress. House. Committee on Financial Services. Subcommittee on International Monetary Policy and Trade.
World Bank and IMF activities in Africa: hearing before the Subcommittee on International Monetary Policy and Trade of the Committee on Financial Services, U.S. House of Representatives, One Hundred Seventh Congress, first session, May 15, 2001.
Published/Created: Washington: U.S. G.P.O.: For sale by the Supt. of Docs., U.S. G.P.O., [Congressional Sales Office], 2001.
Description: iii, 119 p.; 24 cm.
ISBN: 0160662656
Notes: Distributed to some depository libraries in microfiche. Shipping list no.: 2002-0025-P. "Serial no. 107-15." Includes bibliographical references.
Subjects: World Bank. International Monetary Fund. Public health--Africa--Finance. Africa--Economic conditions.
LC Classification: KF27 .B5368+

United States. Congress. Joint Economic Committee.
Reform of the IMF and World Bank: hearing before the Joint Economic Committee, Congress of the United States, One Hundred Seventh Congress, second session, February 14, 2002.
Published/Created: Washington: U.S. G.P.O.: For sale by the Supt. of Docs., U.S. G.P.O., [Congressional Sales Office], 2002.
Description: iii, 27 p.; 24 cm.
ISBN: 0160691079
Notes: "Printed for the use of the Joint Economic Committee." Distributed to some depository libraries in microfiche. Shipping list no.: 2003-0030-P.
Subjects: International Monetary Fund. World Bank. International finance. Development banks.
Series: United States. Congress. Senate. S. hrg.; 107-716.
Variant Series: S. hrg.; 107-716
LC Classification: KF25 .E2 2002d
Govt. Doc. No.: Y 4.EC 7:R 26/4 Y 4.EC 7:S.Hrg.107-716

United States. Congress. Joint Economic Committee.
Reform of the IMF and World Bank: hearing before the Joint Economic Committee, Congress of the United States, One Hundred Seventh Congress, second session, March 6, 2002.
Published/Created: Washington: U.S. G.P.O.: For sale by the Supt. of Docs., U.S. G.P.O., [Congressional Sales Office], 2002.
Description: iii, 57 p.; 24 cm.
ISBN: 016068577X

Notes: "Printed for the use of the Joint Economic Committee." Distributed to some depository libraries in microfiche. Shipping list no.: 2002-0245-P. Includes bibliographical references.
Subjects: International Monetary Fund. World Bank. International finance. Development banks.
Series: United States. Congress. Senate. S. hrg.; 107-478.
Variant Series: S. hrg.; 107-478
LC Classification: KF25 .E2 2002e

United States. Congress. Joint Economic Committee.
Reform of the IMF and World Bank: hearing before the Joint Economic Committee, Congress of the United States, One Hundred Seventh Congress, first session, March 8, 2001.
Published/Created: Washington: U.S. G.P.O.: For sale by the Supt. of Docs., U.S. G.P.O. [Congressional Sales Office], 2001.
Description: iii, 112 p.: ill.; 24 cm.
ISBN: 0160658683
Notes: "Printed for the use of the Joint Economic Committee." Distributed to some depository libraries in microfiche. Shipping list no.: 2001-0268-P. Includes bibliographical references.
Subjects: International Monetary Fund. World Bank. International finance. Development banks.
Series: United States. Congress. Senate. S. hrg.; 107-51.
Variant Series: S. hrg.; 107-51
LC Classification: KF25 .E2 2001

United States. Congress. Joint Economic Committee.
Reform of the IMF and World Bank: hearing before the Joint Economic Committee, Congress of the United States, One Hundred Sixth Congress, second session, April 12, 2000.
Published/Created: Washington: U.S. G.P.O.: For sale by the U.S. G.P.O., Supt. of Docs., Congressional Sales Office, 2000.
Description: iii, 311 p.: ill.; 24 cm.
ISBN: 0160610737
Notes: "Printed for the use of the Joint Economic Committee." Distributed to some depository libraries in microfiche. Shipping list no.: 2001-0016-P. Includes bibliographical references.
Subjects: International Monetary Fund. World Bank. International finance.
Series: United States. Congress. Senate. S. hrg.; 106-575.
Variant Series: S. hrg.; 106-575
LC Classification: KF25 .E2 2000
Dewey Class No.: 332.1/52 21
Govt. Doc. No.: Y 4.EC 7:R 25/2

United States. Congress. Senate. Committee on Banking, Housing, and Urban Affairs. Subcommittee on International Trade and Finance.
Reforms of the World Bank and other multilateral development banks: hearing before the Subcommittee on International Trade and Finance of the Committee on Banking, Housing, and Urban Affairs, United States Senate, One Hundred Sixth Congress, second session on whether the policies and practices of the multilateral development banks (MDB's) are helping developing countries achieve economic growth and development, June 8, 2000.
Published/Created: Washington: U.S. G.P.O.: For sale by the U.S. G.P.O., Supt. of Docs., Congressional Sales Office, 2001.
Description: iii, 56 p.; 24 cm.
ISBN: 0160660122
Notes: Distributed to some depository libraries in microfiche. Shipping list no.: 2001-0305-P. Includes bibliographical references.
Subjects: World Bank. Economic assistance, American--Developing countries. Development banks--United States.
Series: United States. Congress. Senate. S. hrg.; 106-1031.
Variant Series: S. hrg.; 106-792
LC Classification: KF26 .B3946 2000a
Govt. Doc. No.: Y 4.B 22/3:S.HRG.106-1031

United States. General Accounting Office.
World Bank: management controls stronger, but challenges in fighting corruption remain: report to Congressional committees / United States General Accounting Office.
Portion of Management controls stronger, but challenges in fighting corruption remain. World Bank management controls.
Published/Created: Washington, D.C. (P.O. Box 37050, Washington, D.C. 20013): The Office, [2000]
Description: 57 p.: map; 28 cm.
Notes: Cover title. "April 2000." "GAO/NSIAD-00-73." "B-282152"--Text header. Includes bibliographical references.
Subjects: World Bank. International Development Association. Corruption--Prevention. Political corruption--Prevention. Loans, Foreign--Developing countries. Conditionality (International relations)
LC Classification: HG3881.5.W57 U55 2000
Dewey Class No.: 332.1/532 21

Vedeld, Trond.
Participation in project preparation: lessons from World Bank-assisted projects in India / Trond Vedeld.
Published/Created: Washington, DC: World Bank, 2001.
Description: ix, 64 p.; 28 cm.
ISBN: 0821349325
Notes: Includes bibliographical refences (p. 63-64).

Subjects: World Bank. Economic development projects--Citizen participation--Case studies. Strategic planning--Case studies.
Series: World Bank discussion papers; no. 423.
Variant Series: World Bank discussion paper; no. 423
LC Classification: HG3881.5.W57 V43 2001
Dewey Class No.: 338.954/0068/4 21

Verbeek, Jos.
The World Bank's unified survey projections: how accurate are they?: an ex-post evaluation of US91-US97 / Jos Verbeek.
Published/Created: Washington, DC: World Bank, [1999]
Description: 29, [30] p.: ill.; 28 cm.
Subjects: World Bank. Economic surveys--Developing countries. Economic forecasting--Developing countries.
Series: Policy research working papers; 2071.
Variant Series: Policy research working paper; 2071
LC Classification: HG3881.5.W57 P63 no. 2071

Webster, Leila, 1950-
World Bank lending for small enterprises, 1989-1993 / Leila M. Webster, Randall Riopelle and Anne-Marie Chidzero.
Published/Created: Washington, D.C.: World Bank, c1996.
Related Authors: Riopelle, Randall, 1965- Chidzero, Anne-Marie, 1960-
Description: ix, 128 p.: ill.; 28 cm.
ISBN: 0821335189
Notes: Includes bibliographical references (p. 123).
Subjects: World Bank. Small business--Developing countries--Finance. Loans--Developing countries.
Series: World Bank technical paper, 0253-7494; no. 311
LC Classification: HG3881.5.W57 W433 1996
Dewey Class No.: 332.1/532 20

Wolfensohn, James D.
The challenges of globalization: the role of the World Bank / James D. Wolfensohn.
Published/Created: Washington, D.C.: World Bank, 2001.
Related Authors: World Bank.
Description: 16 p.; 23 cm.
Notes: "Address to the Bundestag, Berlin, Germany April 2, 2001."
Subjects: World Bank. Globalization.
LC Classification: HG3881.5.W57 W64 2001
Dewey Class No.: 332.1/532 21

World Bank literature / Amitava Kumar, editor.
Published/Created: Minneapolis: University of Minnesota Press, 2002.

Projected Pub. Date: 0212
Related Authors: Kumar, Amitava, 1963-
Description: p. cm.
ISBN: 0816638365 (alk. paper) 0816638373 (pbk.: alk. paper)
Notes: Includes bibliographical references and index.
Subjects: World Bank. International Monetary Fund. Globalization.
LC Classification: HG3881.5.W57 W6917 2002
Dewey Class No.: 330 21

World Bank.
Guidelines: selection and employment of consultants by World Bank borrowers. Portion of Selection and employment of consultants by World Bank borrowers
Published/Created: Washington, D.C.: World Bank, 1999.
Description: vi, 52 p.; 22 x 10 cm.
ISBN: 0821346555
Notes: "January 1997, revised September 1997 and January 1999"--Cover. "These Guidelines ... replace the 1981 Guidelines: use of consultants by World Bank borrowers and [by] the World Bank as executing agency"--P. vi. Includes bibliographical references.
Subjects: World Bank. Consultants. Loans, Foreign--Developing countries.
LC Classification: HG3881.5.W57 I57 1999
Dewey Class No.: 332.1/532 21

World Bank.
Guidelines: selection and employment of consultants by World Bank borrowers. Portion of Selection and employment of consultants by World Bank borrowers
Published/Created: Washington, D.C.: World Bank, c1997.
Description: iv, 52 p.; 23 cm.
ISBN: 0821341472
Notes: "January 1997, revised September 1997"--Cover. "These Guidelines ... replace the 1981 Guidelines: use of consultants by World Bank borrowers and [by] the World Bank as executing agency"--P. vi. Includes bibliographical references.
Subjects: World Bank. Consultants. Loans, Foreign--Developing countries.
LC Classification: HG3881.5.W57 I57 1997
Dewey Class No.: 332.1/532 21

World Bank.
Making sustainable commitments: an environment strategy for the World Bank.
Published/Created: Washington, D.C.: World Bank, [2001]
Description: xii, 234 p.: ill., maps (some col.); 28 cm.
ISBN: 082134935X
Notes: Includes bibliographical references (p. 221-234).
Subjects: World Bank. Sustainable development. Economic development--Environmental aspects.

LC Classification: HC79.E5 W6659 2001
Dewey Class No.: 338.9/27 21

World Bank.
The World Bank policy on disclosure of information.
Published/Created: Jakarta: World Bank Office Jakarta, [2002]
Description: iv, 22, 12 p.; 26 cm.
Notes: "June 2002."
Subjects: World Bank. Disclosure of information.
LC Classification: HG3881.5.W57 W65 2002
Dewey Class No.: 332.1/532/0684 21

Young, Zoe.
A new green order?: the World Bank and the politics of the Global Environment Facility / Zoe Young.
Published/Created: Sterling, Virginia: Pluto Press, 2002.
Projected Pub. Date: 0211
Description: p. cm.
ISBN: 0745315534 (hb: alk. paper) 0745315488 (pb: alk. paper)
Subjects: Global Environment Facility. World Bank. Environmental policy--Political aspects. Environmental policy--International cooperation. Environmental policy--Evaluation.
LC Classification: GE170 .Y685 2002
Dewey Class No.: 363.7/0526 21

INDEX

G

H

I

N

O

P

Q

R